D1228705

*FOUNDATIONS OF POLITICAL CULTURE: political socialization in Canada, ed. by Jon H. Pammett and Michael S. Whittington. Macmillan of Canada/Maclean-Hunter Press, 70 Bond St., Toronto, Ont., M5B 1X3, Canada, 1976. 318p. 15.95 ISBN 0-7705-1465-0; 9.95 pa ISBN 0-7705-1466-9. C.I.P.

A collection of 15 previously unpublished essays on political socialization in Canada. Edited by two accomplished scholars in the field of political behavior who have contributed the introduction and an article each, the book deals with both theory as well as empirical findings. Four separate sections are included: a critique of current approaches to the subject; the development of political attitudes among young people; socialization of elites and activists; and attitudes toward Canada and its political system on the part of various groups. All the authors are professional academics, most of them political scientists. Since there is virtually no systematic material available on the topic, this volume represents something of a ground-breaking effort, especially in its presentation of new data. However, interest in it is likely to be confined to specialized groups — advanced undergraduates or graduate students in Canadian politics and political socialization and researchers in these areas. At the same time, its utility is likely to be restricted by the absence of a bibliography and an index.

FOUNDATIONS OF POLITICAL CULTURE

Foundations of Political Culture

Political Socialization in Canada

EDITED BY

JON H. PAMMETT

AND

MICHAEL S. WHITTINGTON

Macmillan of Canada
Maclean-Hunter Press

Canadian Cataloguing in Publication Data

Main entry under title:
Foundations of political culture

Includes bibliographical references.

ISBN 0-7705-1465-0 bd.   ISBN 0-7705-1466-9 pa.

1. Political socialization. 2. Canada—Politics and
government. 3. Children and politics. I. Pammett, Jon
H., 1944–   II. Whittington, Michael S., 1942–

JA76.F68   301.5′92′0971   C76-017117-3

Printed in Canada for
The Macmillan Company of Canada Limited
70 Bond Street, Toronto
M5B 1X3

Contents

Preface

Political socialization is a new name for a subject which has long been of concern to students of politics. It is, essentially, the study of political learning. It is concerned with, as one author puts it, "who learns what from whom under what circumstances with what effect?"* While social scientists have certainly not produced definitive answers to any of these questions, they have been, in the last two decades, attacking with empirical methods many of the important research problems in the field. In Canada, research in political socialization has been developing rapidly in recent years. We have been pleasantly surprised, in assembling this volume, to find a wide variety of studies in progress in all regions of Canada, and a keen interest on the part of Canadian scholars in contributing their findings and ideas to this book. The result, presented here, is a collection of articles, all previously unpublished, which illuminate many of the important problems in the study of Canadian political socialization.

The volume is rather loosely divided into five parts. The Introduction is essentially an overview article which attempts to define the connection between socialization and political culture, and to set the study of socialization within the Canadian context. The following section includes articles which are theoretical rather than empirical and draws our attention to some of the conceptual problems one might encounter in attempting to study political socialization. John Shiry argues for an increasing focus on the political elites, those who are most important in formulating the policies which affect Canadians. Political socialization must not concentrate its attentions only on the learning of political orientations by the mass public: hence our inclusion of several articles in this volume on the socialization of political elites and activists. Ronald Landes, in an examination of the uses of role theory, finds that the distinction between the roles themselves and the particular persons inhabiting them has often been blurred, and suggests an "interaction" model whereby both of these

*Fred Greenstein, "Political Socialization," *International Encyclopedia of the Social Sciences*, vol. 14 (New York: Macmillan, 1968), p. 552.

elements can be taken into account. Finally, John Woods strongly presses us to develop distinctively Canadian theoretical approaches, and not to adopt uncritically the culture-bound frameworks of studies done in other societies.

In Part Two, we have assembled three studies of the development of political attitudes in Canadian children. These articles are all data-based rather than theoretical, and they focus upon attitudes as dependent variables. Terry Carroll shows how children develop a conception of a hierarchy of roles within the political system based on their affection for, confidence in, and perceptions of the power of, the authorities in the system. Magnus Gunther undertakes the difficult but vital task of investigating the place of personality variables in the development of political attitudes. He finds that the personality characteristic which researchers label "dogmatism" is an important intervening variable between a person's social characteristics and the attitude of political efficacy. The article by Stuart Proudfoot and Jon Pammett takes a set of hypotheses derived from the work of the controversial "guru" of mass communications, Marshall McLuhan, and finds some support for the notion that the particular medium through which children receive their political knowledge may have effects on the type of learning which takes place. Obviously, no firm conclusions should be drawn at this point, but the results point the way to an intriguing area of future research.

The socialization of political activists and elites is the particular concern of the articles in Part Three. By contrast to Part Two, this section includes articles which consider the possible linkages between political attitudes and specific political roles. Here the basic attitudes considered in Part Two are viewed as independent variables which have an impact on the way elites and activists perform in various political roles. Thelma Oliver, in a theoretical note which is guiding her current research on community activists, presents a model which distinguishes the pattern of "socialization" (which she considers to mean acceptance of the existing system) from one of "politicization," which leads to a commitment to the transformation of that system and participation in political movements to accomplish that goal. Jon Pammett's study of Action-Trudeau provides a detailed examination of the motivations for participation in a mass political movement. Besides providing insights into the "Trudeau phenomenon" in Canadian politics, it places political socialization within the general socialization process and points out how participants in a political movement used their experiences to further their personality development and the evaluation of their roles within society.

Part Three also includes two articles dealing with the subject of "post-incumbency socialization." Both involving studies of freshman members of Parliament, they show how actual experience in a role plays an important part in moulding the way persons come to perceive it. Jack Cramer shows that freshman M.P.'s see some of their roles quite differently from veteran M.P.'s. In a much more elaborate study, Richard Price, Harold Clarke and Robert Krause examine the extent of role socialization and the important agents of socialization at three periods— the pre-nomination period, the election campaign and the short time between the election and the interview. The authors show how the members' perceptions of their roles shifted at each of these time-periods and reveal the agents who produced the shifts.

The final section of the book includes four articles, all of which focus upon attitudes towards the Canadian political system as a whole. Michael Whittington's article looks at the rather remarkable phenomenon of childhood affection for a key personalized symbol of the system, the monarchy. The author goes on to speculate about the implications of supportive attitudes to such symbols in terms of diffuse support for the regime and the political community. Don Higgins looks at Canadian children's attitudes to Canadian authority roles relative to American ones. He finds that while the most visible Canadian roles overshadow American ones, the less salient of the domestic political figures are not as well known or as well liked as are key American authorities such as the president.

In the final two articles, the authors look at divisive or negative attitudes to Canada on the part of subcultural groups. Steve Ullman analyses the differences in orientation to Canada between white and Micmac Cape Bretoners. He points to a significant decline in affection for the Canadian political system which occurs among older Indian children. Don Forbes reveals the differences which exist between French and English Canadians in their perceptions of national identities, and concludes that at least for English Canadians the "mosaic" conception of our political community may be an illusion.

Many people have assisted us in the preparation of this manuscript. Most notably we must thank our contributors who often embarrassed us by meeting our deadlines. Our editor, Diane Mew, was invaluable in improving the manuscript. We appreciate the efforts of Pearl Fisher, Val Foley, Ellen Leleu and the rest of the secretarial staff of the Department of Political Science at Carleton for the long hours spent typing and re-typing the manuscript. Finally we must thank the students in our graduate seminar on political socialization here at Carleton who assisted us with perceptive criticisms of many of the articles.

JON H. PAMMETT
MICHAEL WHITTINGTON

Introduction:

Political Culture and Political Socialization

JON H. PAMMETT

MICHAEL S. WHITTINGTON

The sixties witnessed a flood of literature in political science and sociology which attempted to define and explain the relationship between individual attitudes and political behaviour. Primarily motivated by a search for a reliable set of criteria for cross-national comparison, this body of literature attempted to relate the structural and behavioural idiosyncrasies of discrete political systems to the collective attitudes of their citizenry. The aggregate of the political attitudes of the individuals in a society has come to be described rather loosely as its political culture; and while the term is often used without any conceptual precision, it has provided a stylistically manageable shorthand for the collective social-psychological determinants of individual political behaviour.

The impetus for much of the research into the nature and impact of political culture has come from the United States, and while other social science communities have made some limited contributions, the theoretical underpinnings of the concept remain predominantly American. Certainly there has been a marked paucity of such research in Canada, and it is a primary aim of this collection to gather together some of the material which has been produced. However, to understand the potential significance of the articles included in this volume, it is necessary to elaborate upon the concept of political culture and its theoretical relationship to the process of political socialization.

While the definitions of political culture are many and varied in emphasis,[1] there seems to be a common starting point in the assumption that attitudes (or orientations) and action are separate but related foci for political analysis. As Howard Scarrow has stated:

... Action and orientation are to be seen as two sides of the same coin, even though the analyst's focus is usually on one side of the coin or the other. When the analyst identifies a pattern of action, he can be sure that there is a pattern of orientation which underlies this; and when he identifies a pattern of orientation, he can be sure there are action patterns reflecting it. . . .[2]

Moreover, it has been argued that the utility of "the political culture approach"[3] in the comparative analysis of political systems rests on this basic dichotomy between behaviour and "in-the-mind" phenomena such as attitudes. In structural terms, therefore, political culture is viewed as being composed of attitudes, orientations, values, beliefs, emotions, images,[4] and in functional terms it is viewed as a determinant of political action or behaviour.

There are three major approaches to the study of political culture, each of which is distinguished by a particular analytical focus. The most obvious focus is the attitudes that make up that culture. In other words, it is possible to establish which attitudes are characteristic of a given political culture simply by asking people directly what their attitudes are. Secondly, it is possible to speculate about the predominant attitudes of a political culture by observing the patterns of political behaviour which are typical of the political system. With this approach, the researcher works backwards, deducing the likely attitudinal causes from the observed behavioural patterns. Finally, it may be possible to uncover the attitudinal components of a political culture from the institutional framework of the political system itself. Constitutions, legislation and the actual structure of government may prove to be fairly accurate indicators of the basic values implicit in a political culture.

While all three of these approaches are employed in cross-national comparisons of political systems, there may be a fourth approach to the analysis of political culture. By analysing, in their formative stages, attitudes that define a political culture, it may be possible to understand its social and psychological origins. In other words, it can be hypothesized that important clues to a clear understanding of political culture may lie in the nascent political attitudes of children. Furthermore, while all may not agree that the medium is the message, most would agree that the medium can certainly affect the content and intensity of the message. In this view, it seems likely that the process whereby individuals acquire the attitudinal components of political culture surely has a significant effect on the substance and intensity of their attitudes, and thus, on the political culture itself.

POLITICAL SOCIALIZATION: THE PROBLEM OF DEFINITION

The process of socialization, while usually defined as having to do with the transmission of attitudes and behaviour patterns from one generation of a particular society to the next, has been viewed differently by the three major social sciences which have employed the term. As Robert A. LeVine describes in his book *Culture, Behaviour and Personality*,[5] anthropology, psychology and sociology have taken different approaches to the ultimate question of the importance and meaning of socialization.

Anthropology takes the view that is perhaps widest in scope of all the social sciences, for it is concerned with the transference of the attitudes and values of a culture from the older members of a society to the younger. Socialization is seen by the anthropologist as enculturation, a process through which all aspects of a culture are acquired and internalized by successive generations of a society. However, the disciplines of anthropology and psychology merge to some extent in the writing of psychologists such as Erikson and Kohlberg, who seek to combine theories of cognitive development with theories of enculturation.[6] According to these authors, this enculturation process occurs within certain distinct stages in cognitive development.

Psychology has contributed many important ideas to a definition of the concept of socialization. The notion that an individual's attitudes towards authority, whether political or social, are rooted in his attitudes to his father has its origin in the writings of Freud.[7] Particularly in his social and political writings, such as *Civilization and Its Discontents*, Freud adds a distinctly psychological flavour to the concept by viewing socialization as the acquisition of the ability to harness and control the instinctual drives and impulses which all humans possess. The socialization process is thus a kind of societal defence mechanism against the passionate urges of its citizens. This control is essential for the existence of a civilized society: it is a modern psychologists' theory of the "social contract" which posits that individuals must surrender some of their primordial freedom of action to facilitate civilization and social order. The socialized individual, then, is someone who has curbed the free expression of his personal drives and aggressive impulses in order to exist in a state of mutual toleration, if not harmony, with his fellows.

Sociologists have been most concerned with how society trains the individual to take up certain roles within it. Thus, the socialization process enables the social system to persist over time by transferring various social norms from generation to generation and by fitting the individual into certain slots within it. The use of role theory in sociology has led to a conception of society as a series of these slots which need to be filled, and of the socialization process as essentially a mechanism of recruitment which operates to do so. In functional terms, effective socialization, placing most individuals in previously determined roles within the social system, is seen as necessary for systems maintenance and the exercise of social control. In *The Social System*, Talcott Parsons sums up the place of the socialization process as follows:

The acquisition of the requisite orientations for satisfactory functioning in a role is a learning process, but is not learning in general, but a particular part of learning. This process will be called the process of socialization, and the motivational process by which it takes place, seen in terms of their functional significance to the interaction system, the mechanisms of socialization. These are the mechanisms involved in the processes of "normal" functioning of the social system.[8]

This sort of formulation has led sociologists to place as much importance on the family as a socialization agent as do psychologists, because it is the family which provides the child with his initial niche in the social stratification system and which provides him with the initial information about role requisites and possibilities outside the family.

Political science has, for the most part, used the conception of political socialization favoured by the sociologists. However, instead of looking at how society trains the individual to fill a great many different roles, political scientists have concentrated on a subset of social roles, those relating to the political system. Thus, political socialization studies, including many of those in this collection, have looked at such things as the inculcation in the young individual of support for the political community and the regime, of attitudes regarding the desirability of political participation, and of patterns of allegiance towards political parties and other politically oriented groups. Profitable as these studies are in terms of generating basic knowledge for political scientists to ponder, they are an indication of the nascent state of the field of political socialization, especially in Canadian political science. We are still reasoning inductively in the study of political socialization; we are groping for a way to make basic generalizations out of an array of scattered bits of knowledge.

POLITICAL AND NON-POLITICAL SOCIALIZATION

The student of political socialization, indeed the student of political science in general, must be careful not to assume that politics is a central concern to most people. Although not nearly enough research has been expended to find out the salience of political attitudes in the belief systems of the general public, we do know that the amount of consistent ideological thinking is rather low[9] and that the level of information about basic political institutions, roles and personages is at least lower than the ideal requisites of democratic theory. It behooves us, then, to take a realistic view of the salience of politics when we come to develop our theories and models of the political socialization process, and when we design our research about socialization. There is, to put it bluntly, little evidence that, for most people, there is anything special about their political attitudes and, by extension, that there is likely to be anything special about the process by which they acquired them.

This point seems obvious enough, and yet our habit of extracting certain roles (the "political" ones) from the role theory of sociology, and detailing what children may know and feel about these, has led us to construct an implicit model of political socialization as being somehow separable from socialization to other roles in society. By ignoring non-political roles, and by failing to place political socialization in any other context than that of the political system, we have managed to create a subfield of political science when what we really should be doing is contributing to a general subfield of social science.

Learning theory postulates that the child learns by imitation, and by getting positive reinforcement (rewards) for behaviour patterns considered desirable by influential adults with authority over him, and by getting negative reinforcement (punishment) for behaviour patterns considered undesirable by these authorities. It seems reasonable to assume that political orientations are learned through this same process of positive and negative reinforcement. The young child who becomes aware of the existence of the nation is going to develop feelings towards it that are rewarded rather than punished by parents, teachers and friends having some sort of authority over him. When we see substantial subcultural variation in such attitudes, such as that demonstrated in American studies dealing with the attitudes of black Americans or of those in economically depressed areas,[10] or the differences detailed in the articles by Forbes and Ullman in this volume with regard to children in Quebec and Cape Breton, we are dealing just as much with similarities as with differences; for the ways in which these attitudes were socialized are likely to be quite similar no matter what subculture is being scrutinized.

Not only may the methods by which political attitudes are learned be the same as those by which other attitudes are learned, but these different orientations may fulfil the same sorts of functions for the individual. In a pioneering study, Smith, Bruner and White[11] inquired into the opinions of a small group of men on the subject of Russia, subjecting them to intensive interviews to try to determine the functions which their attitudes towards Russia served for them. These authors determined that there are three functions served for a person by his holding of an opinion: object appraisal, or a way of providing a judgment against which new objects and events may be measured; social adjustment, or a way of shifting to meet the demands of society; and externalization, a way of projecting the person's inner needs and providing some degree of satisfaction of them. This last function of attitudes has been the concern of many political scientists and psychologists.[12] Unfortunately, the credibility of some of these studies has suffered because of an impression they created that they were blaming conservative (or "bigoted") political attitudes on deviant personality development, while implying that healthy personalities were liberal-minded. The scepticism with which it is possible to view some of these studies should not, however, blind us to the very real links between a person's personality development and his political attitudes.

In this formulation, attitudes may be regarded as satisfying needs such as the need to be liked or the need for achievement, or as tools for sorting out a chaotic external world for the individual and for providing him with a previously established base from which to view new events and objects. Political attitudes, while they may be called into play by a special type of event and object in the external world, serve essentially the same functions for the individual as other social attitudes. A basic set of political attitudes will allow an individual to classify an unfamiliar political speaker, just as a set of religious attitudes will allow him to place the doctrine of an unfamiliar preacher in the perspective of the familiar.

It is also possible to view political behaviour as functional for personal-need satisfaction. There is reason to suppose that people engage in political activity for the same sorts of reasons that they participate in other sorts of social action. In a study done in the United States in 1956, Dwaine Marvick and Charles Nixon found a great diversity of motivational aims among party activists. In examining the functions their activities served for these leaders, the authors concluded:

These organizations may serve the latent functions of aiding people to attain a social identity or a social advancement, as well as serving the explicit political functions of carrying on campaigns. . . . To people with only modest claims to social status, it may provide a satisfying sense of position and power. The decline of the old type of machine should not lead us to assume that the social function of the campaign organization has disappeared. Rather, the details of its social functioning may have changed, in order to suit the status-conferring needs of the middle-class group from which it draws its strength.[13]

We might also make a brief reference here to the study in this volume of the motivations of the young Action-Trudeau workers of 1968 and the consequences of their political activity for their personal development (pages 160–94). A major point made in this article is that these young campaigners appear to have used their political behaviour for the same personal purposes that psychoanalytic theory tells us adolescents use other social role experimentation. The overall point to be taken here, therefore, is that political attitudes, and by implication the process through which those attitudes are acquired, may be significant causative agents in the development of non-political attitudes, and in the satisfaction of unrelated personal needs.

The opposite side of the coin, however, is that we must recognize that non-political attitudes may precede and in fact even have causal impacts on political attitudes and behaviour. In studies of political socialization, we would be well advised to look for the development of certain non-political personal characteristics from which particular political attitudes and behaviours might be expected to spring. Expectations about the out-puts of the political system, for example, may be closely related to the development of "deferred gratification" in a population. If one expects immediate gratification of one's wants, and acts always in a short-term manner in order to attain such benefits, it is reasonable to suppose such a general orientation would have a powerful effect on the sorts of attitudes a person develops towards the political system. It is quite possible that in those societies which Almond and Verba[14] classify as "subject political cultures" (oriented towards political outputs but not to the legitimacy of making corresponding inputs) general patterns of needs for immediate gratification may be present in the population. For a "participant political culture," on the other hand, patterns of deferred gratification may pre-dominate. Changes in the gratification-patterns of a society may be necessary antecedents for the evolution of societies from subject to participant political cultures. For example, if as is widely speculated, Quebec has been undergoing such a change during the Quiet Revolution, the specific political changes may have been but one manifestation of a general cultural shift in gratification-patterns. An equally plausible hypothesis would reverse the causal arrow and state that political initia-tives may have come first and provoked general societal changes later.

Political scientists have been aware for some time that it is probable "deeper" attitudes underlie specific political opinions and reactions to particular political stimuli. Attempts to label these attitudes have resulted in concepts such as political efficacy (the feeling a person has that he can comprehend and affect the political process) and civic competence (people's beliefs that they can influence the political system). For instance, two noted political scientists have looked at the early existence of feelings of political efficacy in children, and concluded from their findings that children in the United States learn early in life attitudes which are basically supportive of the American political system.[15]

Similarly, Almond and Verba conclude that those nations which have high degrees of civic competence possess political cultures which are likely to be supportive of democracy. One noted social psychologist, however, has suggested that these concepts of political competence may only be particular parts of the more general conception of competence, which is an integral goal of the general socialization process.[16] The child, in this view, develops many skills to enable him to cope with, and participate effectively in, various aspects of modern society. The individual is motivated to achieve this state of subjective competence in all areas of the social system in which he is likely to act, including the political.

There are three aspects to this general development of competence. First, the individual learns to develop the ability to use a number of alternative pathways or behaviours to reach a certain goal. Secondly, the individual learns to be able to understand and use a number of the subsystems of the society, and to move freely among them. Thirdly, the individual learns to perform effective reality testing, developing a "positive, broad and sophisticated understanding of the world."[17] This is, it needs to be said, a rather idealistic statement of the sort of learning which actually goes on, for if most people in a society achieved such a level of general competence, the degree of understanding and effective behaviour in society would probably be a good deal higher than it actually seems to be. Nevertheless, it still seems reasonable to conclude that people reach levels of competence that they consider sufficient, in many aspects of the social system. If people happen to be more interested in some areas than others, and consequently strive for relatively higher degrees of personal competence there, this does not negate the possibility that they consider themselves to have achieved a level of competence in the neglected areas that is sufficient for the lower levels of activity they are likely to undertake there.

We should recognize, then, that the development of a degree of competence in dealing with and acting within the political system is part of general development which is a main outcome of the socialization process. Furthermore, the same basic personal qualities and the same aspects of a person's location in the social structure which affect the development of non-political types of competence may also play important parts in developing political competence. Smith has suggested "that attitudes of hope and of self-respect are at the crux of competence."[18] If the socialization process instills these basic attitudes, then the foundation for the development of social competence is laid. If enough political competence is learned to engender self-respect, and respect by others, for one's political attitudes and behaviour, the political socialization process has done its job.

DIMENSIONS OF POLITICAL ATTITUDES

Attitudes can be seen to have two broad dimensions, subjective and objective. The former categorizes attitudes in terms of the manner in which an individual perceives a real world object; here variations in attitudes towards reality are viewed more as a product of the "perceiver" than of the "object perceived." By contrast, the objective dimension views variations in attitudes as products of different objects being perceived.

Perhaps the best set of categories breaking down the subjective dimension of attitudes is described in the *Civic Culture*. Taking their inspiration from Parsons and Shils, Almond and Verba identify three types of political orientations: cognitive, affective and evaluative. Cognitions, or cognitive attitudes, are the simplest and in some ways the most fundamental attitudes. These are acquired through our perception of what goes on around us and they consist of knowledge and beliefs[19] about real world phenomena, their characteristics, relationships and so on. While cognitive attitudes are not likely to be perfect reflections of the real world, the mood in which we acquire them is empirical and objective rather than *a priori* or subjective.

Figure 1   Subjective Dimension of Political Attitudes

Type	Form	Mood	Mode of Expression
Cognitive	knowledge, beliefs, information	empirical, objective	is/is not statements
Affective	feelings, preferences	emotional, aesthetic	like/love (not) statements
Evaluative	value judgments	moral, ethical	should/ought (not) statements

Affections, or affective attitudes, consist of the feelings and the aesthetic preferences we have for objects in the real world. These are secondary to cognitive attitudes in that we must have knowledge or awareness of external phenomena first in order to acquire positive or negative feelings about them. However, because it is possible to develop an emotional commitment to our beliefs about "what is," affective and cognitive attitudes will frequently blend together; in this way the distinction between "what is" and "what we would like to be" is often blurred in our own minds.

Evaluative attitudes consist of the judgments about real world phenomena that we make on the basis of our values, and tend to be expressed as "should" or "ought" statements. Evaluative attitudes are more complex than either cognition or affection, being conceptually founded on an amalgam of our empirical beliefs and our feelings. On the one hand, because values are enduring beliefs about what is good and bad in our environment,[20] they have a large cognitive component. On the other hand, because what we perceive as "good and bad" is often related to what we "like and dislike," values or moral judgments are frequently nothing more than complicated rationalizations of what we feel. Thus, while it is convenient to make an analytical distinction between cognitive, affective and evaluative attitudes, in fact they are closely related. Our values and emotions colour our perception of the real world, our feelings depend upon what we perceive, and our values tend to be rationalizations of what we feel.

A factor which is frequently overlooked or ignored in studies of political attitudes is the intensity of attitudes. Naturally, the degree of certainty or uncertainty surrounding a cognitive attitude will depend upon the reliability of the original source of the information, the extent to which the attitude is consonant with other cognitions, and the extent to which the belief has been reinforced by further experience. The intensity of attitudes, however, is likely a more important variable when we come to consider affective and evaluative attitudes. For example, it is quite conceivable that an individual could indicate a preference for one political party over another, and still have a low regard for political parties generally. In such a case the relative partisan preference might very well be ascribed greater significance than could be warranted in terms of the individual's overall affective makeup. Thus in analysing affective attitudes it is incumbent upon the researcher to consider not only the presence or absence, and direction of feelings about a political object but also the strength of those feelings.

Similarly, when considering the evaluative makeup of an individual's political personality, it is necessary to find out not only what values and sets of values are present but the relative conviction with which they are held. The significance of a political value as a potential determinant of political behaviour may well depend upon the presence or absence of value conflicts and upon the "negotiability" of the values. Not only must we look at individual values in mutual perspective then, but we must also determine the extent to which each is absolute or conditional.

Figure 2   The Intensity of Attitudes

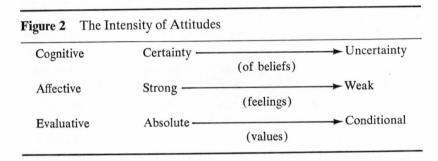

The objective dimension of political attitudes consists of the external phenomena or real world objects reflected by an individual's beliefs, feelings and values. These real world phenomena or political objects for the most part are aspects and characteristics of the political system. What is important in terms of the development of political culture is the attitude towards participation or non-participation in politics. It is the presence (or absence), direction and intensity of beliefs about the possibility of participation, feelings about the political activities per se, and convictions that such behaviour is either good or bad that distinguish parochial, subject and participant political cultural types.

"SELF" AS POLITICAL OBJECT

All attitudes towards political participation or abstinence involve perceptions of a "self-to-system" relationship. The attitudes towards that relationship are obviously affected by the individual's perceptions of the political system, but they are also affected by the individual's perceptions of himself. The basic self-related political attitudes are efficacy and civic competence. These attitudes are behaviourally significant ultimately because they may colour the individual's perceptions of system-related objects and immediately because they may directly constrain or stimulate political activity. The propensity to participate or abstain from political involvement is directly related to the individual's perceptions of himself as a potentially effective participant. Nevertheless, while the likelihood, intensity and the mood of political activity may be set in part by individual attitudinal factors related to self, such behaviour is also directly related to the individual's perception of relevant political roles.

The individual's assessment of the "worth" of the political system and of the efficacy of his active participation in, for instance, the electoral process will depend in part upon his attitudes to the authority roles within the system and to incumbents of those roles. Here our attitudes to the political system are affected by our perceptions of political roles that most of us will never be called upon to perform. Very few persons will ever become prime minister, but most of us will acquire very definite attitudes as to what is appropriate and inappropriate prime ministerial behaviour; in fact, society's expectations of its prime ministers will be an important determinant of the incumbent's behaviour while in office. Elite socialization (the inculcation of the norms of the society in the attitudinal makeup of our leaders and potential leaders) is therefore an important factor in ensuring that the behaviour of the political authorities is in line with dominant societal values.

However, the perception of "citizen roles" is similarly an important determinant of mass political behaviour. Because most of us will be limited to performing such non-elite roles in the political system, the process whereby we are socialized to them will have significant impact on political culture. The role an individual is playing defines for him the parameters of socially acceptable behaviour. It is the expectations society has of the incumbent of a role that tell him what behaviours are appropriate and inappropriate. In the case of political roles, such as "voter," the basic limits have been institutionalized so that the broad behavioural parameters are defined by the Elections Act, the Electoral Boundaries Act and so on. Within these institutional parameters there are also more specific norms of appropriate voter behaviour defined by the region, social stratum, linguistic group and family partisan tradition of which the individual is a member.

Because some minimal political awareness can be expected to precede an individual's actual opportunity to participate in mass political roles such as voting, earliest socialization is anticipatory or vicarious. We acquire some attitudes about political roles long before we are permitted to perform them, and in some cases such pre-incumbency socialization totally determines our behaviour when we come of age. However, it is important to understand that we are not necessarily locked into our earliest perceptions of political roles, and in fact attitudes to what constitutes appropriate and inappropriate role behaviour can change. In this sense, post-incumbency experiences can alter the political role expectations we acquired through pre-incumbency socialization.

THE POLITICAL SYSTEM AS OBJECT

David Easton breaks the political system into three major components or objects: the political community, the regime and the authorities.[21] The political community is the political system seen as a collection of people who share a political division of labour. The political community is the politically relevant aspects of the society for which a given political system performs its allocative function; it is a category whose major significance is that it permits people in one country to identify themselves as politically different from the rest of the world. The regime is the set of structures, norms and ultimate values which determine the form of the state. It includes not only the basic values that determine the broad system goals, but also the institutional mechanisms or the means by which the system goals are attained. The regime within the context of the Canadian political system includes our institutional arrangements such as federalism, parliamentary government and cabinet responsibility. The authorities include the people who occupy the regime roles at any point in time: in other words, the incumbents of offices in the governmental structure. In Canada, these authorities in 1976 include Prime Minister Trudeau, Joseph Clark, the various judges, public servants and members of Parliament.

While this typology was originally formulated to specify different aspects of the political system to which an individual could direct his support for the system, it is being used here to depict different levels or foci for attitudes about the political system. However, it must be emphasized that these categories still remain exceedingly generalized aspects of the political system and that most of our attitudes are in fact directed at much more specific political objects. Hence it is more useful in terms of clarifying the nature of political socialization to categorize specific political objects on one dimension as political community-related, regime-related or authorities-related. Then by adding a second dimension according to whether the object is structural, symbolic or conceptual in form, we can construct a nine-fold system of classification.

Figure 3 The Objects of Political Socialization

Level of Political System	Type		
	Structural	*Symbolic*	*Conceptual*
Political Community (Canada)	Territorial factors . . . the geography of Canada, etc.	Beavers, flags, maple leaves; also personalized symbols such as national heroes	Nationhood or nationality; the Canadian way of life or the Canadian identity
Regime (the government and constitution of Canada)	B.N.A. Act, Parliament, the federal system, the public service, etc.	The Parliament Buildings, the Crown, etc.; also personalized symbols such as the Queen	Ideology: the principles of parliamentary democracy, responsible government, etc.
Authorities (the government of the day; the people in the political system)	Specific roles and (rarely) the incumbents themselves	Symbols of the authorities such as the political parties, and individuals' images	Issues in the current political scene

Structural objects related to the political community include social, cultural and spatial factors which define the territorial, demographic and cultural boundaries of the nation. Awareness of and feelings about such factors constitute our general attitude towards Canada as a physical entity.

Regime-related structures include the basic institutions of the political system: in Canada these would include for example the Houses of Parliament, the judicial system, the public service and so on. The structural objects related to the authorities of the system are in the purest sense the "real" people who occupy system roles at any point in time. However, because what we know of such people is usually limited to their public images we more often simply generalize about them on the basis of the specific role they happen to be occupying, or on the manner in which they are playing it.

Symbols can be genuine objects—"things" which bring to mind an ostensibly unconnected but antecedent phenomenon—or they can be personalized symbols—people who stand for something that transcends their own being. Symbols related to the Canadian political community include objects as diverse as the flag, the Fathers of Confederation, various monuments and the beaver. Unlike the United States or the United Kingdom, Canada lacks a single personalized symbol such as Uncle Sam or John Bull; similarly, with the possible exception of the political figures who participated in the Confederation debates, we have very few national heroes. This lack of widely accepted personalized symbols of our nationhood may be one explanation for the generally low intensity of feelings of nationalism thought to exist in Canada.

Symbols of the Canadian regime are likewise difficult to find unless such objects as the Peace Tower and the Parliament Buildings can be considered as such. On the other hand, in the person of the reigning monarch, Canadians may have a powerful personalized symbol both of the constitutional monarchy and of British parliamentary institutions. However, it might be argued that the Queen as a symbol of the British component of the political community could be a divisive factor, particularly in the militantly non-British segments of Canada.

Authorities-related symbols most commonly would include the images of our political leaders which we receive through the media. It is rare indeed for a citizen to know the incumbents of the regime roles as real people; all we ever see of political figures is a public image, and it is on the basis of this that our general attitudes towards them are formed. It is partly because of the difficulty of "knowing the real man" in politics that political parties have evolved in our system. Political parties provide us with a symbolic representation of groups of the authorities who are allegedly of similar mind, and eliminate or reduce the need to form attitudes about the specific individuals.

Conceptual objects are complex generalizations that we make about the three aspects of the political system. Conceptualized objects of the political community in the aggregate make up our conscious definition of our nationality. Such political-community-related concepts would include fairly specific ones such as biculturalism as well as broad and ill-defined ones such as "the Canadian identity." The conceptual objects related to the regime are the basically ideological components that define the ends of government and the operational rules of the game. The principles of parliamentary democracy, responsible government and provincial autonomy are good examples of well-defined regime concepts that can be objects of political socialization. Finally, the conceptualized objects relating to the authorities of the political system are the issues for which the individual incumbents stand, or the party platforms on which we base our opinions about such organized groups of politicians.

THE CUMULATIVE NATURE OF POLITICAL SOCIALIZATION

While many of the studies of political socialization have focused either on childhood or adolescence, it must be emphasized that the process is continuous throughout the life cycle of an individual. In fact, it is because political socialization is a lifelong process that it is so difficult to study effectively, for the only truly reliable approach is to follow a group of individuals throughout their lives recording the changes in their attitudes at selected points in their personal development. Unfortunately such longitudinal studies are difficult if not impossible to undertake, and the substitute approach is what is termed "quasi-longitudinal." Briefly, the quasi-longitudinal approach posits that the developmental nature of political socialization can be simulated by examining different groups of people at successive age levels and then assuming that any systematic variation from year to year is evidence of development. The obvious weakness of the quasi-longitudinal approach is that in assuming individual attitudinal change is due to personal development or maturation it assumes environmental and systemic factors have remained fairly constant.

The most obvious aspect of the ongoing or cumulative nature of political socialization is cognitive development. Stated simply this is the tendency for individuals to acquire more political information as they grow older; that this is a valid assumption about the process of political socialization is not only obvious but easily testable empirically. Figure 4 contains the responses of children from a national study by Carroll, Higgins and Whittington which forms the data base for several of the articles in this collection.

The instrument used for this study was a questionnaire administered in the classroom by the teacher during 1971. While the 5,842 respondents are not a sample in the strict sense of the word, the schools and the classrooms in the schools involved were selected to be representative of the various regions, urban-rural differences, linguistic and ethnic variations in Canada. The actual cities surveyed are listed in Figure 7. The primary concern of the study was to look at the impact of exposure to American television on the children's relative cognition of and affection for American and Canadian political authority roles. Hence the selection of communities to be sampled was also determined by the availability of cable television, an independent variable which was to serve as a proxy indicator of exposure to American television.

The part of the study which is relevant to this paper is a series of questions asking for the correct identification of twelve political figures, ranging from the Prime Minister to local officials. The amount of knowledge rises steadily through the grades until by the later grades, over three-quarters of the children are able to identify at least half of the politicians correctly.

Figure 4 Percentage of Students Scoring 50 Per Cent or Better on Twelve Cognitive Questions, by Grade

Score	4	5	6	7	8	9
50% or better (6/12)	20.7	35.2	56.1	63.6	81.5	90.1
N =	816	869	884	845	696	172

A corollary of the assumption of cognitive accumulation is that the intensity of cognitive attitudes and the sophistication of our political knowledge will increase over time. In this sense we can hypothesize that the certainty of our beliefs about "what is" will increase as these beliefs are reinforced with new data. The converse of this assumption, however, may also hold true in some instances. On the strength of new data it is not unusual for us to realize that what we believed to be so at one time is false. Thus a logical implication of a theory of cognitive development is that we not only accumulate new data, but that our currently held beliefs and empirical generalizations may be either reinforced or qualified on the basis of the new information. In other words, while we accumulate new cognitive attitudes all the time and while our cognitive sophistication may continue to increase, the intensity of our existing cognitive attitudes may either increase or decrease over time as well.

In terms of the objects of political socialization, it is apparent that some of the earliest cognitive attitudes involve symbols of the political community such as the flag. For instance, the percentage of children in early grades recognizing political symbols such as the flag is higher than the percentage recognizing significant authority figures such as the Prime Minister. While data are not readily available, it seems reasonable, on the basis of what has been discovered about levels of ideological and issue salience in the United States, to hypothesize that awareness of conceptual political objects is likely developed last. But cognitive development is only one side of the cumulative nature of political socialization. Besides the largely quantitative process of acquiring and modifying cognitive attitudes through the continual assimilation of new empirical data, there is a qualitative developmental process. With age and experience, we move from a predominantly cognitive and affective set of attitudes to ultimately include evaluative attitudes as well. While cognition logically must precede affection, for the simple reason that we must be aware of a political object first in order to have positive or negative feelings about it, this distinction should not be carried too far. As is pointed out below, the earliest medium or agency through which we acquire political attitudes is the family and such information about political objects is usually coloured by the affective attitudes of the parents. Thus, in the earliest stages of the process of political socialization, cognitive and affective attitudes are often inculcated virtually simultaneously.

Evaluative attitudes, however, involve the rational application of value criteria to political objects; in other words, evaluative attitudes are

actively constructed within our heads and in response to our own initia-
tives. Because the values themselves cannot be formed or assimilated
except over a fairly long period of exposure to them, and because children
only gradually acquire the analytical sophistication to apply their values
to real-world phenomena, evaluative attitudes develop at a later stage in
personal development. Figure 5 illustrates the increased ability to evaluate
by looking at children's relative rankings of Canadian authority figures in
terms of power. The table shows that as children progress through successive grades in school they become more perceptive in their evaluation of
the power of authority figures. For instance, 60 per cent of the children
in grade four rated the Queen as the most powerful of the three "head of
state" roles in our political system, and only 29 per cent perceived the
Prime Minister as the most powerful. By contrast, in grade nine, the
figures for the Queen and the Prime Minister had virtually reversed. It
might be hypothesized that the generally exaggerated perception of the
power of the monarch in the earlier grades is a reflection of the strong
affection expressed for her (see Figure 6), and that the increased tendency
in later years to perceive her as less powerful than the Prime Minister was
due at least in part to an increased ability to appreciate and to apply the
concept of power.

The overall point to be taken as a conclusion to this discussion of the
cumulative nature of political socialization is that, although the process
tends to be viewed primarily as an agent of political cultural stability over

Figure 5   Children's Evaluations of Most Powerful of Head of State
Roles (Queen, Governor General, Prime Minister), by Grade

Role perceived as most powerful	4	5	6	7	8	9
Queen	60.5%	55.6%	46.6%	42.9%	35.3%	25.4%
Governor General	10.6	12.2	11.8	11.7	11.4	15.3
Prime Minister	29.0	32.2	41.7	45.4	53.2	59.3
	100.1%*	99.9%	100.1%	100.0%	99.9%	100.0%
N =	559	590	629	557	481	118

*Some percentages vary from 100% because of rounding.

Figure 6 Children's "Favourite" of Head of State Roles, by Grade

Role liked best	4	5	6	7	8	9
Queen	74.0%	73.3%	69.3%	65.9%	59.4%	44.4%
Governor General	9.2	12.8	16.3	20.4	29.3	34.7
Prime Minister	16.8	13.9	14.4	13.7	11.3	21.0
	100.0%	100.0%	100.0%	100.0%	100.0%	100.1%
N =	596	619	655	583	505	124

time, in fact political scientists would do well to consider it as an agent of change as well. In viewing socialization as the instrument of latent pattern maintenance—as a mechanism which permits us to transmit political values and attitudes from individual to individual and from generation to generation—we neglect the even more critical adaptive role it may come to play in ensuring the persistence of the system. As Kenneth Langton points out, it facilitates both pattern maintenance and adaptation:

. . . This process may serve to preserve traditional political norms and institutions; on the other hand, when secondary socialization agencies inculcate political values different from those of the past or when children are raised with political and social expectations different from those of their forebears, the socialization process can be a vehicle of political and social change. . . .[22]

Thus, besides inculcating the norms of the society in the minds of the young, the process of political socialization may lead individuals to change their attitudes at different times in the life cycle, and it may even cause one generation to depart from the basic attitudes of the preceding one. However, in order to fully comprehend this process it is necessary to move to a detailed discussion of the vehicle or the agencies through which attitudinal conformity and change are achieved.

AGENTS OF SOCIALIZATION

The socialization of the child to the various objects in the world of politics is usually thought of as taking place, not through his direct observation, but through the teaching of intermediaries, usually referred to as agents of socialization. It is certainly not true, however, that all political learning takes place through the mediation of agents. Political objects can be, and often are, perceived directly. Watching a sitting of Parliament from the public gallery, or even walking round the grounds of Parliament Hill, can be very influential in providing the child with certain orientations towards the political process. Furthermore, direct observations gathered in this manner will often contradict the lessons from other sources; for example, the most often reported perceptions of direct observations of Parliament in session are those involving the lack of attendance of members, the inattention of those who do attend, the dullness of debate and so on. A variation of the process of socialization by direct observation comes when political events are covered directly by the media with a minimum of interpretive comment. A recent example of this was the extensive live coverage of the 1973 hearing of the U.S. Senate's Watergate Committee. Implementation of any of the current proposals for live coverage of parliamentary debates would enhance the operation of the process of political socialization by direct observation of events.

More commonly than through direct observation, however, political objects are presented to the child through intermediaries. These may be agents with whom the child has direct personal contact, such as parents, peers or teachers, or agents like writers or broadcasters who describe and interpret events to their audience. It is useful to classify agents of socialization into two broad types, private agents and public agents. Private agents of socialization are those, like parents and peers, whose contact with children is relatively close, informal and frequent. The style of these contacts is less ruled by societal norms about the form in which they are to be carried on, the types of information that may be legitimately transferred and the opinions that may be expressed. The political knowledge and attitudes which are transferred by such private agents of socialization are often byproducts of contacts which are engaged in for other purposes. Public agents of socialization, on the other hand, are those, such as the schools and the media, whose contacts with children are relatively formal, in that they are charged by society with the responsibility for teaching a particular set of societally approved civic facts, or who are expected to provide such information as a stage-setting for reportage of the news of the day.

By making such a distinction between public and private agents of political socialization, we do not wish to imply that the private agents present children with a slanted, subjective set of personal opinions, whereas public agents provide only the objective facts. Each do both, to varying degrees. Private agents, especially parents, will often see their roles as providing clear, understandable, societally approved descriptions of the operations of institutions and roles in the political system. They also, through the normal expression of political attitudes and opinions in the course of daily conversation with each other and with their children, guide, consciously or unconsciously, the child's affections and evaluations in a direction conforming with their own attitudes. The teaching role of the parents is usually more consciously undertaken than the transference of personal attitudes, but both phenomena occur in the home setting. Peers, as a rule, are much less concerned with teaching as a conscious effort.

Public agents of socialization operate under a societally imposed norm of objectivity, under which it is considered wrong for a teacher in the school context to express partisan opinions to a class. Similarly, school teachers may exhort their audiences to take an interest in things political, to believe in their country or region, to vote and participate in politics, but may not urge them to be apathetic about politics, to support their country's destruction or to believe in ideologies like fascism or communism, considered foreign to our society's interests. In the case of the media, one of the tenets of the "journalist's code" is that the facts should be reported as objectively as possible, with personal opinions reserved for the editorials or other clearly labelled commentaries. However, it is well recognized by those in the media that strict impartiality is more often an ideal than an actual state of affairs; reporters' biases are always present in their work and are sometimes even consciously expressed.

Let us examine some of the evidence about the operations of the agents of socialization, private and public, in the Canadian setting, starting with the family. Many writers have expressed the judgment that the family is the most important agent of socialization.[23] Political scientists, evaluating research from both developed and developing countries, seem remarkably united in this conclusion. In the developed countries basic principles instilled by the family are seen to underlie acceptance of regime legitimacy,[24] whereas in the developing countries the adherence of the family to traditional attitudes is seen as hindering the political, economic and social modernization of the state.[25] Whether the family is regarded as a positive force for system support, or a negative force obstructing the establishment of a modern political system, the power of the family to mould its children in its image has impressed political scientists.

While the question of early establishment in children of attitudes of support (or non-support) for the political community and regime has been of great importance in persuading students of political socialization of the central role of the family as an agent, American writers in particular point as well to the early learning of political partisanship. Identification with a particular political party seems to be learned by most American children by the time they are ten years old.[26] During the first decade of life, of course, the family is the most prominent agent of socialization for the child; if a party preference is learned at this point it is nearly always that of the parents.[27]

Such Canadian evidence as exists, however, places the learning of party identification, indeed of all political perceptions and cognitions, at a later place in life. Canadian children, it has been suggested, are likely to be older than American children when they develop a preference for a party, and consequently such a preference is less likely to be the party preference of the parents.[28] Figure 7 presents the most comprehensive evidence we have to date on children's partisan perceptions in Canada. Tabulated from the study by Carroll, Higgins and Whittington referred to earlier, it presents from all regions of Canada the percentage of children who chose a party in answer to the question, "Which political party do you like the most? Don't know; Liberals; Democrats; Progressive Conservatives; New Democratic Party; Republicans; Social Credit."[29]

Some extremely interesting regional variations in Figure 7 suggest that political partisanship is learned earlier in the Maritimes and Quebec than in other regions of Canada. The results in Trois Rivières and Halifax show substantially higher proportions in the early grades showing a willingness to pick a party that they like the most. In addition, the results in these two cities are relatively free from a phenomenon noted in several other cities, where a fairly high proportion of the younger children, when they did choose a party, chose an American party, particularly the Democrats. In Peterborough, for example, 10.5 per cent of the grade four public school sample and 12.5 per cent of the grade four separate school sample chose the Democrats or Republicans as the party they liked best. In Ottawa, 12.8 per cent of the grade four sample did likewise, and in St. Boniface, 7 per cent of the grade four sample chose an American party.

In many parts of Canada, then, the development of party identification seems to parallel the development of political knowledge in children, building gradually through the child's second decade of life to what by American standards are still rather moderate final levels. This pattern suggests that the other private agent of socialization, the peer group, may be relatively important in Canada. At the ages where politically relevant knowledge and attitudes are being developed in Canada, the child's reference groups are shifting from those within the family to those external to the family, such as friends and groups of cohorts. If the child enters his teens with no firm party loyalty derived from parental socialization, he is more easily influenced by his friends' political partisanship. He is then more likely to end up generating a party loyalty inconsistent with that of his parents, although that attitude may be of relatively low intensity and might therefore be easily switched to some other party.[30]

Turning to the more formal public agents of socialization, the school has often been regarded as an important place for the establishment of

Figure 7   Children Having a Party Preference, by Grade, in Eight Canadian Communities

% Having party preference	4	5	6	7	8	N
Ottawa-Carleton	34.0	40.9	58.6	59.0	59.6	1,163
Ottawa	49.1	42.2	42.9	42.9	53.7	289
Peterborough, Ont. Public	18.4	23.4	34.5	38.2	48.9	395
Peterborough, Ont. Separate	34.3	12.5	16.0	36.4	54.8	126
Lethbridge, Alta.	15.4	25.0	29.9	33.3	33.7	520
Trois Rivières, Que.	40.3	51.7	54.8	48.0	x	232
St. Boniface, Man.	28.1	32.5	44.7	29.8	57.5	419
Port Alberni, B.C.	18.1	30.7	44.6	40.8	x	274
Halifax, N.S.	47.9	56.8	67.8	77.3	80.9	512

x Grades not present in schools studies

the general political norms of a society, as well as for the generation of support for the political system. Formal teaching about a country's history certainly does perform a function of generating pride in and support for the country and its political institutions. There is, however, little conclusive evidence that the teaching of so-called civics courses has much influence in politicizing students or even in providing information that could not otherwise have been obtained. American studies have been particularly discouraging in this regard,[31] although writers on developing countries have been much more hopeful about the effects of the formal education system for producing support for modernizing institutions and for political change in general.[32] In Canada, an influential study by A. B. Hodgetts in the mid 1960s produced a strong indictment of the contribution of Canadian high school history and civics courses to fostering an understanding in Canadian students of the real nature of Canadian society and its problems.[33] Hodgetts concludes:

Most of what is now being done in the Canadian studies classroom must be scrapped and replaced with new instruction materials and practices that by their very nature, indirectly, without any predetermined conclusions, will allow the students to discover a real and vital Canada for themselves. Only in this way can the present deep chasm between promise and achievement in civic education be bridged.[34]

Although some innovations in teaching civics courses have taken place in Canadian schools there is little reason to believe the situation has changed markedly since that time.

The content of the school curriculum, however, is but one aspect of the impact of the school as a socializing agent. The classroom format places the child firmly in the position of being the learner and places the teacher, towards whom all eyes are directed, in the position of being a potentially influential figure. The very formality spoken of earlier enhances the importance, and establishes the legitimacy, of whatever is being taught, or whatever opinions are expressed by the teacher or by other school officials.

However, the relationship of the teacher to the student in the school may in some cases transcend the formality implicit in the educational system, and the teacher may in fact come to play the sort of socializing role which is more common to the private agents. As a friend, parent-substitute and authority figure as well as a public agent of socialization, the influence of the teacher in some circumstances, and at varying stages in the personal development of the child, can be profound. But the influence of the educational system on the development of political attitudes in children may also go beyond the personal impact of a teacher. The very structure of the school as an organization and the conduct of the classroom may reflect a very real and distinctive pattern of authority. The basic attitudes towards authority which are learned by the child through observation and personal experience at school may have an impact on the attitudes he develops towards political authority.

The second public agent of political socialization is the media. As mentioned before, the media in some cases function as simple conductors of information. In this sense they are not agents of political socialization but merely tools which enhance the scope and range of our perceptual organs. However, the media do function as agents of socialization through individuals who interpret, comment upon and edit the coverage of political events in newspapers and on radio and television. In this way our perceptions of political objects are affected not only through conscious editorializing by media personalities but also through the preferences and biases which unconsciously creep in to colour allegedly objective reporting.

While most academic discourse goes no further than to discuss the four agents—family, peers, school and media—it must be recognized that there are many minor agencies through which we can acquire political attitudes. Of these minor agents one that bears brief mention is the organizations and associations with which an individual becomes affiliated. In our early years clubs such as the Boy Scouts, Girl Guides and church organizations can all play a significant role in teaching the values of public service, community involvement and good citizenship. They consciously instruct young people to be loyal, law abiding, respectful of others, all of which are values which if effectively inculcated can have an effect on our political behaviour as adults. In a similar vein, as we mature we tend to expand our organizational commitments. Membership in an organization puts us in an institutional framework where not only are we exposed to the ideas of our peers, but also we begin to internalize the norms of the organization itself.

Obviously, the biggest impact of the organizational agents on the development of political attitudes will be upon the incumbents of roles within specifically political clubs or associations; institutions, political parties, interest groups and even governmental institutions can have a big impact on their members. Besides the influence of group norms and informal standards of behaviour on newcomers to the groups, most such organizations imply a complex set of operational norms with which the members must comply. Two studies of this phenomenon of post-incumbency socialization are included in this volume. However, given that the habitat of man becomes more and more an organizational one,[35] the influence of organizations of all types on the process of socialization can only increase. As students of the process, it is incumbent upon us to consider more carefully organizational agents as interpreters and conductors of images of political objects.

POLITICAL CULTURE AND NATIONAL IDENTITY

The media, as well as formal civics teaching in the school, appear to be the primary agents for transferring to young people a feeling of their political history and the common feelings and symbols which bind them to others within the same culture. They create a national pride, a belief in the country that forms a basic attachment upon which the more specific attitudinal components of political culture can be built.

It is, of course, just such a basic set of beliefs which many observers have found to be lacking in Canada. Differences in the focal points of loyalties (to locality, province, region, county, not to mention the governments of these units) have been apparent to many researchers. The papers by Forbes and Ullman in this volume provide dramatic illustrations of these differences. There is no clear consensus among Canadian social scientists about whether Canada has one, two, five or ten political cultures. The Bilingualism and Biculturalism Commission, as well as several French-Canadian writers, favour the two nations view. Others divide Canada into the standard five regions of British Columbia, the Prairies, Ontario, Quebec and the Atlantic provinces.[36] Still others maintain that we should consider Canada as having ten political cultures, corresponding to the provincial boundaries.[37] Whatever the divisions, they are deep enough to warrant the conclusion that there is no single Canadian political culture.

One conception of the state of national commonality of feelings in Canada is that those which do exist are centred around Canada's relations with other countries, particularly countries like the United States, which are perceived in some undefined way as threats. A feeling of being unjustly exploited or encroached upon will often bring a temporary closeness which lasts until the threat subsides. Perhaps the most recent instance of the phenomenon has been the expression of feelings of economic nationalism (though how widespread these feelings are is debatable) caused by a perceived threat from foreign ownership and thus control of many of Canada's industries. In more quiescent times, however, Canadians often do not feel a great deal of kinship with their fellow countrymen.

Canada, in this formulation, may be seen as an underdeveloped nation in terms of its political culture. The private part of the socialization process produces Canadians who often feel little in common with other Canadians, who have loyalties to provinces or regions which take precedence over their loyalties to the nation, and who support provincial governments in their efforts to reserve more policy clout for the province. While we would resist the charge that we are centralizers or federalists, it does seem likely that too extensive control of resources by the provincial governments runs the risk of perpetuating economic inequalities between regions and citizens, and of so weakening the hand of the federal government that when action becomes necessary in a crisis that government will be unequal to the task. If national symbols, national myths and various concrete realizations of the connections between Canadians are to be created and disseminated, we will probably have to depend on the public agents of socialization to do so.

There are a number of common myths that are emphasized by the media and school systems in their efforts to create this national feeling. The trouble with Canada's myths is that, even if they are widely cited and publicized, they seem related to particular regions and not to the country at large. The myth (and bear in mind that our use of the term myth here bears no necessary relation to the degree of actual truth involved) of the colourfulness of our early politicians centres largely around Sir John A. Macdonald, an Upper Canadian to the core. The myth of the frontier and its peaceful conquest, with the emphasis on the role of the RCMP and the building of the CPR, relates mainly to the West, though as with all frontier myths many can identify with it vicariously. The myth of the development of Quebec from folk to industrialized society strikes few common chords in Canadians from other parts of the country. However, even if personal identification with myths keyed to other regions is difficult for many Canadians, a realization of their existence provides a unifying force. The media play an important role not only in propagating and reinforcing the regional myths but also in creating "national" events. This is particularly so in the case of sports events; it is no exaggeration to say that the Saturday and Wednesday night hockey games of the Canadiens, Maple Leafs and Canucks, the Wednesday night baseball games of the Expos and the Grey Cup game, are important cultural events for Canadians. They bring us together in common experience and reactions as few events do.

Equally as important as the media in creating a shared past are the actual attempts to physically reconstruct it. Creations such as Upper Canada Village and restored forts like Louisbourg give Canadians a chance to actually visit and experience a shared awareness of the past. The symbolic importance of national institutions and the buildings housing them, political monuments as they are sometimes called, is also hard to overstate.[38] The efforts to create in Ottawa a genuine national capital with imposing institutions like the National Library, National Museum and the soon-to-be-built National Gallery are vital to the creation, in Canadians and particularly in children, of a sense of national identity upon which a genuinely national political culture could be erected.

The function of this introduction has been to draw in the boundaries of what is still an ill-defined sub-discipline of political science and to point to some of the problems and obstacles which face its practitioners. We have attempted to place the process of political socialization within the context of the study of the political process and of socialization in general. We have also attempted to give political socialization a Canadian domicile. The success or failure of these ambitious endeavours ultimately will depend upon the willingness of more imaginative and industrious colleagues in many disciplines to get down to the business of conducting the research which will overcome the obstacles and problems we have tried to identify.

NOTES

1. In fact definitions of political culture appear to be of two major types. There are those who prefer to define political culture *structurally*; that is they view it in terms of the phenomena such as attitudes, orientations, beliefs, emotions, images, etc., of which it is composed. Then there are those who prefer to define political culture *functionally* or instrumentally; that is, they define it in terms of the effect it has on political behaviour. While most would agree that it is not a *behavioural* category, but rather a *determinant* of behaviour, some, such as Robert Presthus, define it as both attitudinal and behavioural: "Political culture consists of [among other, predominantly attitudinal things] . . . the extent to which they [citizens] participate in political affairs . . ." (*Elite Accommodation in Canadian Politics* [Toronto: Macmillan, 1973], p. 20). While we agree that the attitudes towards participation are important components of political culture, we will stick to the more traditional view that separates the causative agents such as attitudes from the actual behaviour.

2. Howard Scarrow, *Comparative Political Analysis* (New York: Harper, 1969), p. 35.

3. "The political culture approach enhances our ability to describe and analyse the interactions between the political system and its culture. By distinguishing between behaviour and attitudes, we are able to explicate differences in performance across political systems and structures in terms of the culture . . ." (Dennis Kavanagh, *Political Culture* [London: Macmillan, 1972], p. 13).

4. A cursory glance at the multitudinous literature in political science and social psychology reveals that there is a lack of any clear consensus about the meaning of such terms. While it is commoner in social psychology to view the term *attitude* as referring to a specific type of in-the-mind phenomenon, the literature dealing with political socialization specifically seems to view the term as a generic one that includes values, emotions, cognitions, beliefs, images, etc. For our purposes it would appear to be simpler to view *attitude* and *orientation* as synonymous and to refer to all other in-the-mind phenomena as categories of attitudes or orientations. Thus, attitudes are to be distinguished simply as "of the mind" rather than behavioural, and as internal to an individual rather than external or environmental. We do, however, intend to maintain the use of the term *values* as a distinct concept, referring to the important moral and ethical qualities of the individual.

5. Robert A. LeVine, *Culture, Behaviour and Personality* (Chicago: Aldine, 1973), pp. 61–68. This section owes much to LeVine's account.

6. Erik Erikson, *Childhood and Society* (New York: Norton, 1950 and 1963). See also Lawrence Kohlberg, "Stage and Sequence: The Cognitive-Developmental Approach to Socialization" in D. Goslin, ed., *Handbook of Socialization Theory and Research* (Chicago: Rand McNally, 1969). See also Lawrence Kohlberg and Carol Gilligan, "The Adolescent as a Philosopher" in J. Kogan and R. Coles, eds., *Twelve to Sixteen: Early Adolescence* (New York: Norton, 1972).

7. For the most comprehensive review of the psychologists' conceptions of socialization, see Edward Zigler and Irwin I. Child, "Socialization" in Gardner Lindzey and Elliot Aronson, eds., *The Handbook of Social Psychology* (Reading, Mass.: Addison Wesley, 1969), vol. 3, pp. 450–589.

8. Talcott Parsons, *The Social System* (New York: Free Press, 1964), p. 205.

9. See Philip Converse, "The Nature of Belief Systems in Mass Publics" in David Apter, ed., *Ideology and Discontent* (New York: Free Press, 1964).

10. See Dean Jaros, Herbert Hirsch and Frederic J. Fleron, Jr., "The Malevolent Leader: Political Socialization in an American Sub-Culture," *American Political Science Association*, vol. 62, no. 2 (June 1968), pp. 564–72; Herbert Hirsch, *Poverty and Politicization* (New York: Free Press, 1971); and Edward S. Greenberg, "Children and the Political Community: A Comparison Across Racial Lines," *Canadian Journal of Political Science*, vol. 2, no. 4 (December 1969), pp. 471–92.

11. M. Brewster Smith, Jerome S. Bruner and Robert W. White, *Opinions and Personality* (New York: Wiley, 1956, 1964). See also Daniel Katz, "The Functional Approach to the Study of Attitudes," *Public Opinion Quarterly*, vol. 24 (1960), pp. 163–204.

12. See Harold Laswell, *Psychopathology and Politics* (Chicago: Chicago Press, 1934); T. W. Adorno, Else Frenkel-Brunswick, Daniel J. Levinson and R. Nevitt Sanford, *The Authoritarian Personality* (New York: Wiley, 1950, 1964); Robert E. Lane, *Political Ideology* (Glencoe: Free Press, 1962), and *Political Thinking and Consciousness* (Chicago: Markham, 1969).

13. Dwaine Marvick and Charles Nixon, "Recruitment Contrasts in Rival Campaign Groups" in Dwaine Marvick, ed., *Political Decision-Makers* (Glencoe: Free Press, 1961).

14. Gabriel Almond and Sidney Verba, *The Civic Culture* (Princeton: Princeton University Press, 1963).

15. David Easton and Jack Dennis, "The Child's Acquisition of Regime Norms: Political Efficacy," *American Political Science Review*, vol. 61 (March 1967), pp. 25–38.

16. M. Brewster Smith, "Competence and Socialization" in John A. Clausen, ed., *Socialization and Society* (New York: Little, Brown, 1968), pp. 270–320. In the Clausen volume, see also Alex Inkeles, "Society, Social Structure and Child Socialization," pp. 73–129. See also Robert W. White, "Motivation Reconsidered: The Concept of Competence," *Psychological Review*, vol. 66, pp. 296–333.

17. T. Gladwin, "Social Competence and Clinical Practice," *Psychiatry*, vol. 30, p. 32.

18. Smith, "Competence and Socialization"; this article may also be found in M. B. Smith, *Social Psychology and Human Values* (Chicago: Aldine, 1969).

19. In the purest sense, cognition is simply objectively acquired information about the real world. However, because what we perceive in the real world is always coloured by our values, by what we already believe to be so and by the imperfect nature of our perceptual organs, cognitive attitudes are always in fact our *beliefs* about what is and is not.

20. See Milton Rokeach, *The Nature of Human Values* (New York: Free Press, 1973), chapter 1.

21. See David Easton and Jack Dennis, *Children in the Political System* (New York: McGraw-Hill, 1969), p. 58; David Easton, *A Systems Analysis of Political Life* (New York: John Wiley, 1965), pp. 171–219.

22. Kenneth P. Langton, *Political Socialization* (New York: Oxford University Press, 1969), p. 5.

23. Most of the literature in the field of political socialization bears on this question. Some examples are Fred Greenstein, *Children and Politics* (New Haven: Yale University Press, 1965); M. Kent Jennings and Richard G. Niemi, "The Transmission of Political Values from Parent to Child," *American Political Science Review*, vol. 62 (March 1968), pp. 169–84; Richard E.

Dawson and Kenneth Prewitt, *Political Socialization* (Boston: Little, Brown, 1969), pp. 107–26.

24. Almond and Verba, *The Civic Culture*.

25. Gabriel Almond and James S. Coleman, *The Politics of Developing Areas* (Princeton: Princeton University Press, 1960).

26. See Fred Greenstein, *Children and Politics*; David Easton and Jack Dennis, *Children in the Political System*; Robert Hess and Judith Torney, *The Development of Political Attitudes in Children* (Chicago: Aldine, 1967); Angus Campbell, Philip E. Converse, Warren E. Miller, Donald E. Stokes, *The American Voter* (New York: John Wiley, 1960). The stability of these early identifications to party is questioned by Pauline Vaillancourt, "Stability of Children's Survey Responses," *Public Opinion Quarterly* (Fall 1973), pp. 373–87.

27. For an interesting account of what happens when the parents differ, see M. Kent Jennings and Kenneth Langton, "Mothers versus Fathers: The Formation of Political Orientation Among Young Americans," *Journal of Politics* (March 1969), pp. 329–58.

28. Jon H. Pammett, "The Development of Political Orientations in Canadian School Children," *Canadian Journal of Political Science,* vol. 4, no. 1 (March 1971), pp. 132–141.

29. In Quebec, the alternative answers "Parti Québécois, Union Nationale, and Créditiste" were also included.

30. For an account of the instability of party identification in Canadian adults, see Jane Jenson, Harold Clarke, Lawrence Le Duc and Jon Pammett, "Patterns of Partisanship in Canada," paper presented to American Political Science Association meetings, San Francisco, 1975.

31. Two American studies that draw such negative conclusions are Edgar Litt, "Civic Education Norms and Political Indoctrination," *American Sociological Review* (Feb. 1963), pp. 69–75; and Kenneth Langton and Kent Jennings, "Political Socialization and the High School Civics Curriculum in the United States," *American Political Science Review* (Sept. 1968), pp. 852–67.

32. See the articles in James S. Coleman, ed., *Education and Political Development* (Princeton: Princeton University Press, 1965).

33. A. B. Hodgetts, *What Culture? What Heritage?* (Toronto: Ontario Institute for Studies in Education, 1968). A small but somewhat more hopeful study is reported in Mary Stager and Edward Sullivan, "Conceptions of Canada in Secondary School: An Exploratory Study," *Canadian Journal of History and Social Science,* vol. 6, no. 2 (1970), pp. 21–33.

34. Hodgetts, *What Culture?* p. 87.

35. See especially, Robert Presthus, *The Organizational Society* (New York: Random House, 1962).

36. Mildred A. Schwartz, *Politics and Territory* (Montreal: McGill-Queen's University Press, 1974). See also Richard Simeon and David Elkins, "Regional Political Cultures in Canada," *Canadian Journal of Political Science* (Sept. 1974), pp. 397–437.

37. John Wilson, "The Canadian Political Cultures: Towards a Redefinition of the Nature of the Canadian Political System," *Canadian Journal of Political Science* (Sept. 1974), pp. 438–83.

38. Karl de Schweinitz, Jr., "Growth, Development and Political Monuments" in Muzafer Sherif and Carolyn W. Sherif, eds., *Indisciplinary Relationships in the Social Sciences* (Chicago: Aldine, 1969), pp. 209–26.

PART ONE

Some Critiques of Current Approaches to Political Socialization

Mass Values and System Outputs:

2

A Critique of an Assumption of

Socialization Theory

JOHN SHIRY

Political socialization research . . . begs an important assumption . . . that the values, beliefs and attitudes about politics and political institutions held by the mass population make a difference.

Joseph LaPalombara

INTRODUCTION

It will be my purpose in this paper to step back a distance and ask some simple questions on the topic of political socialization. I propose to look first at the dominant models of political socialization that have come to us from American political science and, secondly, to offer some suggestions on how we might adapt those models to the study of politics in Canada. The analysis is motivated by a basic question: what is it that we are trying to show, and within that framework have we made a defensible and profitable set of assumptions about the nature of politics?

Put briefly, my concern is this: while we have given considerable attention to independent variables, we have done little critical analysis of the dependent variables we have selected. That is to say, we have probed deeply to find the individual and structural factors which appear to explain the existence of a wide range of political orientations, but we have not asked the prior question: whose and which kind of political orientations are important to the operation of the political system, both in the day-to-day matter of determining social policy (what Easton has termed political allocations) and in the longer-term business of the stability, change, and adaptation of the system in a changing environment (the problem Easton called systems persistence).

To preview my argument I shall point out that socialization theorists almost uniformly adopt an allocative theory which assumes, first, that the average man is goal-directed in his political behaviour and, secondly, that his behaviour is a significant factor in the allocative process. I shall label this the "citizen input" assumption. But this view has been discredited by much of the work that has probed adult political behaviour and the theories of the allocation process (and the empirical studies aimed at validating those theories) as well as a long tradition of political and social theory. In place of the citizen input assumption, the literature offers a picture of allocative politics as elite behaviour, relegating the average man to the role of apathetic bystander or powerless constituent. I shall label this the "elitist" assumption. In a following section I shall point out how adopting the elitist outlook would affect socialization theory, with particular reference to socialization to a set of values.

WHAT DO PEOPLE LEARN OR DO THAT IS OF "POLITICAL" IMPORTANCE?: A REVIEW OF SOME SOCIALIZATION LITERATURE

Most students of socialization have selected as a dependent variable some orientation which is assumed to be a significant explanatory factor in the political process. Little effort has gone into investigating how the citizen operationalizes what he has learned or the political consequences which his behaviour might have. The pioneers in the field gave no attention to the selection of dependent variables.

Herbert Hyman's landmark effort is the starting point for the theoretical development of political socialization. His book entitled *Political Socialization* drew together earlier research on voting and national character into a socialization framework. The goals of these earlier research projects had determined the dependent variables: participation, political orientation, and political character. To the extent that he exhibits a theory of politics, Hyman worked within an unsophisticated citizen input framework. He assumed, as did the students of national character, that the masses bear the responsibility for the decay or vitality of their political institutions, and he specifically portrays electoral politics as goal-oriented action. His position is, at the very least, that government policies are related to whether citizens take an active interest in politics and to which party wins office. Hyman can be excused for not presenting a careful defence of the dependent variables since he really had no say in their selection. Later authors who did have this latitude persisted in merely selecting dependent variables which had some assumed, though not demonstrated, significance.

In one of the first projects designed specifically as a study of political socialization, Fred Greenstein indicated that he was guided by a series of basic questions. Among these were:

What is the nature of political awareness and involvement during these years [age 9–13]? What do children learn about politics? . . . Of what relevance is political development during this period for the individual's later political participation and, more generally, for the political system?

He condenses this to the simple statement: "(1) Who (2) learns what (3) from whom (4) under what circumstances (5) with what effects," and offers his own conception of how the content of the socialization process could be classified. From the basic mass-elite dichotomy he derives:

. . . learning connected with the citizen role (partisan attachment, ideology, motivation to participate), learning connected with the subject role (national loyalty, conceptions of the legitimacy of roles and institutions), and learning connected with the recruitment to and performance of specialized political roles.[1]

It follows that these categories reflect (1) socialization of the mass into its role in allocative politics, (2) mass socialization to system politics, and (3) elite socialization to both allocative and system political behaviour. Though he links the generally benevolent response to political authority to system stability, thus implying a concern with systems persistence, Greenstein makes repeated references to the citizen role which indicate that it is related to allocative politics. For example, he refers to the learning of the citizen role and party identification as antecedents of adult political behaviour, asserting that socialization tends to perpetuate the existing social cleavages and that electoral politics is the primary method for expressing these differences. I conclude that Greenstein considers voting and public attitudes on issues to be a significant factor determining policy, and therefore that he, too, has a citizen input view of politics.

A few more illustrations will complete the discussion. Hess and Torney point out:

The franchise is a central feature of a democratic government, and the preparation of children to exercise this right as adults is one of the key elements of the socializing process. In the relationship between a citizen and his government, the right to vote is the power to effects change and to exert control.[2]

In a brief reference to allocative politics, Easton and Dennis cite "ideological positions, policy preferences on issues and [partisan] . . . conflict" as relevant citizen orientations. Finally, in an imaginative effort to incorporate Piaget's child development theories into socialization research, Richard Merelman points to the learning of an ideology as an important phenomenon. He makes it clear that in his view the direction of politics is intimately tied to the extent to which mass publics develop and implement an ideology.

The essential features of the theory of political allocations implicit in socialization research as it has been undertaken in North America are portrayed in Figure 1.

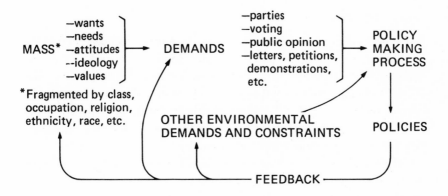

Figure 1   Simplified Version of the Citizen Input Model

This research examines socialization in reference to political attitudes, ideology, party attachment, class, ethnic or religious identity, the inclination to become politically active, and so on.

Some of these orientations may be important social phenomena; however, until they have been shown to be related to political allocations, we would be wise not to assume so. My own inclination is to view them as different ways in which the citizen adapts to the political and social life of his society. In this manner these orientations contribute to the integration of the system.

A basic problem with the citizen input model is the high operational complexity it attributes to adult behaviour. It assumes that the citizen can and does express sophisticated political preferences, and that these choices are a major factor in the political policy-making process. Voting, I shall contend, is primarily a systems persistence type of behaviour and is not part of the allocation process. To date, most political socialization theory has chosen not to specify the significance of the dependent variables; instead it has been concerned with independent variables. Its emphasis has been on explaining how the socialization process works rather than on examining the political consequences of the orientations which are taken as the end product of the socialization process. I shall turn now to consider this issue by noting some findings of research which was designed to discover the factors which appear to cause particular policy outcomes.

THE VIEW OF THE CITIZEN
IN RECENT POLITICAL RESEARCH

In the last section we looked at the implied theory of politics found in the literature on political socialization; the citizen is viewed as making demands of the state chiefly through the electoral system. The assumption is that different levels of political participation, different electoral outcomes, and, in general, the representation of conflicting viewpoints and interests among citizens have major consequences for what the state does. A large body of research casts this assumption into doubt. This work, based on a citizen input model of politics demands that we re-examine many other fields of political research.

John Wahlke has drawn together a wide range of research on adult political behaviour that demonstrates the impotence of institutionalized modes of political expression. He examines the role of the citizen in a number of what he terms demand-input models of representation. "It is . . . not surprising . . . that theorists and researchers alike have for so long taken it for granted that the problem of representative government centers on the linkage between citizens' policy preferences and the public-policy decision of representative bodies."[3]

He outlines three different models of representative government, and in each case the supposed role of the citizen as a participant in policy determination is refuted by research in the areas of public opinion and mass electoral behaviour. It would serve little purpose for me to repeat here the evidence Wahlke reports,[4] and at any rate most of it is known to students of political behaviour. Furthermore, Converse and others long ago discredited the view of the citizen as an active and informed participant in the political process, yet the contrary assumption still underlies much political research, particularly that on political socialization.[5]

Less well known to students of political behaviour is the research which sought to find which political and socio-economic factors were most useful in predicting the policy outputs of American state systems. The most comprehensive work is by Thomas Dye, who measured the policy impact of such political factors as level of party competition, level of voter turnout, degree of malapportionment, and party in office.[6] In all cases these factors were *not* predictive of the levels of expenditure across a wide range of policy areas.

Wahlke summarizes this literature:

. . . the policy-environment correlation studies imply that stimuli which have been thought to be policy demands are really just automatically determined links in a chain of reactions from environment to policy output, a chain in which neither policy demands, policy expectations, or any other kind of policy orientation plays any significant role. There is no room, in other words, for any . . . policy-related behaviours and attitudes of citizens . . . to enter into the policy process.[7]

His conclusion is to redirect attention away from politics as an allocative activity and instead to emphasize the integrative functions served by mass political behaviour. For this he sees the Eastonian concept of "support" as a promising place to begin, and he offers some suggestions.

A similar view has been put forth by Professor Edelman. He sees the basically integrative nature of mass behaviour:

Political analysis must, then, proceed on two levels simultaneously. It must examine how political actions get some groups the tangible things they want from government and at the same time it must explore what these same actions mean to the mass public and how it is placated or aroused by them. . . . For the spectators of the political scene every act contributes to a pattern of ongoing events that spells threat or reassurance. This is the basic dichotomy for the mass public.[8]

On the latter point he concludes that many of our conventional notions about politics comprise what people want to believe about politics. "Clearly, beliefs like these serve functions other than the description of a country's political institutions. They help hold men together and help maintain an orderly state."[9] Once again we are led to reject any model of socialization which sets out to explain how people come to learn the attitudes and skills employed in determining policy, since most people do not play such a role. Edelman's view would tend to reject using party attachment, inclination to participate in electoral politics, and policy attitudes as important dependent variables for studying the political socialization of the masses within a framework which intends to explain political allocations.

Another writer, reflecting on the theoretical significance of the literature on comparative state outputs, declares:

The profound implications for political scientists of the pioneering study by Dawson and Robinson have not altogether been realized. What they showed, and what Hofferbert, Dye, and others have subsequently confirmed and elaborated, is that the principal variables with which we have traditionally been concerned, e.g., demand patterns reflected in party competition, do not "explain" variations in the authoritative outputs of a polity. . . . No doubt the political system constitutes a kind of "black box" through which system resources are processed in order to result in policy decisions, but the implications of these studies is that, except for its own sake, analysis of the black box will yield little of interest respecting outputs or policies.

This, I submit, is a devastating set of findings and cannot be dismissed as not meaning what it plainly says—that analysis of political systems will not explain policy decisions made by those systems.[10]

He might well have added that the findings require us to reassess many other areas of political research in the light of our revised conception of the policy-making process.

In this section I have noted a number of adult orientations which socialization theory assumes are important modes of policy expression by the citizen in a democratic society. I have also cited a growing body of research which questions this assumption. Citizen attitudes, and the structures through which they are expressed, either do not have the influence on policy outcomes which they are thought to have, or they have an impact which is independent of any political intentions by the public expressing them. Thus, party attachment, participation in elections, and membership in politically relevant groups cannot be taken as indicators of involvement in the political allocation process. Their use as dependent variables in the study of political socialization, with the aim of explaining a system's policy performance, must be reassessed.

To this point my attention has focused almost exclusively on American literature, and until parallel study turns up similar findings in Canada, it would be precarious to assume that the same situation exists in Canada. It would also be foolish to ignore these American findings. Political scientists have examined the operation of the American political system far beyond the scope attained in Canada. Their findings are in the process of forcing major revisions in the models used to investigate political phenomena. It is no virtue to adhere to the dominant models until we have proved them deficient, and there is much wisdom in applying a range of theoretical options in a time of rapid change.

However, my point is not to determine to what degree the mass of people in Canada have significant opportunities for exerting political power. Let us suspend that judgment; but let us also adopt as an hypothesis the pessimistic view of this section as an accurate reflection of reality. This is conceptually no different from assuming the opposite (as the political socialization literature has tended to do), and it has somewhat more support in the state policy-making literature. The adoption of this elitist perspective requires that we challenge the conventional notions about social values and political articulation in Canada. It is to that task that the remainder of this paper is dedicated. In the following section I shall offer a critique of the literature on Canadian values, suggesting that more attention should be paid to structural factors. Since values are taken to be one of the important outcomes of the socialization process, the argument requires a different type of socialization research from that which we are accustomed to undertaking.

Figure 2 outlines the view of politics which I have adopted in making the argument of the next section. I hope that it does no injustice to assert that it is the model of the allocation process implied in the literature I have cited in this section.

Figure 2   Simplified Version of "Elitist" Model of Politics

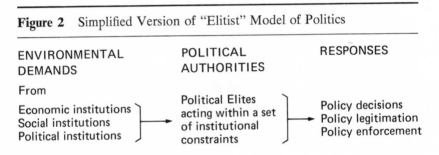

ENVIRONMENTAL DEMANDS

POLITICAL AUTHORITIES

RESPONSES

From
Economic institutions
Social institutions
Political institutions

Political Elites acting within a set of institutional constraints

Policy decisions
Policy legitimation
Policy enforcement

Implicit in this alternative view is the assumption that only institutions or institutional changes are viable sources of political demands. Many of the responses of the authorities can be thought of not as decisions but rather as the legitimation and enforcement of choices since the role of the authorities is one of overseeing the operation and change of the system.[11] I would argue that, most often, this is a more profitable way to conceptualize the political process. The political system is society's main social control mechanism. It does not assert that this should be so or that this is a good thing; it asserts only that for political analysis it is a model that is just as valid as the citizen input model and that for many problems it may be substantially more profitable.

Easton argues that an allocative theory of politics is premature. I agree with him on that point. But what we know about the allocation process, as evidenced by the two models presented above, permits us to say some important things about socialization research. Clearly it is an error to ascribe an active role in policy determination to the public.

Citizens are bystanders who are only rarely aroused. But if human actors are to be assigned a part in the allocation process, then it is a relatively small elite who have such a role. If socialization research can contribute to our understanding of the allocative process, then it should explain how these elite actors come to behave the way they do: how they perceive the environment within which they have to operate, the options open to them, the relative importance of demands from different sources, and the personal and system costs inherent in different courses of action.

The mass can be conceived to play a role in this process only if we assume that it possesses a set of values within which the elite feels it must operate. Social values, then, set the general direction and limits on elite behaviour to the extent that they accept those boundaries.

CANADIAN SOCIAL VALUES:
IMPLICATIONS FOR SOCIALIZATION RESEARCH

Up to this point I have outlined two broad political problems which might motivate our interest in political socialization: the process of deciding political allocations and of systems persistence. Within an allocative theory of politics I have suggested that the existing political socialization literature incorporates a citizen input model to explain the allocative process. Subsequently, I showed that there is a significant body of research about adult political behaviour (and more broadly the correlates of policy) which suggests that an alternate model might be a more defensible way of conceptualizing the policy-making process. I have designated this an elitist model, and at the end of the last section I indicated the role which the values of the masses might play in deciding political policy.

If we are interested in explaining the performance of the Canadian political system through socialization research within this elitist model, then we must examine the socialization of elite actors to whatever patterns of behaviour they exhibit which are shown to have policy consequences. We must also analyse the process by which the masses come to hold a set of values which act as a constraint on those elite actors, if indeed such is the case. In the remainder of this paper I want to consider just how good a starting point the literature on Canadian values provides for that undertaking.

One problem for the student of politics is the tendency to rely on economic values and behaviour, leaving unproved the case that these same values find their logical counterpart in political values and political behaviour. The classic work on Canadian values is by S. D. Clark, and most other writers have followed his lead though they have abandoned his method. Professor Clark sees Canadian values as resulting from differing structural features (primarily economic conditions) in different places at different times. In this respect the main thrust of his argument is that a given set of institutional constraints permits and encourages a distinctive range of acceptable behaviour. Social values take their definition from the implied choices in those patterns, but they are not really choices that were ever actually made by any significant part of the population. Hence there is no motivational doctrine at this level of his analysis. Values are not held by individuals. They are not taken as the antecedents of social action; hence a citizen input model of society is not assumed.[12] Values are, rather, an attribute of social structure, which is in turn a product of elite responses to institutional demands.

Within this set of assumptions Clark portrays the different effects of the frontier in the formation of Canadian and American values. The following passage serves as a convenient summary of both his elitist methodology and his notion of "Canadian character."

Whereas in the United States the development of separatist political movements meant freeing the expansive energies of the frontier and thus strengthening the political society as a whole, in Canada it meant exposing the frontier to forces of American expansion and threatening thereby the separate political existence of the Canadian community. . . .

Canada maintained her separate political existence but only by resisting any movement on the part of her population which had the effect of weakening the controls of central political authority. The claims to the interior of the continent were staked not by advancing frontiersmen acting on their own, but by advancing armies and police forces, large corporate economic enterprises and ecclesiastical organizations, supported by the state. The Canadian political temper, as a result, has run sharply counter to the American. Those creeds of American political life—individual rights, local autonomy, and limitation of executive power—which have contributed so much to the political strength of the American community have found less strong support within the Canadian political system.[13]

This elitist perspective is abandoned by Clark's colleagues who deal with Canadian values in the present tense. As the two passages below indicate, there has been a complete shift of position. The concept of "values" has become primarily motivational in nature, and social patterns are assumed to result from the implementation of those values by large portions of the public. In this paradigm, current values are assumed to sustain present institutions, and hence a citizen input model has been substituted for Clark's elitist one.

Vallee and White offer the following summary of the conventional view of Canadian values:

On the basis of rather inadequate data, sociologists have arrived at a consensus on the outstanding traits of Canadian national character. It can be described succinctly as a *conservative syndrome*, made up of a tendency to be guided by tradition; to accept the decision-making functions of elites, many of whom virtually or actually inherit their positions; to put a strong emphasis on the maintenance of order and predictability. Such values are regarded by many sociologists as incongruent with the requirements of an advanced industrial or a post-industrial society.[14]

This "conservative syndrome" is taken by the authors to explain Canada's dependence on American investment capital and technological expertise. Virtually everyone from John Porter to the editors of the *Financial Post* echoes this interpretation of the Canadian quandary. Commenting on Canadian character, Porter concludes:

Thus, imported capital and imported skills have helped to make modern Canada, a fact which suggests that industrialism is in, but not of Canada, or at least that the values necessary to support industrialization are not as strong in Canada as in the United States. Egalitarian values, particularly applied to education, are essential to high levels of industrialization, because they serve the search for talent that every society must make.[15]

His argument stands on the same citizen input assumption we outlined above. It draws its primary causal arrow from values to social structure, indicating that Canada's economic institutions are a consequence of the underlying values of the mass of Canadian people. To be sure, this position is in stark contrast to the view Porter put forth in *The Vertical Mosaic* (1965), where he seems to argue that the performance of the political system is controlled by elites with no particular regard for the needs, aspirations, and values of the Canadian public.[16]

What is lost is an appreciation of the wider structural context of these patterns of behaviour. In his article on Canadian character, Porter evinces a notion of the relation between political values, educational opportunities and upward mobility that is perplexing. He argues that the lack of egalitarian values among the masses has resulted in an absence of demands for the democratization of education with the result that Canada has failed to produce sufficient numbers of skilled people to manage an industrialized economy. Yet only paragraphs earlier he documented the extremely high levels of out-migration that have been characteristic of Canada. Since 1945 many of these emigrants (mostly to the United States) have possessed high capability levels. Hence, it is difficult to sustain the thesis that we have insufficient native skills.

Clearly, what we do have is insufficient opportunity to utilize our managerial and technical personnel, and an explanation of the high incidence of foreign-born managers in Canadian business must be sought in structural rather than individual-motivational factors. It remains an open question as to whether or not the values of the population bear any causal relationship to the expenditures on education, but educational opportunity cannot be taken as the explanation of the nationality of those who manage the Canadian economy. As the Gray Report points out:

> . . . a significant number of foreign controlled companies operating in Canada lack some of the decision making powers and activities of a normal Canadian controlled business enterprise . . . [this means] less challenging jobs for the Canadian techno-structure which must frequently look to the U.S. for more challenging job opportunities . . . [the effects] go beyond reducing the number of challenging jobs for the relatively small group of Canadian entrepreneurs and managers . . . [it] tends to engender a mentality of the second best with horizons and vision constantly centred on headquarters abroad.[17]

The pattern of behaviour observed is not the materialization of the population's values, it is merely the pattern which is prescribed and permitteJ by the particular institutions. This being so, we cannot rely on the evidence of economic behaviour to conclude that Canadian mass values are not particularly egalitarian and that this deficiency explains the existence of elitist forms of political behaviour. The same criticism can be made of writers who choose political variables as "manifestations" of the values of the masses.

Professor Lipset appears to have originated the argument that educational expenditures can be taken as an indicator of a nation's mass value system. Though he has drawn on Clark's findings, his own formulation is within a citizen input notion of politics to which Clark would never subscribe.[18] The same problem is evident in the other measures Lipset uses as indicators of the consequences of a set of political values. He notes the legacy of social welfare legislation in the United States and attributes the adoption of these measures to the "egalitarian ideals of the Revolution." However, when he concedes that the same policies have been implemented in Canada, he rejects the possibility of an ideological explanation and uncritically cites Porter's argument that:

. . . the haphazard development has come about more by the "demonstration effect" of their existence in other countries, than because they have formed the social philosophy of either of the two parties which have been in power at the federal level.[19]

My point in this paper is not to argue that Canadian politics is more or less ideological than the situation south of the border, but only to say that Lipset has not shown that either is the case: he has merely assumed a model of politics from questionable data, then used equally tenuous facts to validate that view. This problem with Lipset's thesis is made clear in a recent article by Tom Truman.

Professor Truman's critique shows that in a number of important political manifestations Lipset is just plain wrong. Truman cites different data (which are, however, of an equivalent character) to show that the policy outcomes of the systems in question are quite different from what Lipset represented them to be. He concludes:

If Lipset is correct in assuming this causal relationship [between mass values and political behaviour], then the data indicate that he has ranked the four countries wrongly on the equalitarian-elitist dimension. But the evidence could just as well be interpreted to show that equalitarian values are either not the cause of [this political behaviour] . . . are an insufficient cause of [that behaviour], . . . or again have some causal relationship to one or other and not the rest. Much more rigorous methods would have to be used to determine which of these alternatives is correct.[20]

Clearly, my own solution to the problem is evident from the argument of this paper: to reject the assumption of a causal relationship between mass values and political behaviour. These patterns can be explained, without resort to any motivational doctrine, as the range permitted and encouraged by the existing institutions, with the latter seen as related to elite decisions. Mass values can safely be assumed to range far beyond the limits of acceptable expression. They cannot be measured by the uncritical use of behavioural data. If Canadian values are significantly different from those of the United States or other comparably urbanized industrial societies, then it may well be that that situation stems from the peculiar opportunities of the Canadian social structure. One of the basic pillars of learning theory is that no value or attitude can be sustained if the social opportunities for its implementation are denied. Values ought to be considered to be much less durable than they are. Values attain importance only when they are given clear institutional expression (as in the case of the new middle class capturing the government in Quebec),[21] and even here there are important structural limits to the policies such institutional power can realize.

This being the case, the study of socialization to a set of values is meaningful only if done in the context of the existing social structure. If there are not institutional mechanisms for implementing particular values, or if such mechanisms are severely restricted, then it should not surprise us when the socialization to these values "fails to stick." It would be a healthy move for socialization research to reject the assumption that values are the antecedents of social behaviour. Instead, we might profitably put the problem in another form. If we assume that observable patterns of behaviour are largely prescribed by the dominant institutions, then we can examine the process of socialization as the legitimation of those institutions. Instead of looking for the causes of stable patterns of behaviour in individual motivational factors, we should examine the way people learn to accept those patterns as suitable or even desirable ways of doing things. The explanation of why those particular patterns exist is not a behavioural question; it is an institutional and a structural one. It can be answered only when the institution is seen in its historical context. The apparent motives of present behaviour are part of the sustaining mechanism of the particular social structure, but they might profitably be treated as rationalizations for accepting social norms rather than causes of the behaviour they purport to explain.

When we set out to study a nation's value system, therefore, it follows that we ought to pay more attention to the historical development of institutions (which are largely the products of decisions made by elite actors in response to changing circumstances) and the manner in which those structures have been legitimated. The field of political socialization has less to learn from probing the social psychology of the individual than it has from the literature on myths and social control. To the researcher who is interested in the question: What are the values of Canadians or of some group of Canadians? I think a prior question must be posed: Why study values? Are we really sure that that is a profitable starting point for explaining the social phenomenon we are interested in understanding? My own feeling is that in many cases it is not.

It is clearly an error to argue, as Lipset and others have, that the levels of expenditure on education, relative size of police force, crime rates, divorce rates, and levels of investment are the end product of a particular set of mass values. They are not; they are the responses of elites to a set of structural demands. For this reason socialization research ought to tread very lightly, if at all, where the dependent variables are assumed to indicate a role in allocative decisions for the mass of people.

Educational expenditures, as one example, are clearly related to structural features such as the level of industrial development and the financial capability of the system. This latter factor is related to the general economic conditions, but an important part of it may be the particular division of legislative and taxing powers among levels of government. Given a set of needs from the social structure, the elites must match these institutional demands to the resources at their disposal. The situation may or may not afford them some latitude in ordering their priorities. It is highly unlikely that the electorate could substantially alter the allocative pattern even by changing the elected personnel in the elite.

Similar problems are present in non-expenditure policies such as divorce. Initially, divorce rates would have to be compared in relation to the divorce laws in different systems. Different laws could be the result of different mass demands, but other factors should be explored first. Again the level of jurisdiction could be important: if divorce is a provincial or state power, then variations are likely to occur, and the demonstration effect of these differences could be a force making for a greater rate of change throughout the system than would be the case where changes in the law must be made at the national level. In Canada, where divorce is a federal responsibility, it may be that the perception (or mis-perception) by national leaders that liberalized grounds for divorce would be unacceptable to Catholic Quebec prevented change from happening faster than it would have under a different constitutional division of powers.

Divorce laws are made by elites partly in response to their perception of the demands of the mass. Even controlling for differences in the law and financial costs, we must remind ourselves that divorce rates are not necessarily comparable. Statistics show only formalized behaviour. In this instance we are measuring the rate at which family units are dissolved. It may be that in different social settings this is accomplished differently, for example by desertion or by extra-marital affairs. When set in this wider context it seems to me that there can be considerable debate as to just what values are implied by people who divorce. Much more could be said on both of these examples, and clearly I have offered interpretations and not proof of the validity of a particular interpretation. My purpose is simply to demonstrate some of the problems of using social statistics to represent behaviour which is assumed to portray the implementation of particular values either indirectly at the level of influencing the policy outputs or directly at the level of observable behaviour.

Finally, I do not argue that it is never profitable to analyse social values at the mass level. What is needed is a healthy regard for the fact that most of what happens in society takes place without conscious reference to the values of most of the people. It is fair to suggest that these actions may be related to the values of the elite actors involved, but it is theoretically unsound to praise or blame the public for them. My own feeling is that mass values are articulated either as passive acceptance of the status quo, or as the active attempt to veto some aspect of that system of arrangements. That is to say, little room is left to the citizen for making any positive contribution to deciding political allocations. Mass values should be seen as a residual category to explain differences which cannot be accounted for by structural explanations. The matter of systems persistence (the stability and change of a system over time) may be very different.

If our concern is not with political allocations but with this more general kind of political analysis, the persistence of some sort of system for making political allocations, then socialization theory is equally clear in giving us a view of the role of the citizen. Greenstein's characterization is the learning of national loyalty and of a sense of the legitimacy of society's authority roles and political institutions. Easton terms it the development of support for the political community and the regime. Miliband calls it the learning of a legitimating ideology. All of them agree that for this type of political analysis the relevant topic of research is the nature of the bond between the citizen and the social and political system.

Easton has provided the most comprehensive formulation of socialization research within this type of framework, but his effort remains just a beginning. We need much more precise indicators of mass values than are provided by the concepts of efficacy, positive affect, alienation, and so on. This is, as Wahlke points out, a major area for theoretical elaboration and empirical investigation. Canada provides quite different structural features from those in the United States; consequently, we should find that the generation of support, the management of discontent, and institutional change are achieved differently in the two countries. It is to understanding these processes that we might profitably direct our research into political socialization.

For example, Clark, Porter, and Lipset agree that symbols like the crown, the British connection, the American threat, and the Canadian national state have been used throughout Canadian history to mobilize the masses or to control their discontent. It is likely that on many occasions elites have used these responses to curb the demands of the masses, but at other times it could be that expected reactions have limited the options that elites could contemplate. To explain the growth of our institutions it is necessary to show the process of interaction between the elites and the masses, and an important link is the learning of responses to these symbols by the masses. But we should be careful not to overestimate the role of mass values in *shaping* social change. It is interesting, for example, that in studies of three Canadian mass movements at different times and at different places, the common factor of an elite which has effectively organized the population is present. In the case of the two agrarian protest movements, it seems to me that this organizational component may be more influential than the ideology of the respective elites. The particular solutions may have been less important to the success of the movement than the security offered to the masses by simply belonging to an organization which at least claimed to have some answers to the social plight.

Similarly, class, region, ethnicity, and at times religion have been attachments with important consequences. Our understanding of Canadian politics as an adaptive process could benefit from knowing how different members of the community come to have different responses to these symbolic identities. The existence of third parties at the national level and their attainment of power at the provincial level can be understood, in part, as the absence of a set of political symbols with uniform meaning in all parts of the country or across ethnic divisions. Socialization research may yield interesting data by showing why these symbolic identifications mean different things to Canadians who grow up in different structural settings and may thus cast light on how social conflicts are sustained over generations. Perhaps these variations are indicative of different value systems, but it is equally plausible to assume that the values of these antagonistic groups are the same but are given different behavioural expression because of differences in their institutional position. Clearly, a good deal of work remains to be done before we can say with certainty what Canadian values really are. At this point, all we can do with confidence is to treat values as the choices implied by our institutions. We really do not know very much about either the content or consequences of mass values.

The more specific job of understanding how the authorities come to make the decisions they do is an equally interesting problem, and, as I indicated above, this is where our highly elaborate models of socialization are appropriate. Here more specific values can be assumed to be operative. Here belief systems and ideologies can be taken to be significant factors for explaining behaviour. The application of socialization research to this process may indeed cast considerable light on just what the allocative process is all about and in this manner may contribute to our fuller understanding of how political systems operate. But studying the socialization of elite actors is not so simple a problem as it sounds.

We are still left with one of the most difficult questions in the study of politics: how are policy decisions made? Within the general elite category it becomes necessary to specify who the relevant actors are. We would have to formulate or adopt some theory of policy-making to give us guidance in selecting whom to study. Having done this, we would then be able to proceed with the more complex issues of deciding what characteristics determine how decision-makers behave: ideology, personality, role structure, elite norms and values, and so on. These are not easy problems, and socialization is only one of the processes which has consequences for the allocative behaviour we seek to explain. It may be that Dye's work is correct even to the extent that elites do not have a significant influence on policy outcomes. But if elites do matter, some questions for research are evident: What kind of socialization contributes to having elite aspirations? What are the mechanisms of elite recruitment? How does socialization contribute to our understanding of the type of decision-makers a system has? How do these factors combine to show us how elite socialization contributes to the policy outputs in the system? In terms of Easton's model of the political system, "the public" is only one source of demands. It would be interesting to know how elite members perceive the system's environment: what do they see as important and how does that affect their behaviour?

The key point that I want to make is that an allocative theory of political socialization will, in the nature of the problem, be examining the origins of elite behaviour. An early stage in the development of this theory will involve research to discover what elite orientations are predictive of allocative outcomes, and only later will the theory explore the origins of those characteristics in socialization processes. To the extent that elites pay attentions to the values of the masses, the socialization of the average citizen to a set of politically important symbols is a topic for research.

NOTES

1. Fred Greenstein, *Children and Politics* (New Haven: Yale University Press, 1965), pp. 1, 12–13.
2. R. Hess and J. Torney, *The Development of Political Attitudes in Children* (Garden City: Anchor Books, 1968), p. 69.
3. J. Wahlke, "Public Policy and Representative Government: The Role of the Represented," *Report 9*, The Laboratory for Political Research, Iowa, 1967, p. 2.

4. He cites the following standard works to show the lack of consistency in the political thinking of the average citizen: Almond, Gabriel A., and Verba, Sidney, *The Civic Culture* (Princeton, New Jersey: Princeton University Press, 1963); Berelson, Bernard, Lazarsfeld, Paul F., and McPhee, William N., *Voting* (Chicago: University of Chicago Press, 1954); Campbell, Angus; Converse, Philip E.; Miller, Warren E.; and Stokes, Donald E., *The American Voter* (New York: John Wiley & Sons, Inc., 1960); Campbell, Angus et al., *Elections and the Political Order* (New York: John Wiley & Sons, Inc., 1966); Cantril, Hadley, *The Pattern of Human Concerns* (New Brunswick, New Jersey: Rutgers University Press, 1965); McPhee, William N., and Glaser, William A. (eds.), *Public Opinion and Congressional Elections* (New York: Free Press of Glencoe, 1962).

5. See Converse, "The Nature of Belief Systems in Mass Publics" and "Attitude and Non-Attitudes." Similar conclusions follow from Rokeach who points out that attitudes on most things of a political nature fall in the intermediate or peripheral zones of a belief system and are therefore quite fluid (*The Open and Closed Mind* [New York: Basic Books, 1960], pp. 31–53).

6. Dye's *Politics, Economics and the Public* (Chicago: Rand McNally, 1966) has become the summary work. For other contributions to this literature see: R. Dawson and J. Robinson, "Interparty Competition, Economic Variables, and Welfare Politics in the American States," *The Journal of Politics*, vol. 25 (1963), pp. 265–89; R. I. Hofferbert, "The Relation Between Public Policy and Some Structural and Environmental Variables in the American States," *The American Political Science Review*, vol. 55 (1966), pp. 73–82; and I. Sharkansky, "Economic Development, Regionalism and State Political Systems," *The Midwest Journal of Political Science*, vol. 12 (1968), pp. 41–61.

7. Wahlke, "Public Policy and Representative Government: The Role of the Represented," pp. 28–29.

8. Murray Edelman, *The Symbolic Uses of Politics* (Chicago: University of Chicago Press, 1964), pp. 12–13.

9. Ibid., p. 192.

10. R. H. Salisbury, "The Analysis of Public Policy: A Search for Theories and Roles," in A. Ranney, ed., *Political Science and Public Policy* (Chicago: Markham, 1968), pp. 163–64.

11. This view is more fully developed in the writing of Amitai Etzioni, though he would probably object to my characterization of his model as "elitist." See Etzioni, "Toward a Theory of Societal Guidance," *American Journal of Sociology*, vol. 73 (1967), pp. 173–87; and *The Active Society* (New York: Free Press, 1968).

12. Brian Barry, in his *Sociologists, Economists and Democracy* (Toronto: Collier-Macmillan, 1970), explores this distinction between a structural and a motivational conception of values (pp. 86–98).

13. S. D. Clark, *The Developing Canadian Community*, second edition (Toronto: University of Toronto Press, 1962), p. 214.

14. F. G. Vallee and D. R. Whyte, "Canadian Society: Trends and Perspectives," in B. Blishen et al., eds., *Canadian Society*, third edition abridged (Toronto: Macmillan, 1971), p. 559.

15. John Porter, "Canadian Character in the Twentieth Century," *Annals*, 370 (1967), p. 55.

16. This is not the place to enter into a lengthy analysis of Porter's political thought, but a brief comment is needed. In *The Vertical Mosaic* the main thrust of Porter's *analysis* is that Canadian politics is dominated by elites. Underlying his criticism of Canadian society is

the assumption that significantly broader participation in social and economic decision-making is possible and desirable. He sees part of the remedy to the poverty of Canadian social policy to lie with a greater politicization of the masses so that they are more persistent in pressing their demands on policymakers. It seems unfair to place that kind of expectation on the Canadian public and optimistic to assume that we would suddenly evolve toward utopia if only the impulses of the masses could be given political expression. Porter lets this bias show by equating his concept of "creative politics" with progressive measures. I would differ with him in this one fundamental way: I do not regard the policies of a society to be inseparable from the social characteristics of its leaders. It is one point to argue that Canadian society has a relatively closed structure for upward mobility, but it is a separate question to engage in a criticism of the decisions of the elites. This citizen input "ideal-type" of Porter's is evident in his article on Canadian character where he takes institutional patterns to represent mass values.

17. *A Citizen's Guide to the Gray Report* (Toronto: New Press, 1971), pp. 90–91.

18. S. M. Lipset, "Revolution and Counterrevolution: the United States and Canada," in O. Kruhlak et al., eds., *The Canadian Political Process* (Toronto: Holt, Rinehart & Winston, 1970), pp. 13–38. It is an awkward fact for my assertion of a difference between the two authors that Lipset and Clark cite each other with apparent approval. Clark's two most widely read articles on Canadian values show many similarities to Lipset's work. My differentiation of the two authors is based on how each conceives of the relationship between values and institutions within the larger work that each has produced. I take Clark to be chiefly concerned with docu-

menting how particular institutions came to exist in response to various economic and social conditions. Values, for Clark, are primarily a descriptive attribute of these institutional forms though, of course, he concedes that values in one sense contributed to the emergence of the institutions. Lipset seems to me to place the emphasis on this latter conception of values. For him, values are held by people who are guided by them in how they set about building or changing social structures. For Lipset to say that an institution reflects a certain value (say egalitarianism) is part and parcel of the assertion that it was created by people holding a belief in that value. There is little point in documenting this difference since quotations could be selected that show either or both characterizations are false. However, Lipset comes face to face with the issue in his rejection of the materialistic interpretation of social change: "the value system is perhaps the most enduring part of what we think of as society, or a social system. . . . Thus it is necessary to work out the implications of the value system within a given material setting." (*The First New Nation* [Garden City: Anchor Books, 1967], p. 140). The general observation I have made is based on a comparison of Clark's work on the development of different types of social structures in early Canada and Lipset's equivalent treatment of the developing American nation where the emphasis is on the materialization of "American values."

19. S. M. Lipset, "Revolution and Counterrevolution: The United States and Canada," p. 28.

20. T. Truman, "A Critique of Seymour M. Lipset's Article, 'Value Differences, Absolute or Relative: The English-Speaking Democracies'," *Canadian Journal of Political Science*, vol. 4 (1971), pp. 509–10. Truman is highly critical of Lipset's

findings; however, he does not attack Lipset's theoretical and methodological assumptions. Truman's own case could be made easier simply by arguing that the indicators Lipset uses are not a measure of the values of a population. Both articles are efforts to compare some dimensions of different societies, but neither of them examines in sufficient detail the factors which have given rise to these differences to be able to say that value differences are responsible.

21. Unlike English Canada, postwar Quebec has not sought occupational opportunities through emigration and has been forced to come to terms with the problem by making institutional changes. Professor Hubert Guindon offers a penetrating analysis of the consequences of economic dependence for the new managerial-technical class in Quebec. "The constraints to the growth of the new middle class are a function of the specialized character and the smaller scale and size of the bureaucracies it staffs. . . . Given these two constraints, one can view the new middle class as seeking and needing space for expansion, occupationally and organizationally. . . . To overcome the restricted social mobility of its small bureaucratic pyramids, it has adopted a twofold strategy: (1) a bureaucratic transformation of traditional institutional institutions, and (2) a reaffirmation of linguistic identification, so that by expanding linguistic space and ethnic jurisdiction, it can also increase job outlets". (*Two Cultures*, p. 87). A similar view of the social impact of the economic changes in Quebec is taken by Leon Dion, in "The Origin and Character of the Nationalism of Growth," *Canadian Forum*, 43 (1964), pp. 229–33.

The Use of Role Theory in Political Socialization Research

3

RONALD G. LANDES

The importance of role theory for political socialization research can be easily seen if we consider recent definitions of the concept of a "political system." Mitchell and Mitchell, for example, define a "polity . . . as those sets of roles which are concerned with the making and implementing of public choices."[1] A similar view is seen in the following description by Almond and Powell of the basic units of the political system.

Beginning with the concept of role as one of the basic units of a political system, we may speak of a subsystem (for example, a legislative body) as consisting of related and interacting roles; and of the political system as a set of interacting subsystems (for example, legislatures, electorates, pressure groups, and courts).[2]

As these definitions indicate, a basic unit of political analysis is the concept of role. It is not surprising to find, therefore, that in political socialization research the primary emphasis to date has been on how children, as they mature, perceive and become attached to the political roles in their particular political system.

A role is a pattern of expectations defining typical behaviour for an individual position in society.[3] Examples of political roles in the Canadian system include the Prime Minister, Governor General, provincial Premier, or Member of Parliament. Notice that the definition of role refers to the office and not to the individual who happens to occupy that position at any particular point in time. In other words, no matter who is Prime Minister, we expect that certain actions will be carried out (for example, the selection of the cabinet), because these actions are definitive of the office regardless of who the incumbent may be.

An important corollary of role theory is that each person simultaneously fulfils many roles. For example, Pierre Trudeau is not only Prime Minister of Canada, but also Member of Parliament for the Mount Royal riding in Montreal and leader of the Liberal party, in addition to filling such nonpolitical roles as husband and father. An interesting instance of this can be seen in the practice of several former prime ministers of holding a specific cabinet portfolio in addition to that of Prime Minister. Sir John A. Macdonald was his own Justice Minister at one time, and Alexander Mackenzie made use of his training as a stonemason in becoming his own Minister of Public Works. Nor is the practice so ancient; for his first two years as Premier of British Columbia, Mr. Barrett was his own Minister of Finance.

The fact that each individual may fill many roles leads to the problem of role conflict—in other words, the situation in which a person finds that the roles or positions which he fills have behavioural expectations which are mutually contradictory. For example, the roles of husband and father have expectations associated with them which emphasize the privacy and sanctity of the family unit, while the role of the politician is patently public: the politician and his family are under constant scrutiny by the public and the news media. Another typical example of role conflict which most politicians face is the need to raise money for election campaigns, while at the same time remaining independent of interest groups and the wealthy segments of society. In a democratic political system, one aspect of the public's expectations regarding politicians is that they represent and are responsible to the public, and not to special interest groups of any kind. Thus the role of political candidate and his need to raise money to pay for campaign expenses are often in conflict with the public's role expectations of the elected politician.

Despite the fact that each person simultaneously fills multiple roles, role conflict is seldom so pronounced that we are prevented from fairly accurately predicting our politicians' behaviour when they are in their public capacity. By knowing the formal office a particular individual is filling, we can be fairly certain what the individual's broad behaviour pattern will be. By knowing an incumbent's political role we infer a number of conclusions regarding his expected and actual behaviour pattern. No matter who the Governor General is, we can be pretty sure that he will be on hand to open Parliament and read the Speech from the

Throne. Expectations, then, define the limits of acceptable behaviour for each political role.

Within the constraints that public expectations place on the behaviour of any particular role incumbent, there is, however, considerable room for variation in role enactment or performance. And this individual variation may have an important impact on how other members of the political system perceive and evaluate that political role. Particularly when we consider a child's developing perception of the political system, it seems logical to suggest that the role occupant (whether the Prime Minister is Diefenbaker, Pearson, or Trudeau) may be an important factor in the child's perception of the political role of Prime Minister. Especially for elective roles at the top of the political system, it is likely that the office or role will become associated to some extent with the unique characteristics of a particular role occupant. This essay will suggest, therefore, that an important distinction needs to be made in political socialization theory and research between perceptions and evaluations of the role itself and of the particular person occupying the role at the moment.

THE USE OF ROLE THEORY IN PREVIOUS RESEARCH

This brief review of some of the main ideas of role theory suggests the need for the introduction of a role-occupant distinction in political socialization research. In this section, therefore, we will consider the specific use of role theory evident in several empirical investigations. Particular focus will be centred on the work of David Easton and Jack Dennis because of their explicit use of role theory and because of their subsequent influence on later research in the political socialization field. After reviewing the work of Easton and Dennis, plus a brief look at a recent Canadian investigation, we will suggest the need for an "interactionist" interpretation of our role-occupant distinction. We will conclude our analysis with a discussion of the implications of such an interpretation for future research in the political socialization area.

The basic assumption of Easton and Dennis is that children relate directly to roles rather than to particular role occupants:

From the earliest grades we shall find that our test children typically see the incumbents of these positions as representative figures and that their attitudes pertain to the role, not to the persons who occupy it. From this we shall be able to conclude that our children are in the process of constructing an image of the structure of political authority.[4]

Included within this conception is their view that certain personality characteristics are associated with particular political roles. In other words each role is characterized by certain personal qualities which each role occupant would exemplify—what Easton and Dennis refer to as role personality. This role personality accounts for the personalization of political orientations that develop among children as they mature, particularly as they relate to the American President. However, it is important to remember that the personalization of authority refers to role personality and not to the personality characteristics of any particular role occupant. As Easton and Dennis interpret this distinction: "to say that the child personalizes authority is not the same as asserting that he sees only the person or incumbent in the authority role."[5] In the Canadian context, the Easton and Dennis view would be that children relate directly to a political role and its associated role personality. In other words, the role occupant would have no significant impact on what the child perceived about the political system.

In viewing the child's evaluations of the authority figures as judgments about roles and not specific incumbents, Easton and Dennis make the following inferential leap.

The children, especially those in the earlier grades, have little knowledge about the Presidency. It is unlikely that they have enough information about the personal qualities of a given individual to make judgments about him. *They must therefore be making assumptions about the characteristics of all Presidents as persons who hold this office.* In effect they are describing what they see as aspects of the typical personality in that role, the role personality. (Emphasis added.)[6]

However, we find it difficult to accept the view that a child who does not have enough information about the most visible and salient political leader in the system to know about his personal qualities, will at the same time be able, at least implicitly, to understand and to make a rather sophisticated evaluation of role personality.

The term or concept of personalization suggests a possible resolution of this dilemma. Note that we are using the term personalization to refer to the characteristics of the role occupants and not to the role characteristics referred to by Easton and Dennis as role personality. If the children become attached to the structure of political authority through a process of role personalization, might it not also be logical to assume that their role evaluations are likewise formed? In other words, the particular incumbent and his personality mediate between the child and his perception of the characteristics of the role itself (including the role personality). For example, we are suggesting that children in the Canadian system may first perceive the incumbent or the role occupant, such as Pierre Trudeau. Once this connection is established, the children then generalize from what they see and learn about Trudeau to an understanding of the role of the Prime Minister of Canada.

We are suggesting, then, the addition of at least another variable between the child and his perception and acceptance of the structure of political authority. The children first view political authorities (i.e., occupants) in personal terms, which are then transferred into more general role perceptions and evaluations. It is interesting to note that Easton and Dennis considered this possibility and rejected it.

If we had been driven to the alternative conclusion that the children in our group were evaluating only the personal characteristics of Kennedy as President, we would be required merely to add another link in our interpretive chain of reasoning. . . . But if we are forced back to this interpretation, it would prohibit us from drawing direct inferences from our findings about the way in which the child feels about the structure of authority. *Yet it is exactly statements about the child's relationship to the structure of authority that we would like to be able to make, and have in fact made.* (Emphasis added.)[7]

However, it should be evident to most observers that the necessity to interpret data in a particular way to keep one's theoretical assumptions intact is a highly suspect methodological procedure.

In reviewing the final test questionnaire used by Easton and Dennis (Library of Congress Document 9365) for their data collection, their view of the role-occupant problem becomes readily apparent. The as-

sumption that children relate directly to roles and not to the role occupants is incorporated within the questionnaire without a demonstration
of its validity. For example, the children are never asked to name the
President or to describe his political role. Instead, they are asked to
evaluate the President on the assumption that their responses refer to the
generalized role and not to the personal characteristics of any particular
president. This procedure becomes more questionable when we find that
a likeness of President Kennedy appears three times before the first set of
questions dealing with the President and one additional time before the
second set of rating items. The rationale for this methodology is described
by Easton and Dennis as follows:

Transparently most younger children at any rate are not able to distinguish
consciously between the Presidency and the role occupant. For this reason
in designing our questionnaire *we felt free to use a hand-drawn sketch of
President Kennedy to represent the general role of President* without fearing
that the child would really be relaying to us his image of only Kennedy the
man. (Emphasis added.) [8]

However, we would have to stress that this view of the role-occupant
distinction is an assumption that appears to be untested by Easton and
Dennis. To include a drawing of a particular president and then to infer
that the children are evaluating the characteristics of all presidents (i.e.,
the role characteristics) is a highly suspect methodological technique.

This brief review of the major assumption utilized by Easton and
Dennis in their interpretation of role theory indicates, in relation to our
role-occupant distinction, that they place almost total emphasis on the
role side of the role-occupant dichotomy. In our next example we will see
an almost contrary point of view.

In a paper presented at the Canadian Political Science Association's
annual meeting in 1971, Terence Carroll, Donald Higgins, and Michael
Whittington presented a preliminary report of an ongoing study of the
political socialization process in Canada.[9] Our concern here is with their
interpretation and application of role theory in relation to our role-
occupant distinction.

In reviewing their use of role theory we find that many of the assumptions already discussed in relation to the work of Easton and Dennis are

likewise incorporated in their perspective. The basic approach utilized is how children perceive and relate to authority roles. As the authors view their analysis they are attempting "to indicate who is learning what about which authority roles, when, and to a limited extent, how."[10] The pattern of authority roles is referred to as the "Canadian political authority hierarchy," a perspective which is similar to the "structure of authority" concept as used by Easton and Dennis. With their main focus "on a few symbols and a number of specific authority roles," a total of nine Canadian political authority roles and one symbol were finally selected for inclusion in their analysis.

In relation to our role-occupant dichotomy, we should note that an important contribution to the use of role theory in political socialization research is evident in this research project: that is, an explicit recognition of the influence of role occupants on perceptions by children of political roles. In explaining a child's cognition of political roles, Carroll suggests that three factors must be accounted for. These factors include the perceived structural characteristics of the role, the perceptions of past incumbents, and the perceptions of the present incumbent. Noting that the first two elements are usually associated, Carroll indicates that "the only distinction which seems capable of meaningful operationalization, then, is that between perceptions of the personality and behaviour of the present incumbent and the other two elements in role cognition taken together."[11] While recognizing the influence of the role occupant, the authors note that their purpose is not to make a comparison of the perceptions of the personality of the role occupant with role expectations. Instead, the influence of the role occupant is significant in people's recognition of political roles, and "if the individual perceives only the behaviour and personality of a present role incumbent, then that is all there is to his perception of that role."[12]

Our basic criticism of this conception of the role-occupant problem is that it lays undue stress on the occupant side of the dichotomy. While Easton and Dennis stress role over occupant, Carroll and his colleagues stress occupant over role. There is more that needs to be taken into account than the simple recognition of role occupants. If a person perceives "only the behavior and personality of the present role incumbent," can we really then infer that this recognition is an indication of his understanding of specific roles in a rather complicated type of political structure?

As a way of summarizing our interpretations of the use of role theory in the above two research projects, we present in Figures 1 and 2 a schematic portrayal of both the Easton and Dennis and the Carroll models of role theory. In Figure 1, the Easton and Dennis model, the child perceives and relates directly to the political role (including the role structure and the role personality). As indicated in our previous discussion, very little, if any, attention is given to the role occupant as a factor influencing the child's perception. In Figure 2 we see the Carroll interpretation, which views role cognition as being screened primarily through the child's view of the present incumbent and secondarily through the child's perception of past incumbents and structural characteristics.

As our earlier discussion of role theory indicated, both the role requirements and the role occupant's personal characteristics have a bearing on how people perceive and relate to various political roles. It is the interaction between role prescriptions and individual occupant variation that is the key for understanding how people perceive political roles. On this basis we must reject both the Easton and Dennis and the Carroll conceptions of the role-occupant dichotomy. Both viewpoints, we suggest, are examples of a misuse of role theory in political socialization research. Instead, an interaction approach to the role-occupant dichotomy should form a more adequate base for future research in the political socialization area.

AN INTERACTION APPROACH TO
THE ROLE-OCCUPANT DICHOTOMY

As we have indicated, the interaction between role prescriptions and occupant predispositions is the key point on which the role-occupant problem can be resolved. In contrast to these previous approaches, which seem to pose the problem as an either/or dichotomy between the importance of role and the role occupant, we are suggesting that it is the interaction between these two elements which can significantly influence a person's perception of and attachment to the political system.

Given this significant conclusion concerning the role-occupant interaction nexus, how can we modify the use of role theory in future political

Figure 1   The Easton and Dennis View

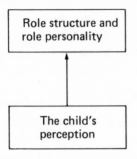

Figure 2   The Carroll View

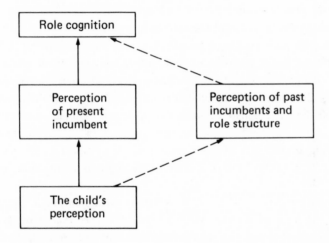

socialization research? In Figure 3 we present our proposed interaction approach to the role-occupant problem. In our view the child may perceive and develop orientations toward both political role expectations (arrow AB) and the role occupant (arrow AC). For example, arrow AB would be concerned with the child's perception of such items as the selection of the cabinet by the Prime Minister, while arrow AC would represent the child's view of the personal and unique characteristics of

Pierre Trudeau. In addition, the interaction between the role occupant and role expectations (arrow BC) provides us with an interpretation of the style of role performance or role enactment which may also be recognized by the child (arrow AD). An example of this relationship would be the handling by a particular role occupant of a crisis situation facing the political system, such as Trudeau's handling of the October Crisis of 1970.

The most obvious conclusion to be drawn from Figure 3 is that the child's perception of and attachment to a political system is influenced by his growing awareness of all three linkages evident in this diagram. For example, the linkage AB could represent a change in the public's expectations concerning a particular role's legitimacy and requirements (i.e., the debate over whether Canada's parliamentary system is becoming more "presidential" in nature). The linkage AC would represent a person's view of an individual that is called upon to fill a political role (i.e., the characteristics of a specific role occupant, such as his sex, religion, and ethnic group membership).

Particularly for a political system such as the Canadian one, where there is a split between major ethnic groups, we are suggesting that the linkage of the child to the role occupant may have a significant impact on the child's resulting view of the political system. In other words, does it make any difference on the child's perception if the Prime Minister happens to be an English Canadian or a French Canadian? Previous research would lead us to answer this question in the affirmative. In investigating the impact of ethnicity on the perception of heroes and historical symbols, Jean Pierre Richert came to the following conclusion:

The findings generally . . . showed, first of all, that children overwhelmingly identified with historical symbols of their own culture, and that their ethnocentric perception of historical figures increased with age. Second, the data showed that Francophone and Anglophone children identified with different eras of Canadian history.[13]

Although the above research dealt with historical figures and symbols, a number of other studies have also stressed the differences between English-Canadian and French-Canadian students' views of the political system.[14] In terms of our discussion of role theory, we feel that the above research suggests the importance of the ethnic group membership of both

Figure 3 An Interaction Approach

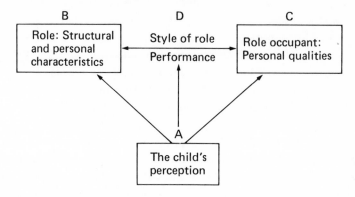

Figure 4 A Pattern of Positive Support

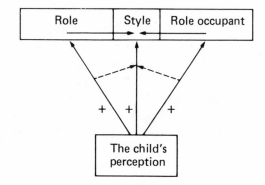

the role occupant and the child as formative influences on the child's emerging perception of the political system.

A second characteristic of the role occupant (and of the child perceiving the role occupant) which may influence the child's perception of the political system is the sex of the role occupant. Whittington's study of children's evaluations of the monarchy (Chapter 12 of this volume) shows important male-female differences, and leads him to speculate that a male monarch might produce a quite different pattern of allegiances.

Returning to a consideration of Figure 3 we see that the final linkage BC (style of role performance) and the person's view of that linkage (arrow AD) represents our interaction approach to the role-occupant dichotomy. The importance of the role occupant's personality on his resulting role performance in the Canadian system has been noted by a number of researchers. For example, in analysing the results of the 1968 and 1972 elections John Meisel makes the following assessment of the effect of Trudeau's personality on the election outcomes.

It is always difficult to assess the respective influences on the outcome of particular election issues, events, long-standing party attachments, personalities of candidates and leaders, but the Liberal victory of 1968 and the party's 1972 stumble *can be explained largely in Trudeau terms. His was the victory and his the fall.* . . . The answers are many and complex. One of the principal explanations may lie in the combination of the general style of the government party *with the particular style of its leader.* (Emphasis added.) [15]

The significance of personality considerations has also been discovered in other contexts in the Canadian political system. In studying the bases of party support in the 1968 election, Meisel also found that for "Canada as a whole . . . the leader was the most important factor, among those suggested, in the voting decision." [16] The importance of role-occupant interaction in relation to the Prime Minister of Canada is nicely summarized for us by Peter C. Newman's comment about the office in his analysis of the Diefenbaker years:

Although Canada's political system culminates in this one man, and the arsenal of his authority is indeed huge, both the basis and boundaries of that authority are ill defined. . . . What the Prime Minister of Canada is not is established by legislative checks and the circumscribing realities of Canadian politics. What he is depends on him. The office is reconfigured by its occupant. [17]

These brief reflections on each of the linkages in Figure 3 point to the need to consider each of them as possible determinants of the child's view of the political system. In addition, the child's overall view of and attachment to the political system will be the resulting mix of the interaction among all of the elements contained in Figure 3.

Initially the young child will have little if any knowledge about any of these linkages. As he matures he will begin to acquire orientations to all three elements. We would speculate that the linkage AC might develop first, then the linkage AB, and finally the linkage AD. We would also suggest that as the children mature a connection will be established among these separate identities. Borrowing an idea from "balance theory" in social psychology, we speculate, as an hypothesis for further study, that supportive attitudes for the political system will be most likely to develop where the perceptions of all three linkages are positive and in congruence with one another. Whenever negative linkages appear the level of positive support for the political system will decline. For example, if a person comes to dislike the particular role occupant, these negative feelings may be transferred into a dislike of the office of Prime Minister and even eventually into a rejection of the legitimacy of the entire political structure. In Figure 4 we indicate one of these possible patterns of development, where attitudes toward each of these linkages are positive and congruent and where they begin to coalesce into the child's supportive perception of the political system.

We will now briefly consider, as a way of concluding our discussion, the implications of our role-occupant distinction for future research in the political socialization area.

The first and most obvious theoretical result is that the child's perception of and attachment to the political system is a considerably more complex phenomenon than has been previously assumed. Children's perceptions of and orientations about a number of political objects (i.e., roles, role occupants, outputs) influence his growing awareness and possible attachment to a particular political structure. More importantly, it is the interplay between the views of these various objects that will determine the child's overall level of support for the political system. In other words, the child's view of particular political objects such as political roles and role occupants (often described as "specific support") will help to determine his overall level of acceptance of the entire political system (usually described as "diffuse support for the structure of authority"). Negative views of a particular role occupant, we are suggesting, may be transferred, at least in part, into a dislike of the political role that occupant is performing.

A second theoretical implication of our role-occupant distinction is that much of the previous research in the political socialization area may be "timebound," due to a failure to distinguish between role and occupant influences on the child's perception of the political system. While all survey research is in a sense timebound, we are using the term here to refer to a very specific problem. If the child's view of the political system is heavily influenced by the role occupants of the major political offices, then it becomes very difficult to generalize from the data collected when a specific incumbent was in office. In other words, are the findings about the political socialization process when Pierre Trudeau is Prime Minister the same as they would be if the same type of data were collected under former or future prime ministers?

A third outgrowth of our analysis is that levels of political support may be subject to short-run changes in any political system. Rather than being a problem of "political generations," we suggest that the development and maintenance of levels of support is a continuous problem in any political system. By viewing the political socialization process in terms of roles, occupants, and styles of performance we can introduce the possibly radical notion that what governments and political occupants actually do might have some bearing on the level of support created for the political system. Instead of concentrating on how attitudes learned in childhood will affect the political system in ten, fifteen, or twenty years when these children may become actual participants in the political process, a more immediate task is to demonstrate the impact of specific outputs on the child's perception of the political system. In other words, how does a change of role occupants, an election campaign, or a crisis such as the October Crisis of 1970 influence the child's perception of and support for the political system?

A fourth theoretical implication that results from our role-occupant distinction is that the political recruitment process (i.e., the selection of role occupants) becomes significant in considering the creation of political support for any political system. The type of person filling the major roles in a political system will help to determine how a society views its politicians (i.e., whether politics is seen as a legitimate profession or as a "dirty business"), a factor which may influence how new members begin to perceive the overall political structure.

In addition to these theoretical concerns two important methodological points need to be recognized. First of all, questions must be designed to test not only each linkage in Figure 3, but also the interaction effects among these component elements. As a result our second methodological implication becomes evident. Longitudinal research (research which reinterviews the same person several times during a given period—say once a year for three years) could make a significant contribution to the political socialization area. In contrast to previous suggestions for introducing such research (that cross-sectional samples at one point in time in several grades may not reflect an individual's specific developmental pattern), our recommendation is based on the need to see the interaction effects of the three linkages in Figure 3. Only in a longitudinal study will we be able to assess how different role occupants influence an individual's view of a particular political role. Changes in evaluation between a person as candidate and as a role-occupant and between role evaluations at different points in time would lend weight to our interpretation of the role-occupant distinction.

With these theoretical and methodological implications of our analysis, the investigation of political socialization phenomena will certainly become a more difficult and complex undertaking. However, if these added difficulties can be overcome, our theoretical understanding of how people perceive and become attached to their political system will be greatly enhanced.

NOTES

1. Joyce M. Mitchell and William C. Mitchell, *Political Analysis and Public Policy: An Introduction to Political Science* (Chicago: Rand McNally, 1969), p. 332.
2. Gabriel Almond and G. Bingham Powell, *Comparative Politics: A Developmental Approach* (Boston: Little, Brown, 1966), p. 22.
3. See Theodore R. Sarbin and Vernon L. Allen, "Role Theory" in Gardner Lindzey and Elliot Aronson, eds., *The Handbook of Social Psychology*, vol. 1, second edition (Reading, Mass.: Addison Wesley, 1968), pp. 488–567.
4. David Easton and Jack Dennis, *Children in the Political System* (New York: McGraw-Hill, 1969), p. 66.
5. Ibid., p. 199.
6. Ibid., p. 197.
7. Ibid., p. 194.
8. Ibid., p. 199.
9. T. G. Carroll. D. J. H. Higgins, and M. S. Whittington (1971), "The Development of Children's Perceptions of Political Authority Roles: Some Preliminary Findings." Paper presented at the annual meeting of the Canadian Political Science Association, St. John's, Newfoundland.
10. Ibid., p. 4.
11. Ibid., p. 18.
12. Ibid., p. 19.

13. Jean Pierre Richert, "The Impact of Ethnicity on the Perception of Heroes and Historical Symbols," *Canadian Review of Sociology and Anthropology* (May 1974), p. 156.

14. See John Johnstone, *Young People's Images of Canadian Society* (Ottawa: Queen's Printer, 1969). See also the article by Forbes in this volume.

15. John Meisel, *Working Papers on Canadian Politics*, enlarged edition (Montreal: McGill-Queen's Press, 1973), pp. 229–30.

16. Ibid., p. 31.

17. Peter C. Newman, *Renegade in Power: The Diefenbaker Years* (Toronto: McClelland and Stewart, Carleton Library edition, 1973), pp. 80–81.

History, Culture and Political Socialization:

4

The Canadian Setting

JOHN WOODS

How we acquire the knowledge and attitudes which fit us for membership in a political order is an ancient concern with an abundant if diffuse literature.[1] Despite this, however, the study which we are now calling "political socialization" is a new field marked by its own style, methods and specific concerns. Its practitioners tend to stand aside from the pertinent classics and call upon their own muse, so far with mixed results. Canadian scholars who take up the question must meld these unsympathetic traditions, the ancient one rich but obscure, the modern one familiar but sparse.

Political socialization is in the social science tradition, where the meaning of "science" is to be taken rather strictly.[2] We usually think of science as set apart by the universality of its formulations, but as a scholarly enterprise its peculiarity is its accessibility. Everything has to be in the open, and this places unique demands on the scientist. For him, as distinct from other scholars, there comes a critical moment in any investigation when the wealth of accumulated knowledge and insight is winnowed down to a series of spare and simple statements about how certain isolated and readily observable properties of things relate. From this point forward he can accept information only in its elements, each datum representing a single property of something viewed in its context. He must for the moment be utterly intolerant both of the ambiguity which invites us to penetrate appearances, and of the eccentricity of new insights, even though there could be no science without these. To reconstruct understanding in such terms is no easy task and deep involvement leads many to confuse the atypical character of this one phase with that of the entire enterprise—an understandable mistake, because, being the final step, this one is easily misconstrued as the sole contributor to the outcome. Weights and measures thus often replace imagination as the basis of it all.

The study of political socialization suffers particularly from this problem because it emerged as a field at the very moment when the behavioural revolution was redirecting the study of politics along more scientific lines.[3] In their concern for the revolution's success, devotees of the new approach conveyed to their students—often but not always unwittingly—the impression that anything cast in the traditional modes was valueless. Many not only failed to assimilate but also came to despise the fund of understanding which goes back to classical times. Traditional political science was presented in personalized styles, and it comprised idiosyncratic and, in "scientific" terms, unexamined thought. Its base of information was complex or obscure and its discussions were conducted in figurative rather than "operational" language—all things "unscientific." To the detriment of the field of political socialization, technique and substance were thus confused in the minds of many.

On the one hand, political socialization is in danger of being cut off from its heritage; on the other, it has as yet developed no clear directions of its own.[4] Since the behavioural revolution, political science as a whole has been rather rootless, and so it can provide us with little firm guidance. Socialization proper is more firmly established as a field, but it has not yet found the common ground on which all its adherents might stand together. Failing unanimity among those most able to guide him, it is particularly hard for the newcomer to employ this or that approach to the special problems of his own research concern; the common ground of a heterodox political science and an only slightly less heterodox study of socialization is doubly hard to chart.

THE VALUE QUESTION

One of the thornier problems in charting the ground is that of values. Questions of social value dog all nominally independent inquiry, but particularly the social studies, and this field most of all because it is concerned with values people are learning and on which they will therefore found the societies of the immediate future.

Every choice of research topic holds the promise of some eventual action. At the very least it implies that the area selected is of more practical importance than those which the researcher has passed over. Researchers are touched both by the value implications of their disciplines and by the problems and aspirations of the communities in which they live. The scholar must know how each of these forces has come to shape his thought so that he can decide the extent to which he will permit them to direct his efforts. This concern is particularly pressing at this time because of the role Americans are playing in the field as it develops. Like everyone else, American scholars find their work influenced by the problems and prospects of their own country; but, unlike the typical case, this tendency was out of control at the height of the behavioural revolution because access to the stabilizing heritage of social thought was cut off. As excitement subsides, impediments in the way of the investigators' good sense are more easily overcome and the broader perspectives are regained; but barriers remain in by now habitual antipathies and in the "behavioural" literature of the past fifteen-odd years, a literature which now tends to guide the discipline.

THREE PHASES OF THE SCIENTIFIC ENTERPRISE

The upshot of all this is that we do not presently have anything approaching an adequate tradition of political socialization as a field of study. Each of us must either accept on faith whatever is handy, or sort it out for himself. The latter course involves three quite distinct tasks; defining the field, framing research and constructing theory.

The first task therefore is to set the bounds of what we will consider "the political" and achieve a sound understanding of it in relation to society as a whole. Only with this in hand can we intelligently consider the range of learning events which support or serve to change the political process.[5] This requirement cannot be satisfied short of sustained and serious study. But this is not simply a plea for liberal education. It is true that we must strive to acquire the perspective and sensitivity which makes for responsible professionalism but we must also face questions of validity. The explicit formulations which follow upon our understanding will surely be miscast if they are rooted in fragmentary or superficial intuition.[6]

Furthermore, we must recognize that the words appropriate to this intuitive mode illuminate the heart of a thing, rather than differentiating it with the precision necessary later on. Someone who demands on scientific principle that we substitute a precise but anemic term like "system affect" for a broader term such as "loyalty" is demonstrating the superficiality of his own understanding. That term belongs to another mode of thought and another phase of science.

All this may sound too obvious to warrant mention, but it is precisely this obvious first step that is most difficult to accomplish and where the failures of contemporary political science, as well as its successes, are most apparent.[7] Its omission accounts for much that is trivial or absurd in the more "scientific" phase of political socialization as it has developed to date; but once a researcher does have this broad grasp of the field he can frame specific research concerns with a sure sense of his potential contribution to the field.[8]

When this setting is finalized, however, a whole new set of preparatory tasks emerge. Once again they are frequently and disastrously skimped. The loose conceptualizations adequate for a personalized understanding of the field, however profound, will not bear the weight of a sound research design. It is at this point that the transition to "science" in the narrow sense must be made and, just as the prior, intuitive phase is not only legitimate but essential, so is the second, technical phase. Each style of thought must be respected and employed in its proper place.[9] Before the researcher can gather "data" as opposed to information, for instance, he must rebuild the working portion of his imagined political world in terms which will provide both unmistakable guidance for the data-gathering operations and a basis for making sense of the outcome.

Even if this shift in perspectives is successful, things can go awry because the task of operationalization forces the researcher to narrow both his scope and the meanings he assigns to terms. If he, or worse still, an entire school of thought comes to value the strict, elegant but unavoidably simplistic operational model over the less disciplined but richer conceptions of the intuitive stage, they may substitute this part for the whole. The outcome is the same as if they had missed the first and fundamental stage altogether.

For instance, one useful simplifying assumption which unfortunately appears to have been accepted as true in a larger context is that socialization is prior to policy. According to this view, people first learn preferences for certain social conditions, and for ways of conducting the policy process. Their consequent expectations determine both institutional forms and the substance of policy. Despite an even more common and of course far sounder but less manageable working assumption—that all political processes are interdependent—this obviously conditional position, that learning comes first and policy later, seems to have worked its way back to shape our conventional understanding, so that political socialization is sometimes not regarded as itself affected by policy decisions. As a consequence, the traditional concern for political *education* as a policy matter has been a surprisingly rare theme in the political socialization literature.[10] We need not only to develop a sound grasp of the entire field at the outset, but also to husband that understanding once we have it. Fascination with "scientific" research, its techniques and its cumulative character can smother commonsense understanding at any stage of the enterprise.

Finally, research results must be accommodated within the wider body of understanding; this constitutes a third step to be undertaken as advisedly as the first two. The hope is that direct appreciation, or intuition, will be backed up through accretion of statements cast in the strict terminology of science, leading at last to theory. In this the final phase, successful efforts must be both rigorous, as in the second stage, and fully representative of the phenomena, as in the first. Our failures take the forms of uselessly simplistic theory on the one hand, and the mere reduction to jargon of pre-existing thought on the other.

One way to avoid the errors which characterize these three phases is to keep them distinct. If we move to the second stage without adequate attention to the first, we risk misperceiving the matter. To move directly to the final, theoretical phase requires vast factual knowledge and insight for any degree of success, and if successful, leaves a trail difficult for others to follow.

Examples of both kinds of error abound. People select some area of interest within the field and without any prior consideration of how their way of setting up the study might relate to larger views or purposes, plunge into months or years of work, drawing students and colleagues with them. However, graduate studies in recent years have tended to encourage the other error. Because the graduate curriculum has been dedicated to method and conceptualization since the behavioural revolution, students fresh from their undergraduate training are encouraged to essay criticisms of people like Max Weber. Too often they thenceforth think that they can make a career of disputation at the highest theoretical level. But Weber's theoretical work capped a career of intense historical investigation and was based on staggering erudition. The social sciences are far from the deductive elegance of the physical sciences they tend to take as their models, and anyone who expects to work in the realm of pure thought just now must turn elsewhere. Both the construction of general theory and its criticism are endpoints of a lengthy process of insight, data collection and hypothesis testing. We are still in the initial phases of this process (assuming that success in it is a reasonable expectation for the social sciences). We have each to start close to the beginning today and cannot expect to move directly to theoretical concerns, or even to the technical concerns of the second phase.

PROBLEMS, GUIDELINES AND VALUES

One of the phrases quite justifiably in the air at the moment is "systems theory"; unfortunately it is one of those terms frequently used by the mediocre to mystify in lieu of challenging us, and its very use has consequently come to give offence. Our distaste should be for those who would debase such notions, however, and not for the notions themselves. Systemic views have always characterized the most lasting social thought. Although most research is done on the basis of narrower conceptions, the final phases of a science's development, those of encompassing theoretical representations, are today best understood by the term systems theory. In the initial phases, the word "theory" hardly applies, but the published attempts to be theoretical are nevertheless most useful in establishing fruitful perspectives. In particular, Easton's series of three books on the systems approach provide a useful checklist of components and processes.[11] So, of course, do Bagehot, Tocqueville or any number of other classical writers who adopted a systemic viewpoint; but the less explicit style of the classics can leave the unmindful with gaps in his private, mental representation of the political process. The danger for our students in the contemporary works, on the other hand, is that they are couched in seductively weighty-sounding terms which can divert attention—even commitment—to themselves. But formally systemic approaches are available to guide students of political socialization in attaining a broad cultural and institutional perspective and to neglect them would be as irresponsible as to consider their terms magical.

Even in the initial stage, where perspectives are most general, Canada's peculiarities, notably federalism and the regional and ethnic multiplicity underlying it, should be considered; but it is in the second phase that national peculiarities become truly of central concern. As we move toward operational models we encounter questions of purpose and method which can be fully answered only in the light of specific information about the case in question. Among these, the thorniest and most recurrent are the value questions which arise from the policy implications of research choices. Fortunately, what has been the most vexatious of recent value controversies is easily laid to rest. This is the matter of "value-free" social science.[12]

First of all, there obviously cannot be a value-free study of political socialization in the sense that it stands independent of all desires. Anyone selects substance and method because he so chooses, which is to say that he acts with reference to his valuations. Just as obviously, though, there can be a value-free science in the sense that it pursues purposes independent of "the values" characterizing the scientists' own society. Freedom from the values is classic to intellectual endeavour and certainly not a new issue raised by exponents of formal science; but it is particularly important to political socialization because values are part of the substance the scholar addresses in this field. He must be sophisticated enough to transcend the conventional in adopting the values which will guide his work. Finally, the terms of scientific statements must obviously be value-free in the sense that two oranges plus two sour oranges are just as surely four as if the second two were sweet.

The principles underlying the value controversy are as simple as their applications are complex. The important thing is to distinguish between the vastly overblown debate over value-free science (now hopefully at an end) and the crucial matter of how fact and value are to be related in the pursuit of understanding. This is an inextricable part of the entire question of what is to be studied and how.

THREE BASES FOR CHOICE

There are three sources of both values and optimization criteria for the field: the classical heritage, society's concerns and the discipline's own impetus. This last is presently the most treacherous guide because there is so little seasoned tradition in which to ground further research with any security. The directions in which the more mature sciences are moving have emerged after thousands of years of investigation and consideration. Directions have been verified by countless tests. No rich history of cumulative research and refinement of conceptions, such as mark the older sciences, supports our choices of concern or method. The heritage of social insight, rich as it is, remains the province of the humanities. It does not fall easily into the neat configurations of a science, and does not point collectively in any particular direction for research; its messages are not easily unravelled by the impatient, and social scientists consequently tend to rely instead on the rudimentary developments which have occurred to date in their own fields.

There is, however, no reason to assume that initial directions in a new field should be followed. Most of the work being done in the broadly delineated field of political culture and socialization follows American concerns in selecting research topics. It was also in the United States that the mistaken belief most held sway that a value-free science stands independent of valuation. Believing values were no concern of theirs, American researchers naturally failed to consider them and hence could have no control over their place in research planning. The upshot is that most research to date has been based on American conditions, concerns and aspirations. This is not an acceptable foundation for our own work.

Greenstein's work with American children, for instance, concentrates on symbols and legitimation of authority and on the ways in which participatory norms and party preferences are learned.[13] His concerns are underlaid by the assumption that the truly fundamental political learning is that of roles within a large mobile, pluralistic and boisterously participant state such as the United States. The stability of a vast, shifting, heterogeneous, unruly populace must be secured through their intense response to national symbols, their submission to authority, and through upholding partisan political commitments which provide continuity and stability by overriding factional involvement, changing aspirations and frequent relocations. These concerns would appear eccentric in a tribal society, and even in traditionalistic Canada they should not be given the priority they deserve in the United States. Here, concern has rightly been with the substance of our ethos, rather than its fulfilment. Psychologically, Canada is still made up of colonial communities, ethnically and economically distinct in many ways, but with a tempered loyalty to one another expressed through acknowledgment of an over-arching power. Loyalty is not at the forefront of our minds but there is a bedrock of virtually unquestioned allegiance to some hazy conception of a nation—whether regional or national in scope. Thus, despite the deep and lasting antipathy of French Canada to English-Canadian domination, the events of October 1970 remain for all Canadians a shocking and baffling interlude. Whatever our differences, the collapse or suspension of civil order strikes us as distinctly out of place and to many Canadians is incomprehensible. Especially for English-speaking Canada, the focus of our allegiance may occasionally be in question but not allegiance itself. It is our destiny which is unclear, while Americans, sure of their mission, suffer from outbursts of impatience for fulfilment.

American revolutionary individualism has always been equivocal about submission to civil authority, which seems fundamentally at odds with the nation's genius. The respect for authority acquired by children is thus a matter of paramount importance for the system's stability. We have seen innumerable examples of the tenuousness of civil authority in contemporary U.S. history and Greenstein's concern is understandable in the American context; but the same focus would be inappropriate for a Canadian study. The Quebec case can be seen as only superficially similar. The issue for the vast majority of those concerned is not the acknowledgment of civil authority itself, but of specifically English-Canadian authority.

The inappropriateness for Canadian researchers of a primary concern with partisan loyalties can be seen in this same light. Canadian history has provided for the regional-ethnic loyalties which focus and regularize our political competition without dependence on political parties as clearly visible and continuing poles about which to cluster and focus interests.

THE CANADIAN SETTING

Our own national purposes and problems rather than the impetus of the discipline should provide the first-hand guidance for our research, just as

American concerns have guided the work done in the United States. But we must accept this guidance on the understanding that methods developed and inferences drawn apply only here in Canada until their broader applicability is clearly established.

There is a substantial body of literature touching on the nature of our country. Some of the best is rooted in the Laurentian thesis of Canadian national development. It presents or implies innumerable related hypotheses regarding our ideologies, lifestyle and political processes, a sound understanding of which must ground our selection of concerns in the study of political socialization. The Laurentian thesis holds that Canada developed around the extension of trade routes, first from Europe and then from the settlements on the St. Lawrence.[14] Our cultural heritage is thus one of virtually unbroken reliance on an established order which simply extended itself into the wilderness. There has been no disordered frontier, no break with tradition, no rugged individualism on the American model. This is not to say that historians think we have had an easy time of it. The hostility of the Canadian Shield and the prairies to agriculture has been a constant threat, one which in the early days could only be met by maintaining constant contacts with a secure home base. Co-operation is thus built into the nation's fabric and a sense of essential, if not always willing, mutual dependency into the spirit of the communities which sprang up along trade routes and at their end-points. Individualism has been minimized as compared with the American case. A sense of the European cultural roots has been maintained, and lines for the flow of cultural substance from Europe have tended to remain open. A rather hierarchical style of community life, for the modern world, is acknowledged here, even if not entirely accepted, and government is generally regarded as a participant rather than simply an overseer of community life. Our allegiance to the regime is a comfortable one. We have never decided upon allegiance and thus have no reason to question such a decision (at least in English-speaking Canada). Our allegiance is simply found in the nature of things: hence, our lesser concern over authority, over the dilemma of individual freedom versus collective order and over legitimacy. This also tends to explain the direction of loyalties through communities rather than through parties. My point is that all of this is drawn primarily from the work of Canada's historians and social commentators, certainly not from that of prior students of political socialization, nor even from that of social scientists, as we understand the term today. Its significance for a responsible choice of research topics in political socialization is nonetheless obvious. Socialization is the transmission of a culture and the culture is an historical development.

The culture is also revealed in our novelists' and poets' insights, and for the scientist to suppose, as many appear to do, that he stands apart from, or even above, their work is both arrogant and foolish. The relevance of Hugh MacLennan's or Gabrielle Roy's work, for instance, is so obvious that it hardly needs to be mentioned, but there is much to be found elsewhere. To cite a recent example, some critics have found in Robertson Davies' *Fifth Business* a characterization which illuminates an important English-Canadian cultural thread, the Gaelic. In fact, there is a lot of Lester Pearson about the hero. He is a critical but sympathetic observer of failing and excess, a moderator and conciliator, but seldom an initiator. He is a realist but not in the modern tradition which elevates technological advance to an ontology. His realism is profound but quaintly narrow, bridging frugality and mysticism. For me, this odd combination of philosophic roots points up characteristics of the Canadian cultural panorama which are essential to a thorough understanding of political upbringing in this country.

The point I am trying to make is that while these speculations are, on the face of it, a bit removed from the developing subdiscipline of political socialization, they can yield valuable clues as to what we should look for and why. Davies may be saying nothing about Canada and his interpreters may be far from the mark, but some authors and some interpretations provide keys to our culture and our social forms. Unless we search for this understanding wherever it might be found, we cannot claim to study political socialization responsibly.

COMPARATIVE STUDY

To study a nation's political socialization effectively one must understand that particular nation. The rule applies with the same force to comparative studies. Comparison is fruitless if the cultural characteristics, still worse the ideals, of one nation are thoughtlessly taken as parameters for the study of others. One must first develop an adequate representation of each culture and its patterns of socialization as they relate to its own political institutions and processes. Only with adequate descriptions in hand is it reasonable to undertake the search for a comparative theory, linking those points of similarity between countries which illuminate their differences. The enterprise is confounded if the points of similarity have been assumed beforehand and built into the fabric of the research.

Providing the lead for political culture and socialization, American scholars have tended to project an image of their own society onto those which they study. The classic case in point is Almond and Verba's five-nation study of political cultures and the theory of the "civic culture" they presented in reporting it.[15] The questions they asked were for the most part familiar to scholars in the "public opinion" stream of American behaviouralism, having to do with the underpinnings of participant, pluralist democracy in the modern industrial state.

The civic-culture thesis has been correctly construed by its critics as an apology for the United States' having fallen short of the liberal-democratic ideal of rational and self-interested, yet civic-minded, men governing themselves, as provided for in the American founding myths. In the civic culture, stability is ensured by a proper balance of this kind of behaviour as against passive non-involvement, depending on the times and the issues. By this measure, the modern political system is one which does not quite live up to the criteria originally laid down for the United States. Needless to say, Almond and Verba also found that the four other countries they studied compared unfavourably with their own country in one or more regards and were thus somehow less attuned to the contemporary world. Because American conditions were held up as the standard, the United States naturally approached them more closely than did the other nations.

At present, American scholars in the field are shaking free of these limitations. *The Civic Culture* was published in 1963 and its authors' more recent work (in comparative politics) are from a far more cosmopolitan viewpoint.[16] It would be doubly a shame for Canadian scholars to follow faulty precedents just as they are being set aside by their own earlier proponents.

Such pitfalls are more readily recognized than avoided, however. The discipline as we see it practised is seductive. It is hard to make one's way from the basics to the finished product, and the cumulative character of a formal science can be comfortably misconstrued as a constraint on the initiative of scholars nominally "scientific" in much of their work. It is easily assumed that one's work should follow on what has gone more or less immediately before in the same nominal interest area, that it should adopt the same perspectives and terms and thus, unavoidably, the same concerns. Furthermore, there is undeniable social pressure within any discipline to further existing lines of research. The influence of a former thesis supervisor may continue to provide the bench-mark for work many years removed from a scholar's graduate study. To adopt the style, concerns and interpretations of someone earlier in the field is a legitimate way to evade the difficulties and potential embarrassment of confronting colleagues with one's own position, derived from the rudiments.[17]

There is also a great temptation to get in on the ground floor of a new intellectual edifice; certainly, no one wants to be left out. Finally, the early attempts are crude and easily attacked; the findings are minimal and easily improved upon; the techniques in a new field are unsophisticated, easily learned and easily discarded as we move on to something a little bit better. All these things promise easy fame to those who will set aside properly prior considerations of what is both viable and valuable. A moral as well as an intellectual commitment is required to avoid the pitfalls.

Recent political science has shown more concern for the survival of systems than for the well-being of people. As Macpherson points out, we have achieved value freedom by relinquishing values.[18] But social science is first a humanity. Its proper concern is enhancing life. Canadian scholars in the field today must set a standard for study rooted in this concern and not in the scientific or governmental technologies which may advance it.

The early years are particularly important because, try as we may, we cannot entirely escape precedents. Just as there is a culture and socialization of society at large, so there is a culture and socialization of each discipline and subdiscipline, which grows out of its history. The work of the next few years will set the baseline for growth in the study of political socialization because the premises of initial debates becomes a new field's rudiments. They should be drawn from the Canadian experience, the heritage of the humanities, and only the best that the established social sciences can offer.

NOTES

1. See, for example, Aristotle on child-bearing and upbringing, Book 7, chapter I of the *Politics*. The director of education is to see that children are raised to be suitable citizens and the curriculum is to be organized so as to optimize learning processes relative to stages of the child's development and so that "The citizen should be moulded to suit the form of government under which he lives" (Book 8, chapter I). Aristotle also provides a counter to the compartmentalization of the social sciences. "He does not forget in the *Ethics* that the individual man is essentially a member of society, nor in the *Politics* that the good life of the state exists only in the good lives of its citizens." W. D. Ross, *Aristotle* (New York: The World Publishing Co., 1959), p. 183. See also Plato, *The Republic*, Part II, chapter IX.

2. See, for instance, the style and technique of a well-known and comprehensive American study by Robert D. Hess and Judith V. Torney, *The Development of Political Attitudes in Children* (Chicago: Aldine, 1967).

3. Fred I. Greenstein, one of the early and significant workers in the field, dates the study of political socialization from the late 1950s and early 1960s, in David L. Sills, ed., *The International Encyclopedia of the Social Sciences* (New York: The Macmillan Co., 1968), vol. 14, p. 551. In political science, the behavioural revolution is often nominally dated from the publication of David Easton's *The Political System* (New York: Alfred A. Knopf, 1953).

4. An orientation to socialization is provided by Roger V. Burton's article in the *International Encyclopedia*, ibid., pp. 534–44.

5. David Easton and Jack Dennis, *Children in the Political System* (New York: McGraw-Hill, 1969),

pp. 18–19, talk of a "Political Theory of Political Socialization" which will establish the significance of the socialization process. Finding such a position is a step logically prior to much that has already been attempted and which on that account tends to be rootless, or rooted in someone's sound or unsound common sense.

6. Among significant works, Kornberg's use of the term "socialization" to denote the moment at which subjects recall becoming acquainted with national politics is a case in point. Allan Kornberg, *Canadian Legislative Behaviour* (Toronto: Holt, Rinehart and Winston, 1967), p. 50.

7. Examples in the minor journals are easily found. Among notable works, Hess and Torney come to mind. Valuable as the book may be, it appears riddled with ready assumptions about what constitutes an orientation toward the political process. A glance at the table of contents will suffice. It lists what are essentially the power patterns of American national politics, together with the independent effects of some gross social indicators, notably s.e.s., together with the agents of socialization as commonly classified in the U.S. literature. There is little apparent concern for the fit of the implied model to the U.S. case. There is no consideration of possible variation in patterns of socialization; only one is assumed. There is no discussion of the history or resultant culture, without an understanding of which no research design in political socialization makes sense. All is assumed, perhaps quite correctly for the American case, but assumed nonetheless.

8. Even those who subscribe to this view can be faulted for stopping short of a thorough grounding. Compare Weber's massive historical scholarship with the apparent nar-

rowness of Easton's base or that of Talcott Parsons.

9. The current trend toward rejection of formal theory-building on a strict, empirical basis is as foolish a fad as was its earlier exaltation. Formal science is no more a threat to understanding than it was the guarantor ten years ago. The threat is from those who fail to perceive the interdependency of the descriptive or speculative phase and the formal phase, but most especially from those who overlook the former entirely.

In a very sensible paper on Canadian political science, Alan C. Cairns recently observed, "I have the feeling that too little of the recent literature on Canada is a dialogue with what has gone before, and too much is a peripheral dialogue with the American literature" ("Continentalism and/or Nationalism in Canadian Political Science: Is There a Problem?", a paper presented at the ix World Congress of the International Political Science Association, Montreal, August 1973). A "peripheral dialogue with the American literature" in the case of political socialization means one with an excessively formalistic sub-field. "What has gone before," on the other hand, can be thought of as a considerable body of sound historical and speculative literature bearing on the Canadian culture.

10. In a 1969 introduction to a new edition of his own study of 1959, H. H. Hyman (ibid.) points out the loss of a distinction in the field between those aspects of political socialization which are "idiosyncratic in character": the kind of thing learned in a non-institutional setting such as the family, and those aspects which "lend themselves to social and educational policy" (*Political Socialization* [New York: Macmillan, 1969]). The concern for policy was not entirely lost, however. See James S. Coleman, ed., *Education and Political Develop-*

ment (Princeton: Princeton University Press, 1965); in particular see Edgar Litt, "Civic Education, Community Norms and Political Indoctrination" in Litt, ed., *The Political Imagination* (Glenview, Ill.: Scott Foresman, 1966), pp. 86–94; and Richard M. Merelman, *Political Socialization and Educational Climate* (New York: Holt, Rinehart and Winston, 1971).

11. David Easton, *The Political System* (New York: Alfred D. Knopf, 1953), *A Framework for Political Analysis* (Englewood Cliffs, N.J.: Prentice-Hall, 1965), and *A Systems Analysis of Political Life* (New York: Wiley, 1965).

12. Mulford Q. Sibley's essay, "The Limitations of Behaviouralism," provides a fine brief discussion of the value problem and related concerns; it is to be found in James C. Charlesworth, ed., *The Limits of Behaviouralism in Political Science* (Philadelphia: The American Academy of Political and Social Science, 1962), pp. 68–93. Some of the sillier discussion is both described and indulged in by Russell Kirk in "Segments of Political Science not Amenable to Behavioural Treatment," ibid., pp. 49–67.

13. Fred Greenstein, *Children and Politics* (New Haven: Yale University Press, 1965).

14. The names most strongly associated with the Laurentian thesis are those of H. A. Innis and D. G. Creighton, but W. L. Morton's *The Canadian Identity*, 2nd ed. (Toronto: University of Toronto Press, 1972), is its most direct and readable statement.

15. Gabriel A. Almond and Sidney Verba, *The Civic Culture* (Princeton, N.J.: Princeton University Press, 1963).

16. See Sidney Verba's concluding chapter to Leonard Binder et al., *Crises and Sequences in Political Development* (Princeton: Princeton University Press, 1971). Verba is not dealing with political culture and socialization here, but the example

of maturing outlook will nonetheless suffice. He demonstrates a view of the political process that is at one and the same time cogent and admitting of multitudinous forms and ways of arriving at them. This is in the sharpest contrast to the views underlying *The Civic Culture* study.

17. It would be foolish to demand that each study of political socialization must be rooted in the socialization literature. It is the field in its entirety which must maintain the liaison. What rankles is the lip service paid this duty; see, for example, Dawson and Prewitt, *Political Socialization* (Boston: Little, Brown, 1969), p. 42, for a single page which manages a bow both to the literature on socialization and to the classics.

18. C. B. Macpherson, *Democratic Theory: Essays in Retrieval* (Oxford: Clarendon Press, 1973), p. 78.

PART TWO

The Development of
Political Attitudes

Affection and Evaluation in Children's Perceptions of Authority

TERRANCE G. CARROLL

5

The concept of authority, according to Sebastian de Grazia, is indispensable to politics. Indeed, he went on to argue that the very ". . . subject matter of the political scientist is earthly authority and its relation to the divine."[1] While the theological aspects of authority may not have received a great deal of attention from students of politics in recent years, almost every theoretical study and a great many of the empirical works in the field focus directly upon authority. Because basic attitudes about authority have been found to be shaped early in life, interest in this area has been particularly pronounced in studies of childhood political socialization. Such studies have typically tried to discover what sorts of attitudes children from different environments learn about various political authority roles and symbols, and to trace the chronological pattern of this developmental process. Of basic importance, of course, is simple knowledge of the existence of such roles and symbols, and there exists a considerable body of data on children's cognitive development.

Simple recognition of role labels such as "Prime Minister" or "Mayor" in itself, however, tells us nothing about a child's attitudes towards these roles. Cognition is the *sine qua non* for perceptions of authority, but in a sense that is all it is. Central to the concept of authority is the notion of dominance and subordination, and until a child learns to assess different roles relative to each other he cannot be said to have truly developed an awareness of the structure of political authority.[2]

A review of the relevant literature suggests a number of criteria which might be employed in assessing authority roles, but not all of these apply fully in the case of children's perceptions of political authority. Herbert Simon, for example, suggested that authority might be based upon sanctions, confidence, identification and/or legitimacy.[3] By sanctions he

92

meant the subordinate's perception of the ability of the superior to reward compliant behaviour, and to punish non-compliance. It seems probable that this factor, for which we shall use the more familiar term "power," is relevant to childhood socialization. Several studies have indicated that children frequently do have some impression of the power of an authority role.[4] These impressions may not always be very accurate, but they exist nevertheless, and it would seem likely that they influence the extent to which authority is accorded to the role.

By confidence Simon meant a general feeling that the incumbents in particular roles, whoever they might be, were likely to make good, wise decisions. The decisions are accepted as authoritative because one has faith in the source from which they emanate. Confidence would seem to be a significant element in many of the authority relationships in which children participate. When a child takes an adult's hand and permits him to decide when it is safe to cross the street, he is displaying confidence in the adult. He has been taught to accept on faith the adult's superior ability to make such decisions. Children may well acquire similar attitudes towards political authority roles.[5]

The concepts of identification and legitimacy would not seem to contribute as significantly to our understanding of how children picture the structure of authority. Identification with the accepted values of a reference group may help an individual to define his own place in the structure of authority, but it provides no direct assistance in mentally structuring relationships between other authority roles.[6] Legitimacy—the acceptance of an obligation to obey a superior—in a sense subsumes much of our concept of authority itself. For children at least, legitimacy is likely to be the cumulative result of other factors, rather than a separate element in authority. Young children do not as a rule distinguish between those who have the ability to command and those who are worthy of deference.[7] The fact that formal authority and merit do not always co-incide is one of the harsh realities faced later in life.

Children, then, may be expected to accord legitimate authority to those roles which are perceived to have other qualities which justify their superior position. Power and confidence are two of the criteria which might be employed to compare authority roles. Turning to the works of another major writer on the nature of authority, Max Weber, we find that he also suggested four potential reasons for according authority to a superior.[8] Weber argued that self-interest is the immediate motivating factor in compliance with the orders of authority roles.[9] In part this is like our power component; it is based upon the subordinate's perception of the rewards and punishments which are at the command of the superior. Weber also included the subordinate's assessment of the gains and losses which are intrinsic to compliance, but it seems unlikely that children make this type of judgment about the instrumentalities of political authority relationships in which they are not themselves direct participants.

Weber went on to suggest three less variable motives for accepting the legitimacy of an existing authority structure. Two of these depend upon reference to some set of absolute values. People might obey because of a rational belief in the absolute propriety of the authority structure, or on the basis of faith in a set of religious values which justifies compliance. There would not seem to be any common body of religious beliefs in Canada which sets out and underpins the complex web of relationships between various political authority roles, however, and it is doubtful that many children have rationally related the structure of political authority to a system of ethical or aesthetic values.

Weber's final motive, on the other hand, does seem to provide a criterion which is different from those suggested by Simon, and which children might well employ in comparing authority roles. He pointed out that "affectual or emotional surrender" by a subordinate to a superior could lead to a willingness to comply.[10] This seems particularly worthy of consideration in the case of children. If only through the tone of voice used by elders when mentioning a particular authority role, or a vague impression gained while deciphering a newspaper headline, a child may develop positive or negative feelings towards certain roles while knowing relatively little about them.

In this paper, then, we will examine some aspects of the development in children of a picture of the structure of authority through their ability to assess political roles on the basis of affection, and to evaluate them in terms of perceived power and accorded confidence. These three criteria seem to be the aspects of authority which are most relevant to the socialization process during childhood. Political authority is not simply another way of saying "affection" or "power" or "confidence," but taken together these elements are likely to encompass the essence of a child's perception of the authority of political roles.

Many studies have looked at children's affective and evaluative attitudes towards authority roles in an absolute way. That is, they have asked if the respondents liked or disliked a role, thought it was good or bad, or powerful or weak. Relative assessments involving "better or worse" or "more or less" questions relating two or more roles to one another have, however, been remarkably rare. As assessments of this type are clearly central to the development of perceptions of the authority structure as a whole, one can only conclude that the implicit assumption has been that such rank-ordering demands a degree of sophistication not commonly found among young children.

Easton and Dennis's survey of children's attitudes about political authority in the United States remains the best available example of a socialization study which is carefully integrated into a more general theoretical analysis of political life. It explicitly attempts to examine the development of knowledge of and support for the structure of authority.[11] Using a number of specific questions which are similar in nature to the three criteria employed in this paper, they asked their young respondents to give separate assessments of the roles of President, Senator and Policeman, and of such collectivities as the Government and the Supreme Court.[12] Because identical questions with identical response categories were used for each role these assessments are comparable, but no questions requiring the children themselves to compare different roles were asked.[13]

While studies such as this ignored the development of a mental ordering of authority roles, they did cast some doubt upon the assumption that such attitudes towards political authority could not profitably be examined in surveys of children. In addition to having his entire New Haven sample fill in questionnaires, for example, Greenstein also conducted semi-structured interviews with a smaller number of children employing questions eliciting direct comparisons, apparently with at least some success.[14] When pre-testing for the present Canadian study also failed to reveal any great difficulties in getting responses to this type of question, pupils in grades two through eight in what is to be a national sample were asked to give relative assessments of a number of Canadian and American political authority roles. Preliminary data from over 3,600 children in this on-going study strongly suggest that the ability to make such comparisons on the basis of affective and evaluative criteria develops at a surprisingly early age.[15]

The nine political authority roles included in this study are the Queen, Governor General, Prime Minister, Federal Cabinet Minister, Federal Member of Parliament, Provincial Premier, Local Mayor, American President and American Congressman. These roles were presented in pairs, and the children were asked to indicate which of each pair they liked more, which of each pair they thought was more powerful, and in which of each pair they had the most confidence.[16] The average response rate for these questions was 80 per cent, and even at the lowest grade level the incidence of "don't know" and "no answer" responses was less than one in three.

Each role was paired with the office of Prime Minister in questions based upon each of the three criteria.[17] This makes it possible for us to gain a quick overall impression of our respondents' perceptions of the structure of political authority by ranking all of the roles on scales comparing them with the Prime Minister (and, by inference, with each other). The prime-ministerial role was placed at zero, and all of the others were ranked between plus and minus one, depending on how frequently they were selected in direct comparisons with the Prime Minister. Thus if all of our respondents in a given grade chose the Governor General over the Prime Minister on the basis of power, for example, the Governor General would receive a score of one on the power scale for that grade. An even division of responses between the two roles would result in a zero score, and if everybody opted for the Prime Minister the role of the Governor General would have a score of minus one.[18]

Table 1 shows the composite structure of affective orientations for the sample as a whole. The best-liked roles at every grade level are the Queen, the Governor General and the Prime Minister, in that order. While this affective ordering does not change, the relative position of the monarch declines substantially among the older respondents. Indeed, one of the most noteworthy developments traced in the table is the decrease in the distance between roles. The range drops by almost half between grade two and grade eight. In grade two our respondents were in general agreement about which roles they liked and which they disliked, but by grade eight this consensus had dissipated. Relative affection for the role of Federal M.P. follows a U-shaped pattern, starting out almost as high as the Prime

Table 1   Affective Assessments of Authority Roles, by Grade

Role	2	3	4	5	6	7	8
Queen	.773	.757	.603	.543	.485	.514	.320
Governor General	.160	.279	.203	.193	.218	.315	.254
Prime Minister	0	0	0	0	0	0	0
Provincial Premier	−.644	−.642	−.469	−.395	−.201	−.083	−.126
Federal M.P.	−.030	−.199	−.485	−.460	−.231	−.137	−.145
Local Mayor	−.615	−.706	−.601	−.513	−.333	−.228	−.187
Cabinet Minister	—	—	−.534	−.446	−.377	−.257	−.267
American President	−.243	−.421	−.554	−.440	−.400	−.236	−.426
American Congressman	—	—	−.634	−.603	−.508	−.387	−.421

Minister, declining through the middle grades, and then increasing in popularity among older children. The remaining Canadian roles—Provincial Premier, Local Mayor and Cabinet Minister—are all much less liked than the Prime Minister in the youngest grades, but they steadily gain in affection as the respondents mature. By grade eight each of the Canadian roles is better liked than either the American President or Congressman.

The pattern of evaluations based upon confidence is quite different (Table 2). Our respondents had the greatest confidence in the roles of Queen, Governor General and Prime Minister, but by grade eight the office of Prime Minister displaces that of Governor General in relative confidence. While the composite evaluations of these three roles tend to converge as the children grow older, there is relatively little change in the positions of the other roles. The American presidency comes fourth at every grade level, and the role of Congressman last. While the remaining Canadian roles tended to be better liked among the older respondents, none of them gains at all substantially in relative confidence.

Finally, Table 3 shows that among our younger respondents the Queen is seen as having the greatest power, followed by the Governor General,

Table 2   Evaluations of Confidence in Authority Roles, by Grade

Role	2	3	4	5	6	7	8
Queen	.647	.584	.642	.463	.401	.391	.175
Governor General	.227	.269	.106	.033	.051	.072	−.037
Prime Minister	0	0	0	0	0	0	0
American President	−.214	−.283	−.327	−.267	−.173	−.111	−.207
Provincial Premier	−.567	−.589	−.533	−.576	−.545	−.501	−.498
Local Mayor	−.448	−.577	−.527	−.606	−.637	−.595	−.542
Federal M.P.	−.529	−.668	−.579	−.665	−.626	−.616	−.568
Cabinet Minister	—	—	−.690	−.665	−.669	−.652	−.592
American Congressman	—	—	−.708	−.731	−.730	−.702	−.698

the Prime Minister, and the American President. However, the composite evaluation of the monarch declines in the more senior grades, the presidency comes to be seen as equivalent in power to the Prime Minister, and the Governor General falls to fourth position. One might think that the remaining roles are perceived to be less powerful in part because they are less well known, but in fact their relative positions all tend to decline as the grade level of respondents increases.

The tempting conclusion to be drawn from these data is that a sizable majority of children as young as seven years of age were able to apply the criteria outlined above when assessing political authority roles. On the face of it, however, it would seem equally possible that our respondents simply attempted to oblige their interrogators by making random choices when presented with the questions. Our interest in this paper is with children's ability to compare authority roles on the basis of affection, confidence and power, and thus to mentally structure political authority relationships. In order to assess their ability to make such comparisons we must consider the extent to which respondents distinguished between the criteria, and the extent to which their judgments based upon one

Table 3 Evaluations of the Power of Authority Roles, by Grade

Role	2	3	4	5	6	7	8
Queen	.595	.612	.681	.489	.473	.437	.201
Governor General	.387	.278	.097	−.037	−.086	−.043	−.206
Prime Minister	0	0	0	0	0	0	0
American President	−.162	−.271	−.327	−.289	−.139	.043	−.023
Provincial Premier	−.520	−.639	−.539	−.562	−.637	−.642	−.619
Local Mayor	−.427	−.454	−.552	−.649	−.685	−.706	−.713
Federal M.P.	−.517	−.659	−.611	−.676	−.719	−.697	−.766
Cabinet Minister	—	—	−.642	−.652	−.720	−.720	−.753
American Congressman	—	—	−.698	−.760	−.784	−.819	−.801

criterion influenced those ostensibly based upon the others. An examination of the degree of consistency in comparisons of the same roles on the basis of different criteria can help in this regard.

Let us take the comparisons of the offices of Prime Minister and Local Mayor as an example. It should be kept in mind that, as was the case for every pair of roles, these two offices were compared three times—once with affection as the criterion, once using confidence, and once on the basis of power. Suppose that a child indicated that he liked the Prime Minister better than the Local Mayor. If this was a random choice it should not have influenced his selections when the two roles were compared on the basis of confidence or power. On each of the questions based upon these two criteria the probability of selecting either role remained at 0.5. With random selection, in other words, given the choice of a particular role on the basis of one of our criteria, the same role should have been chosen 50 per cent of the time in the questions based upon the other two criteria. As the degree of consistency with the first choice moves above the 50 per cent mark the possibility that the selection process was random declines.

To establish consistency ratings, then, we first determine which role from a particular pair a respondent selected on the basis of one criterion —affection, for example. We then see whether or not he chose the same role when confidence and power were the criteria. The consistency rating would be 100 per cent if the same role was selected in all three comparisons; 50 per cent if it was only chosen one additional time; and zero if the alternative role was selected in the second and third comparisons. We can then sum the consistency ratings for all of the comparisons a respondent has made, and can calculate the average degree of consistency between selections based upon affection and those based upon the other two criteria for all of the respondents in a grade. The same process can be repeated using power and confidence in turn as the base criterion.

In analysing the responses in this survey we find that, regardless of which criterion we pick as the starting point, the consistency of subsequent responses never falls as low as 50 per cent in any grade or for any of the seventeen pairs of roles presented to the respondents. Treating each of the three criteria in turn as the starting point, the average degree of consistency between this first set of choices and subsequent responses is 68.8 per cent. Obviously, therefore, many of the children in our sample were not simply answering at random and, in fact, must have been employing *some* criterion in selecting one political authority role over another.

We still would not be justified in assuming that the respondents were actually employing all three of our criteria. It is possible, for example, that one of the criteria, such as affection, coloured their relative evaluations of the power of roles, and influenced their confidence in them as well. In this case a child who "liked" the Prime Minister better than his Local Mayor, for instance, would also tend to perceive the Prime Minister as more powerful and more deserving of confidence. If respondents' selections were made on such a basis, however, the consistency ratings for affection, power and confidence should all have approached unity. Since this was not the case it seems clear that many of our respondents were able to differentiate between the degree of affection they held for a role, the degree to which they had confidence in it, and the extent of its power.

With an average consistency rate of 68.8 per cent, then, we can be confident that the selections in the aggregate were neither completely random, nor based upon any single criterion. We cannot, of course, see inside the minds of the children to determine positively that the criteria which they employed were those that we had intended. It is possible that their judgments were based upon factors entirely different from those suggested in our questions. The questions were worded simply, however, and were constructed with the assistance of professional educators. Neither in the pre-test nor in the actual administration of the questionnaire were we able to find any evidence of serious doubts among the children about the meaning of the questions. By far the most plausible conclusion is that many of our respondents were able to apply the three criteria in forms very close to those which we had anticipated in making relative assessments of the various authority roles.

Even though many of our respondents do seem to have differentiated between the different criteria in assessing the relationships between the roles, one would still not expect to find that affective and evaluative orientations are entirely distinct. Rather, it might be anticipated that assessments based upon affection, confidence and power influence one another. If, for example, a child had strong positive or negative affective orientations towards a role, it seems likely that this will have influenced the extent to which he displayed general confidence in the same role. Indeed, we might hypothesize that the more important a particular criterion was in the child's mind, the greater the extent to which it can be expected to have influenced his assessments based upon other criteria.[19] This, of course, would lead to a higher consistency rating for the criterion in question, since selections ostensibly based upon the other factors were made to conform with the choice made on the basis of this more important element in authority. Conversely, then, it can also be hypothesized that the degree of consistency between different assessments indicates the importance of each criterion to the respondents.

Calculating consistency ratings as indicated above, again using each criterion in turn as the starting point and measuring the degree of consistency between judgments based upon it and those based upon the other two criteria, we obtain aggregate indicators of the relative importance of each factor in the children's minds. In Table 4 the least influential criterion at each grade level has been given a zero value, and the table entries record in percentage points the extent to which consistency with the remaining criteria is higher. Thus in grade two general confidence was the least influential criterion; consistency with the responses to the affection

Table 4   The Relative Influence of the Components of Authority, by Grade

Criterion:	2	3	4	5	6	7	8
Power	1.0	6.0	1.5	3.7	1.2	6.1	3.4
Affection	0.8	0	0	0	0	0	0
Confidence	0	3.6	0.1	3.6	4.9	7.1	7.3

questions exceeded consistency with responses to the confidence questions by 0.8 per cent; and the most influential criterion was power, as consistency with responses to those questions was 1.0 per cent higher.

The differences revealed in this table are very small, but they are not without import. Although the range of scores within grades varies from a maximum of just over seven percentage points to a minimum of only one, the pattern after grade two is very regular. Power remains the most important element in the children's assessment of political authority through grade five. The greatest spill-over between orientations along our three dimensions is from attitudes about the power of a role to attitudes reflecting the affection and confidence criteria. Confidence is the second most influential factor throughout these grades, and the least important is affection. This relatively weak impact of affective orientations on other types of attitudes continues in grades six, seven and eight, but among these older children diffuse confidence replaces assessments of power as the most influential factor.

This finding is quite different from what had been expected. Our *a priori* hypothesis was that affective orientations would be the most important factor in role assessments, although we anticipated some reduction in their pre-eminence as the children grew older. Implicit in this hypothesis was the assumption that the greater the emotive content of a factor, and the less important its factual component, the easier it would be for children to employ it as a criterion, and the more it would influence their judgments based upon other criteria.

It is true that affection has its greatest impact among the youngest respondents, but except for this relatively minor point our hypothesis must be completely rejected. Generally, affective orientations have the least spill-over of the three types, and even among the younger children power is more important than affection. An examination of response rates, moreover, reveals no straightforward relationship between the degree of ease with which children employ a criterion and the degree of influence it has on their other comparisons.

A possible explanation for the relative importance of the three criteria might be found instead in the contrasting natures of political authority on the one hand, and the types of authority relationships with which children are most familiar on the other. The latter, especially for younger children, are direct personal relationships.[20] The important authority figures are the parent, the teacher, and so on, and here emotive reactions to the personality of the superior might be expected to outweigh any consideration of their actual physical power. Political authority roles, however, are distant, impersonal abstractions for children, and these characteristics are particularly pronounced when the roles are divorced from specific incumbents, as they were in the questionnaire used in this study.

Our respondents appear to have little difficulty in forming emotive orientations about these roles, and in assessing one role relative to another on the basis of these attitudes. It may well be, however, that emotional reactions to roles such as the Provincial Premier, while common, are not very intense, at least not in Ontario and Alberta in 1970. Although our respondents quite clearly prefer the role of Canadian Member of Parliament to that of U.S. President, their affective orientations towards these roles may not be particularly strongly held. This would explain why assessments based upon the criterion of affection have relatively little effect upon the children's confidence in these roles or their evaluations of their relative power. The fact that they think the presidency more powerful, on the other hand, seems to have a more marked influence on the children's affection for and confidence in the two roles. While emotive reactions to the presidency and to Members of Parliament may be relatively weak, then, the impression of a powerful presidency may be a more firmly held attitude.

It is generally true that the more intensely an attitude is held, the greater is the tendency to make other related attitudes harmonious with it.[21] If our explanation is valid, then, we would expect to find a greater internal symmetry in the children's assessments of power than in their assessments of confidence or affection. Here symmetry simply refers to the condition described by the axiom which states that if A is greater than B, and B is

Table 5   Asymmetrical Evaluations of Roles as a Per Cent of All Comparisons, by Grade

Criterion:	2	3	4	5	6	7	8
Power	11.1	12.4	3.9	5.3	3.7	3.9	3.3
Confidence	15.5	9.1	6.5	6.1	5.4	3.7	1.4
Affection	18.3	14.0	7.4	9.9	8.4	6.1	5.8

greater than C, then A must also be greater than C. Thus, if a child sees the Prime Minister as more powerful than the Provincial Premier, and the Premier as more powerful than the Local Mayor, he should also see the Prime Minister as more powerful than the Mayor. Cases which fail to meet this condition will be termed asymmetrical.

Using the comparisons which involve the three roles mentioned above as an example, we can see that our expectations are met (see Table 5). In four of the five earliest grades the proportion of asymmetrical selections is lower among power evaluations than it is among comparisons resting upon confidence or affection. Among the older children whose assessments are more influenced by their attitudes of confidence than of power (Table 4), confidence also replaces power as the criterion which leads most frequently to symmetrical evaluations of roles.

There is a clear tendency for the most influential criterion to also be the one which leads most strongly to internal symmetry in the relative evaluations of different pairs of roles. If one accepts the assumption that it is the intensity with which attitudes based upon a particular criterion are held which determines the degree to which role selections based upon this criterion are symmetrical, then our explanation of the relative influence of the three criteria employed in this study gains a considerable amount of support. The more intensely a criterion is felt, the greater the impact which assessments based upon that factor will have upon the evaluations which are primarily based upon other grounds. And, for our respondents at least, power is the most intensely perceived and most influential factor until the children reach about eleven or twelve years of age, when it is displaced by confidence.

Our *post hoc* explanation for this finding can only be speculative, but its logic seems reasonably convincing. On the whole the children in our sample seem to have affective orientations towards political authority roles, general feelings of confidence in them, and some impression of the power at their command. Each of these criteria can be employed in comparing one role with another. The affective orientations towards these distant, impersonal roles may not be very intense, however, and as a result judgments based upon affection have relatively little impact upon assessments based upon confidence or power. Among the younger respondents power is the most influential criterion, perhaps because they find the seemingly immense control exercised by political roles to be overwhelming. As Easton and Dennis note, a child's first awareness of authority external to his own family is likely to come with the discovery that some political roles can dominate even his parents.[22] As children mature perhaps the limitations upon political authority become clearer and the power of such roles becomes less impressive. By this point, however, the socialization process frequently has engendered general confidence in the political system and its authority roles, and this factor becomes the most important source of authority among our older respondents.

The impact which a criterion has does not, of course, vary only with chronological stages of development. Different political objects may also be expected to lead to variations in the spill-over of influence between the criteria used for evaluation. Thus affective orientations might be expected to (and do) have a greater relative impact when the object is a role such as the Local Mayor than is the case with as distant a role as a U.S. Congressman. Each of the political authority roles included in this study was individually paired with the role of Prime Minister in questions asking for comparative assessments on the basis of our three criteria. Because the prime-ministerial role was a constant in these comparisons we may treat the measures of consistency discovered in each case as a function of the other role.

Affective orientations achieve their greatest spill-over effect on questions dealing with the Local Mayor, the Governor General, and the monarchy. Since these are probably the most personalized roles of those included, this fits neatly with our argument that emotive attitudes achieve their greatest intensity when directed towards this type of authority role. This influence remains confined to the younger children in our sample, however, and by the grade six level both confidence and power are more influential than is affection, no matter what political object is mentioned.

When dealing with the roles of Members of Parliament and Provincial Premier, on the other hand, attitudes expressing diffuse confidence in the political object have more than the usual degree of impact. Power considerations decline in importance, although remaining more influential than affective orientations. This ordering, which also holds for the Local Mayor, may well represent a vague impression that these roles are at the lower end of the political authority hierarchy in Canada, combined with a generally benevolent attitude towards virtually all native authority positions. The reverse side of this coin may be seen in the case of the U.S. Congressman. Here power considerations have a greater than average influence at the expense of feelings of trust or confidence. The American presidency, which is presumably a more familiar role, comes close to the average position, in which assessments of power are most influential in the lower grades and the degree of confidence most important among older children.

By the time children pass into their early teens the relative positions of the three criteria seem to be quite firmly set. As Table 6 shows, affective orientations are the least influential, perceptions of power come next, and attitudes of confidence have the greatest impact. The distance between the criteria depends to an extent upon the political object in question, but regardless of which authority role we consider the rank-ordering of the influence of the three factors remains constant.

Returning to our original description of the respondents' relative assessments of the nine political authority roles, we can now interpret the patterns revealed in Tables 1 to 3 with somewhat more confidence. The evidence suggests that these children, as a group, neither randomly selected one role over another nor based their choices on any single criterion. Rather, they tended to base their selections on the three criteria which we provided. Among younger children power was the most important source of authority. Their perception of the power of a role influenced their confidence in it, and the extent to which they liked it. Confidence replaced power as the most influential criterion in the later grades. This, we have speculated, may be a function of the intensity with which the three types of attitudes are held. The extent to which authority is based upon each of the sources varies somewhat from role to role, but not sufficiently to change the rank order of the three criteria.

Table 6   The Relative Influence of the Components of Authority* for Different Political Roles (Grade 8)

Role	*Federal M.P.*	*Governor General*	*American President*	*Local Mayor*	*Provincial Premier*	*Cabinet Minister*	*American Congressman*	*Queen*
Confidence	9.1	8.8	8.3	8.0	6.1	5.5	5.3	5.0
Power	5.3	2.5	4.9	6.3	1.8	5.0	1.6	4.3
Affection	0	0	0	0	0	0	0	0

*The zeros in the bottom row do not indicate that judgments based upon affect have no spill-over effect upon other assessments. Rather, they indicate that affective orientations have less cross influence than either confidence or power.

So far in our discussion we have treated assessments based upon each of the three criteria separately, but political authority itself is a single concept. The extent to which authority is based upon affection or confidence or power may vary from role to role, and from grade to grade, but the end result is the same; one role is perceived as being more authoritative than another. Judgments based upon these three criteria together create a pattern of dominance and subordination: a structure of political authority.

The spill-over effect which we have examined may be measured in the actual responses which our respondents gave, and might thus be termed the "explicit" ordering of the relative influence of the three criteria. The fact that confidence is more important than affection or power among our older respondents, for example, is reflected in the comparisons which they ostensibly made on the basis of affection and power. But while we know that this explicit type of spill-over takes place, we also know that the children in our sample were, on the whole, able to distinguish between the three criteria. Because no one element came at all close to subsuming the other two the possibility exists that the children also mentally ordered the criteria in a manner which was not reflected in their responses.

Thus affective orientations, for example, may be much more important in children's minds than either of the other types of attitudes, but because they distinguished between the criteria when responding this need not have affected their answers. It is this possibility of an "implicit" ordering of the three factors by children which has thus far forced us to discuss the components of authority separately, without attempting to examine the concept as a cumulative whole. We cannot safely assume that the criteria weigh equally in importance.

One way of roughly estimating this implicit ordering is by returning to our examination of response rates. If we assume that the incentive to answer questions tends to increase as the importance of the criterion employed increases for the respondents, then differential response rates may be used to establish weights for each of the three elements of authority upon which sets of role comparisons were based. Such weights were established for affection, confidence and power at each grade level by summing the response rates for the three types of question and finding the percentage contributed to this total by each of the criteria. The implicit ordering thus discovered is noticeably different from the actual spill-over effect found in the data. Power remains the most important element with an average weight of .340, but affective orientations, with an average weight of .336, replace diffuse confidence (average weight = .324) as the second most influential criterion for assessment.[23]

The scores based upon affection, confidence and power (as reported in Tables 1 to 3) were weighted according to the appropriate response rate and the three weighted scores for each role were combined. Table 7 shows the resulting structure of political authority as perceived by children at each grade level, and the mean position of each role. The three most authoritative roles for children of all ages are the Queen, the Governor General and the Prime Minister, in that order. It is interesting to note how the perceived distance between these roles continually narrows as the children grow older. Immediately following these three roles which converge at the pinnacle of the political system in Canada we find a foreign position. Children of all ages perceive the American President as more authoritative than any of the more specialized or localized Canadian political roles. This ascription of a great deal of authority does not seem to extend to other roles in the American system, however, as the U.S. Congressman is consistently perceived as the least authoritative role of all.

The roles of Provincial Premier and Federal Member of Parliament came next in the ordering, achieving the same average position. The former role is, however, relatively more important in the eyes of older

Table 7 Children's Perceptions of the Structure of Political Authority

Role	Mean Position	Grade						
		2	3	4	5	6	7	8
Queen	.523	.671	.651	.640	.498	.454	.447	.230
Governor General	.129	.258	.275	.139	.063	.064	.111	−.007
Prime Minister	0	0	0	0	0	0	0	0
American President	−.260	−.209	−.325	−.410	−.332	−.240	−.098	−.209
Provincial Premier	−.503	−.577	−.623	−.511	−.510	−.458	−.415	−.425
Federal M.P.	−.503	−.360	−.507	−.555	−.600	−.522	−.488	−.506
Local Mayor	−.542	−.496	−.580	−.562	−.589	−.549	−.515	−.492
Cabinet Minister	−.576	—	—	−.617	−.580	−.586	−.548	−.548
American Congressman	−.667	—	—	−.678	−.698	−.672	−.641	−.648

children. Finally, among the Canadian roles we find two which would seem poles apart; the Local Mayor and the Federal Cabinet Minister. The low assessment of the Cabinet Minister, which improves somewhat among older children, is probably influenced by a lack of knowledge. Data reported elsewhere show that children's cognition of this role is quite low.[24]

No comparable data about adult Canadians' perceptions of the structure of political authority are available, so we are unable to make any inference about how firmly fixed this ordering of the authority roles is. While movement in the precise positions of the various roles is ubiquitous, however, changes in the rank-ordering of the more authoritative roles obviously occur very slowly. Even when the less authoritative and less well-known roles are included there is, on average, only one change in the rank-ordering between each grade.

We have found, then, that even very young children are able to assess political authority roles relative to each other on the basis of affection, diffuse confidence and power. There is some spill-over between orientations along these three dimensions, but not to such an extent as to markedly weaken the distinction between the different evaluations. These assessments typically lead to a symmetrical pattern of authority relationships which can be extended to include most important political roles. From at least the very beginning of the age of literacy children's affection for and evaluation of these roles combine to create a broad picture of the structure of political authority in Canada. The changes which subsequently occur in their perception of this structure are slow and developmental, and fit into their pre-existing framework for thinking about politics.

NOTES

1. Sebastian de Grazia, "What Authority Is Not," *American Political Science Review*, vol. 53, no. 2 (June 1959), p. 321.
2. See Talcott Parsons, "Authority, Legitimation and Political Action" in Carl J. Friedrich, ed., *Authority* (Cambridge, Mass.: Harvard University Press, 1958), pp. 208–20.
3. Herbert A. Simon, Donald W. Smithburg and Victor A. Thompson, *Public Administration* (New York: Knopf, 1954), pp. 188–201.
4. See David Easton and Jack Dennis, *Children in the Political System* (New York: McGraw-Hill, 1969), pp. 220–27 and 359–63.
5. In Easton and Dennis's study, for example, 72 per cent of children in grade four believed that the President rarely or almost never makes mistakes, and a majority took this position even in grade eight. Ibid., p. 186.
6. In fact, if one is able to mentally assign political roles to groups, a process similar to "identification" might help in assessing their authority. This seems unlikely to be the case with children.
7. Rather mixed evidence on this

point is provided by Harrell R. Rodgers, Jr., and George Taylor, "The Policeman as an Agent of Regime Legitimation," *Midwest Journal of Political Science*, vol. xv, no. 1 (February 1971), pp. 72–86. In a comparative study of black and white children, they found that a lack of respect for the police was associated with a disinclination to obey the law, but this relationship could be explained by other factors in the case of black respondents.
8. Max Weber, *Basic Concepts in Sociology*, trans. H. P. Secher (New York: Citadel, 1964), p. 75.
9. Max Weber, "Politics as a Vocation" in *From Max Weber: Essays in Sociology*, trans. and ed. H. H. Gerth and C. Wright Mills (New York: Oxford University Press, 1946), p. 79.
10. Weber, *Basic Concepts*, p. 75.
11. Easton and Dennis, *Children in the Political System*, pp. 4–7 and 49ff.
12. Ibid., pp. 166–71. The non-political role of "Father" was also included.
13. Similarly, Fred Greenstein's earlier New Haven survey included assessments of the roles of President, Governor and Mayor, but did not

ask for an evaluation of one against another. *Children and Politics* (New Haven, Conn.: Yale University Press, 1965), pp. 31–42.
14. Ibid., pp. 33–34.
15. The preliminary data are only from schools in Ontario and Alberta. Full information on the sample and the questionnaire may be found in T. G. Carroll, D. J. H. Higgins and M. S. Whittington, "The Development of Children's Perceptions of Political Authority Roles: Some Preliminary Findings" (a paper presented at the 1971 annual meeting of the Canadian Political Science Association in St. John's). See also the introductory article in this volume.
16. The actual questions asked were: "Which in each set is your favourite?"; "Which in each set is more able to make people do what he wants?"; and "If these people disagree, who do you think is more likely to be right?" Each of these was followed by a list of political authority roles arranged in sets of two.
17. All of the thirty-six possible pairs of roles could not be included because of limitations in available time and in children's attention span. In grades two and three the roles of Federal Cabinet Minister and American Congressman were excluded altogether, and only nine pairs were presented for comparison. In the higher grades every role was compared with that of Prime Minister, and other pairings which seemed intrinsically interesting were included to bring the total up to seventeen. Thus, for example, the role of Local Mayor was paired with that of Provincial Premier, but not with that of Governor General.
18. This technique was developed jointly

by the present writer and D. J. H. Higgins, who also supplied most of the calculations required for its use.
19. A number of psychological studies relating to this point are cited by Jack W. Brehm and Arthur R. Cohen in their *Explorations in Cognitive Dissonance* (New York: Wiley, 1962), pp. 24–27 and 61ff.
20. General socialization studies do not usually include much consideration of the objects of the process of learning authority attitudes. Many do emphasize the unique position of parents and teachers as direct, personal authority roles, however, in their discussions of the socializing agencies. See, for example, Frederick Elkin, *The Child and Society* (New York: Random House, 1960), pp. 45–62; and Talcott Parsons and Robert F. Bales, *Family, Socialization and Interaction Process* (London: Routledge and Kegan Paul, 1956), pp. 114–15.
21. See Brehm and Cohen, *Explorations in Cognitive Dissonance* and also the discussion of the relationship between intensity and consistency in Angus Campbell, Philip E. Converse, Warren E. Miller and Donald E. Stokes, *The American Voter* (New York: Wiley, 1960), pp. 128–36.
22. Easton and Dennis, *Children in the Political System*, pp. 3–4.
23. These figures are averages for all grades, but in practice it is the specific value for each grade which is used in the weighting process.
24. Even by grade eight barely half of the children in our sample were able to identify the role of Federal Cabinet Minister when provided with the names of three prominent incumbents. See Carroll, Higgins and Whittington, "Children's Perceptions of Political Authority Roles," p. 11.

Personality and Political Efficacy: 6

A Study of High School Students

MAGNUS GUNTHER

The study of personality and politics has a long but uneven history as a field of intellectual interest. For Aristotle there was little question of the importance of personality to the polity: ". . . the type of character appropriate to the constitution is the power which continues to sustain it, as it is the force which originally creates it."[1] Generally, however, political and social scientists have remained skeptical as to the degree to which "human nature" is worthy of study in the context of political behaviour.

There are, indeed, many reasons for being cautious about the presumed relationship between personality and constitution and, more specifically, democratic constitution. One can question whether personality in fact makes any sustained and fundamental difference to the functioning of social structures. There is a strong argument (made largely by political sociologists) that, providing one has democratic institutions, democratic behaviour can be induced of even anti-democratic personalities. Personality and behaviour are pliable, once one has an adequate institutional setting for containing what is regarded as personal and idiosyncratic.

Thus any discussion of personality and democratic constitution meets an immediate criticism in the question of whether personality can in fact be used as an explanatory concept in the analysis of a social structure. For the moment we will use the following as working definitions of personality and social structure. Personality deals with "the individual as a system of needs, feelings, aptitudes, skills, defenses, etc.," and social structure deals with the "relations that emerge when two or more persons interact with one another."[2] The unit of analysis when discussing social structure is not the individual but aspects of his interaction with others, such as role relations in dyads or the clusters of roles that make up an organization.

112

Our argument on this point, however, is as follows. Even if we accept the minimal relevance of personality to social structure delineated by some sociologists, the conditions of mass society make the study of personality and democracy particularly pertinent today. If the mass society theorists are correct, then the minimal personality characteristics for simply sustaining a stable (as opposed to a desirable) democratic society are threatened. There is thus a need, not only to study the empirical relevance of personality to democratic structure or constitution in mass society, but also to study what is the desirable personality for the maintenance of the most desirable democratic society.

PERSONALITY AND POLITICAL THEORY

The empirical research presented below is linked to a specific aspect of personality and political behaviour. Our theoretical approach stems from a simple and explicit view of the factors affecting political behaviour. Following Levinson[3] we focus on the concept of political role as a useful way of integrating the mediating effects of personality on both political structures and political behaviour. Our interest, then, is the relationship of personality to political roles.[4] Personality is seen as having a mediating function. What does it mediate? More specifically, which aspects of political and socially relevant structures does it mediate in relation to which political roles and which political behaviour? In order to simplify the ensuing discussion, the following model of the assumptions underlying the research design is relevant.

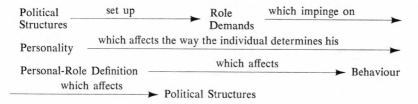

It must be emphasized that this model is a gross oversimplification of actual behavioural processes.

Thus in our transitional democracies we may say that there are fairly clear role demands made by various manifest and latent political structures as to what is required of the citizen.[5] There is little need to list these demands or norms but among them there is one which has been the subject of extensive research and which from the standpoint of the psychology of politics is crucial to the functioning of the fully active democratic citizen. This is the norm of the efficacious citizen.[6] As a norm, political efficacy refers "to the timeless theme of democratic theory that members of a democratic regime ought to regard those who occupy positions of political authority as responsive agents and that members themselves ought to be disposed to participate in the honors and offices of the system. The *norm* of political effectiveness embodies the expectation in democracies that members will feel able to act effectively in politics."[7]

In slowly filling out the oversimple unilinear model set out above we start with political structures which make external demands for effectiveness on the citizen. However, normative demands are hardly ever fully explicit and clear. Not only are they often ambiguous, they may also contradict other norms within a specified norm-set. For the political scientist two related problems are perhaps of greater interest. It is not sufficient for political and social structures to make role demands; role facilities must also be provided. The obvious discrepancies that exist between effective citizenship role demands and the great differences in the facilities afforded to the citizen to carry out these demands have been the source of much personal strain, group conflict and social change.

Closely linked to the problem of differential role facilities is another difficulty discussed also by Levinson.[8] We have already referred to the contradictions which seem to be an inherent part of most human situations. Where such contradictions exist they create role dilemmas for the occupant of a social position. Rosenberg has highlighted some of these role dilemmas in his discussion of the "Threatening Consequences of Political Activity."[9] For example, political activity involves controversy and conflict. Where the social structure is such that controversy threatens interpersonal harmony a role dilemma is created. Or alternatively people can see political controversy as potentially ego-deflating. Here the role dilemma stems more from personality characteristics. The article shows that role dilemmas exist and that they have their source both in the individual personality and in political and social structures.

Thus the linkage between structure and personality is anything but simple. In terms of our model, it is the task of personality to integrate and adapt to the confusing welter of norms, differential facilities and role dilemmas created by external structures. For this kind of adaptation Levinson provides the term "Personal Role Definition." The following quotation clarifies the meaning of this term. It also provides the basis for the hypotheses to be tested in our study.

Just as social structure presents massive forces which influence the individual from without toward certain forms of adaptation, so does personality present massive forces from within which lead him to select, create and synthesise certain forms of adaptation rather than others. Role-definition may be seen from one perspective, as an aspect of personality. It represents the individual's attempt to structure his social reality, to define his place within it, and to guide his search for meaning and gratification. Role-definition is, in this sense, an *ego* achievement—a reflection of the person's capacity to resolve conflicting demands, to utilise existing opportunities and create new ones, to find some balance between stability and change, conformity and autonomy, the ideal and the feasible, in a complex environment.

The formation of a role-definition is, from a dynamic psychological point of view, an "external function" of the ego. Like the other external (reality-oriented) ego functions, it is influenced by the ways in which the ego carries out its "internal functions" of coping with, and attempting to synthesise, the demands of the id, superego, and ego. These internal activities—the "psycho-dynamics" of personality—include among other things: unconscious fantasies; unconscious moral conceptions and the wishes against which they are directed; the characteristic ways in which unconscious processes are transformed or deflected in more conscious thought, feeling and behavioural striving; conceptions of self and ways of maintaining or changing these conceptions in the face of changing pressures from within and from the external world.[10]

A personal-role definition is the outcome of an interaction process between personality and social structure. From our perspective personal role definition is also a mediating factor, mediating between personality and behaviour. It is the impact of personality on a limited yet important aspect of the personal-political-role definition that is the focus of our empirical research.

The research presented below is an attempt to find the relationship between one aspect of personality and a part of that complex whole which can be called the political actor's personal-role definition. Personal-role definition is seen here as the way an actor defines, rationalizes or gives meaning to his location in social or political space.

PERSONALITY THEORY AND POLITICAL THEORY

Most political scientists who have attempted to make use of the personality theories developed by psychologists have found the experience frustrating but often fruitful. The field of personality theory is anything but unified. There is a vast offering of different conceptions of the *elements* of personality, of the *structure* of personality, of the *boundaries* of personality and of the *relation* between personality and other phenomena.[11]

Clearly some choice of politically relevant personality factors must be made. Recently H. D. Lasswell and F. I. Greenstein have discussed the question of appropriate and inappropriate personality types in a democratic political system from a contemporary point of view.[12] For Lasswell there is a democratic personality type who is most appropriate to the sustenance of democratic social and political relations. His democratic personality is an ideal-type, based partly on neo-Freudian concepts of wholeness and mental health. One aspect of Lasswell's discussion of the democratic character type is of central concern to our research. Lasswell distinguishes a cognitive element in personality. In the democratic personality this cognitive element has a certain structure which distinguishes it from the structure of the cognitive elements in the authoritarian personality. In essence the "democrat's" structure is open, tolerant of ambiguity, multi-valued, flexible and relatively anxiety-free. Lasswell does not specifically distinguish between the content of these cognitions and the style with which the beliefs are held.

A major set of studies dealing indirectly with the cognitive elements and structures of the democratic personality have been carried out by Rokeach and his associates in *The Open and Closed Mind*. Rokeach focuses not so much on the content of the belief system as on its structure. His own words are pertinent here: "The axe we frankly grind is simply this: it is not so much *what* you believe that counts, but *how* you believe."[13] We would disagree that content counts for little; but we do agree that how one believes can be a crucial personality determinant of personal-role definitions and behaviour. Rokeach's cognitive approach has other uses for the political scientist. His research, he says, led him and his associates "more and more to view a given personality as an organization of beliefs or expectancies having a definable and measurable structure."[14] This approach to personality is particularly fruitful since it attempts to find a single set of concepts applicable not only to the study of personality but also to the study of ideology and cognitive behaviour such as the ability to synthesize and analyse.

It is unnecessary to summarize in detail each of the theoretical concepts that lie behind the actual items in the Rokeach Dogmatism Scale. The central concept implicit in this measuring instrument is rooted in the various functional approaches to attitude formation which have been developed during the last two decades.[15] According to these approaches a person's cognitive structure serves two main functions: the need to know and understand the world, and the need to fend off threatening stimuli. "To the extent that the need to know is predominant and the need to ward off threat absent, open systems should result."[16] The open mind is very different in its structure and in the content of its beliefs about four crucial areas of social and political life, namely, the self, ideas, other people and authority. As regards ideas, the closed mind is perceptually narrow, defensive of its core beliefs, intolerant of discrepant beliefs. As regards other people, the closed mind is intolerant of out-groups, and disdainful of persons seen as renegades or disbelievers. As regards the self, the closed mind sees man as alone, helpless and isolated. As regards authority, the closed mind sees it as absolute and people are accepted or rejected according to their agreement or disagreement with such authority. By contrast the open mind is one which is relatively free of distorting internal pressures (e g., the need for self-aggrandizement) and of reward and punishment pressures from external authority (whether peers or institutional norms). It is able to evaluate and act on information independently, and is governed by self-actualizing forces rather than by irrational inner forces. In our empirical research these cognitive aspects of personality, as measured by the Dogmatism Scale, are the key intervening variable.

Brief mention must be made of a second personality-type variable we used in the study. Although I.Q. has rarely, if ever, been used in studies of adult political behaviour, it is being used more and more in socialization studies. I.Q. has considerable relevance as a mediating variable. Although intelligence has not been well integrated into other work in psychology, it can, when defined as a dimension of individual differences, be tied to other psychological personality theory. As Hayes has pointed out, intelligence as measured on I.Q. tests consists of nothing more than an accumulation of learned facts and skills.[17] Thus the formal learning experience, especially the curriculum, is more readily mastered by the child with a high I.Q. Since the curriculum involves some civic education, I.Q. may well affect the degree to which the formal political "rules of the game" are learned. But I.Q. tests do not supplement the need for tests which get at what Hayes calls "experiencing drives," which are motives affecting tendencies conducive to learning. These latter drives result from genetic influences and from the nature and variety of experiences available in general to the child. The two factors probably reinforce one another but they may have different effects on different kinds of political attitudes.

POLITICAL EFFICACY

Having discussed the major intervening variables used in the study we turn now to the dependent variable we are interested in. Political efficacy was first investigated in systematic and operational form by the authors of *The Voter Decides*. They defined the concept as follows:

Sense of political efficacy may be defined as the feeling that individual political action does have or can have, an impact upon the political process, i.e., that it is worthwhile to perform one's civic duties. It is the feeling that political and social change is possible, and that the individual citizen can play a part in bringing about this change.[18]

Their scale for measuring political efficacy has been thoroughly investigated, applied in numerous studies, and has found to be a reliable and valid instrument. Recently Easton and Dennis investigated the development of political efficacy among school children from grades three to eight in the United States.[19] They presented an efficacy measure applicable to school children which we in turn have modified and used in our study. We follow Easton and Dennis in assuming that the responses of the child to this index show not only the way the child perceives the adult but also that as he learns from the adult he will think of himself in similar ways. "We can therefore interpret the attitudinal component represented in the index items only as a first but critical step in the child's acquisition of an orientation to political efficacy as *it relates to himself*."[20]

INDEPENDENT VARIABLES

The development of personal role-definitions (in this case of political efficaciousness) depends, then, on personality needs and on structural or environmental factors. We used socioeconomic status as one major structural variable. SES is related not only to political behaviour but also to child-rearing attitudes and practices which have an effect on the behaviour and personalities of the offspring.[21]

We were interested in the impact of the developmental process on political efficacy and thus three groups of high school students were selected for study. The three groups were drawn from a grade thirteen, a grade eleven (five-year) and a grade eleven (four-year) class. Ontario schools have since 1961 permitted a streaming of students by both branch (Arts and Science; Business and Commerce; Engineering; Technology and Trade) and program. All the students in our sample came from an Arts and Science branch, but two groups were in a five-year program ("education for professions") and one group was in a four-year program ("education for employment").[22] As originally conceived, the streaming system was designed "to cut down on the number of 'drop-outs,' and also to provide students who leave school at the end of Grade 12 (this would apply especially to the 11 (4-year) group) with a secondary school diploma which would admit them to positions in industry and commerce; i.e., to provide them with marketable skills."[23]

A number of writers have noted the tendency for education systems to support existing stratification systems. Turner has provided a brilliant theoretical discussion of the way a society's mode of upward mobility shapes the school system and thus the values, personalities and sense of competence and efficacy of the students who pass through the schools. It may be argued that until recently the mobility system in Canada was predominantly a modified "sponsorship system," in which the elite or their representatives call individuals with the appropriate qualities to elite status. A sponsorship system would have a direct influence on the sense of efficacy of the potential citizen, since it involves a system of social control based on "training the masses to regard themselves as relatively incom-

Table 1 High School Students' and Parents' Responses to *Political Efficacy Questions*

Question*	Disagree	Undecided; probably disagree	Undecided; probably agree	Agree	%	Grade†
	%				%	
1. Voting is the only way that people like my Mother and Father can have any say about how government runs things.	18	12	12	59	101‡	Grade 13
	25	8	22	45	100	Grade 11 (5)
	12	2	26	60	100	Grade 11 (4)
	24	5	14	56	100	Parents
2. What happens in government will happen no matter what people do. It is like the weather there is nothing people can do about it.	57	28	12	4	101	Grade 13
	60	15	18	7	100	Grade 11 (5)
	48	33	7	12	100	Grade 11 (4)
	68	14	8	10	100	Parents
3. There are some big powerful men in the government who are running the whole thing, and they do not care about us ordinary people.	26	26	26	24	102	Grade 13
	30	33	27	10	100	Grade 11 (5)
	19	29	29	24	101	Grade 11 (4)
	45	23	17	15	100	Parents
4. My family does not have much say about what the government does.	49	26	10	16	101	Grade 13
	52	20	18	10	100	Grade 11 (5)
	38	24	19	19	100	Grade 11 (4)
	55	16	13	15	99	Parents

	Not at all	Very Little	Some	Very Much		
5. I do not think people in the government care much about what people like my family think.	33	28	18	22	101	Grade 13
	30	27	28	15	100	Grade 11 (5)
	19	37	26	19	101	Grade 11 (4)
	52	17	19	13	101	Parents
6. Citizens do not have a chance to say what they think about running the government.	33	29	18	20	100	Grade 13
	48	23	10	18	99	Grade 11 (5)
	37	26	26	12	101	Grade 11 (4)
	58	18	11	13	100	Parents
	Not at all	Very Little	Some	Very Much		
7. How much does the *average person* help decide which laws are made for our country.	6	47	43	4	100	Grade 13
	5	48	42	5	100	Grade 11 (5)
	2	47	37	14	100	Grade 11 (4)
	5	49	34	11	99	Parents

*The following questions were altered as follows in the Parents Questionnaire:

1. Voting is the only way that people like me have any say about how the government runs things.

4. People like myself do not have any say about what the government does.

5. I do not think public officials care much what people like me think.

†Missing data have been excluded from the calculations. N's are: Grade 13—51; Grade 11 (5)—60; Grade 11 (4)—43 or 42; Parents—177 or 176.

‡Percentages may not add to 100% because of rounding.

petent to manage society, by restricting access to the skills and manners of the elite, and by cultivating belief in the superior competence of the elite."[24] Our grade eleven (four-year) sample is taken as a potential indicator of the degree to which this proposition holds, at least for some Canadian high school students. We interpret streaming of this kind as a hangover from the period of strong sponsorship mobility which seems now on the decline in Canada.

THE STUDY

As mentioned earlier, the sample consists of three classes of high school students drawn randomly from a group of six classes. A questionnaire was administered directly to the students, who were asked to take a modified form of the same questionnaire home to their parents to be mailed back once it was completed. The questionnaire administered to the students included the usual questions on parents' occupation, education and income. Students were asked to respond to the Dogmatism Scale, a set of questions related to Abstract Democratic Principles, an Awareness of Democratic Principles Quasi-Scale and a Political Efficacy Scale. In this paper we are mainly concerned with our high and low dogmatic groups and the impact of dogmatism on political efficacy. The two groups were divided on the basis of their total scores on the Dogmatism Scale. The highest quartile ($N = 38$) in total score form the high dogmatism group, the lowest quartile ($N = 38$) form the low dogmatism group.

We may first note the general distribution of efficacy scores between students and parents. If the responses for students as a whole in Table 1 are compared to those of parents we see that the parents are in general more politically efficacious than are the students. The group of parents is, however, self-selected and there may be an element of bias here; those returning the questionnaire perhaps were more efficacious than those who did not. If this bias is not significant, however, this finding reverses the usual claim made in studies of U.S. political behaviour that students tend on the whole to be more efficacious than their parents.

Table 1 shows developmental changes by grade in responses to the political efficacy items. Age changes as reflected in grade levels are not significant. The overall greater political efficacy of the parents is seen to be due to the generally lower political efficacy of the grade eleven (4) group. Grade eleven (5) and grade thirteen are similar to the parents as a whole and if we collapse the two "agree" and two "disagree" categories, the two grades are similar to each other.

Table 2* Student Characteristics by Grade
(High and Low Dogmatism Quartiles Only)

Grade 11 (4)		*Grade 11 (5)*		*Grade 13*	
Family Income		Family Income		Family Income	
(N = 27)		(N = 23)		(N = 22)	
High	Low	High	Low	High	Low
19%	82%	61%	39%	52%	48%
IQ (N = 27)		IQ (N = 23)		IQ (N = 16)	
High	Low	High	Low	High	Low
19%	82%	70%	30%	75%	25%
Dogmatism (N = 27)		Dogmatism (N = 26)		Dogmatism (N = 23)	
High	Low	High	Low	High	Low
74%	26%	50%	50%	22%	78%
Political Efficacy		Political Efficacy		Political Efficacy	
(N = 27)		(N = 26)		(N = 23)	
High	Low	High	Low	High	Low
41%	59%	62%	39%	70%	30%

*Note that in this table and those which follow the categories used were as follows:
a) High Dogmatic and Low Dogmatic—respondents in highest and lowest quartiles on total scores.
b) High Efficacy Score—respondents getting a standardized score between 500 and 799.
   Low Efficacy Score—respondents getting a standardized score between 200 and 499.
c) I.Q. was measured on a *Dominion Test of Learning Capability*. High I.Q. were respondents whose scores ranged from 104 to 120 (+). Low I.Q. ranged from 80 to 103.
d) High and Low SES was determined by rank on the Blishen *Socio-Economic Index for Occupations*. Low SES were all those respondents whose *Fathers* were scored between 25.36 and 45.51 on the Index. High SES were those who scored between 45.52 and 76.69. See B. R. Blishen, "A Socio-Economic Index for Occupations in Canada," *Canadian Review of Sociology and Anthropology*, vol. 4, no. 1 (1967), pp. 41–53.
e) High Family Income were those respondents who said their family income was above $10,000 per annum. Low Family Income was any respondent whose family income fell below $10,000 per annum.

This pattern is demonstrated clearly when we separate the grades in Table 2 on several of the characteristics we are concerned with in this study. A dramatic difference is apparent between the grade eleven (4) stream and the other classes on all of the characteristics, particularly on family income, I.Q., and dogmatism. These grade eleven (4) students are predominantly from low-income families, lower in I.Q. and much more likely to be in the high dogmatism quartile. They are also more likely to be low in political efficacy, but this relationship, though substantial, is not as strong as the others just mentioned. In comparison to the differences between the two streams, the differences between grade eleven and grade thirteen students in the "academic" stream are rather minor. The only one of any magnitude involves dogmatism, and shows the grade thirteen students lower on the dogmatism scale than the grade eleven (5) students.

As a preliminary step towards sorting out the effects of the structural characteristics of family income, I.Q. and personality (as well as grade) on political efficacy, we present in Table 3 summary measures of the interrelationships of these four variables. The measure used here is Goodman and Kruskal's Gamma,[25] which varies between 1 and −1 depending on the strength of the relationship between the two variables being correlated. In general, gammas of .5 or above indicate quite strong relationships, while those of a magnitude of .2 or below indicate weak relationships. The positive gammas in Table 3 can be interpreted as the likelihood that high political efficacy is associated with high income or I.Q., but low dogmatism.

As can be seen from Table 3, dogmatism and I.Q. show the strongest

Table 3   Gammas Measuring Relationships Between Political Efficacy, Family Income, I.Q., Grade and Dogmatism
(High and Low Dogmatic Quartiles Only)

	IQ	Family Income	Dogmatism	Grade
Political Efficacy	.66	.22	.76	.38
I.Q.		.52	.51	.79
Family Income			.43	
Dogmatism				.78

relationships with political efficacy, dogmatism being slightly the stronger of the two. Family income has a rather weak association with efficacy, and grade a moderate one. As noted with regard to Table 2, grade is strongly correlated with I.Q. and dogmatism. Finally, income, I.Q. and dogmatism are all related quite strongly to each other, low degrees of dogmatism being associated with high I.Q. and high family income.

In order to tease out the directions of association and the nature of the relationships reflected in Table 3, a series of controls were placed on the simple (called zero-order in statistical language) gammas in Table 3. This procedure allows the effect of the predictor variable to be seen on the dependent variable while one or more of the other variables is controlled or held constant. If the gamma is reduced strongly by this procedure, we may conclude that some or all of the effect of the predictor can be accounted for by the control variable, and that the initial relationship was to some degree "spurious."

The decision on which relationships to subject to controls and which variables to use as controls was determined by the theoretical scheme presented earlier. The first test (lines 1, 2, and 3 of Table 4) is whether the relationship between dogmatism and political efficacy is able to maintain its strength when subjected to controls for, in turn, grade, I.Q. and family income. The final column of Table 4, entitled "partial prediction," shows that the relationship between dogmatism and political efficacy is not significantly affected by controlling for any of these structural variables. The middle columns of Table 4 show the result for each category of the control variable, for example line 1 shows the predictive power of dogmatism on political efficacy for each of the three grades studied.[26]

It is clear from Table 4, then, that despite variations within groups, the personality characteristic of dogmatism remains the strongest predictor of political efficacy. The question of how important this predictor is as opposed to I.Q. can be investigated from the data here. Although there are relationships (see Table 3) between both dogmatism and I.Q. and political efficacy, their effect on political efficacy is shown by Table 4 to be distinct and different under alternative conditions of social structure. As noted before, grade eleven (4) is primarily a low I.Q. group, whereas grade thirteen is primarily a high I.Q. group. When, however, we examine the relationship between I.Q. and efficacy within the different grade levels (line 5, table 4) we find that I.Q. is an extremely poor predictor of political

Table 4 Partial Gammas, Subjecting Zero-Order Relationships from Table 3 to a Series of Controls

Zero-Order Prediction	First Partial	Second Partial	Third Partial	Partial Prediction
Dogmatism on Political Efficacy controlling for Grade, I.Q. and Family Income				
1. $\gamma yx = .76$	$\gamma yx.u_1 = .89$	$\gamma yx.u_2 = .59$	$\gamma yx.u_3 = .72$	$\gamma yx.u = .73$
2. $\gamma yx = .76$	$\gamma yx.z_1 = .62$	$\gamma yx.z_2 = .73$		$\gamma yx.z = .77$
3. $\gamma yx = .76$	$\gamma yx.w_1 = .54$	$\gamma yx.w_2 = .90$		$\gamma yx.w = .80$
I.Q. on Political Efficacy controlling for Dogmatism, Grade and Family Income				
4. $\gamma yz = .66$	$\gamma yz.x_1 = .5$	$\gamma yz.x_2 = .64$		$\gamma yz.x = .58$
5. $\gamma yz = .66$	$\gamma yz.u_1 = -.02$	$\gamma yz.u_2 = .83$	$\gamma yz.u_3 = .67$	$\gamma yz.u = .52$
6. $\gamma yz = .66$	$\gamma yz.w_1 = .86$	$\gamma yz.w_2 = .53$		$\gamma yz.w = .63$
Grade on Political Efficacy controlling for Dogmatism, I.Q and Family Income				
7. $\gamma yu = .38$	$\gamma yu.x_1 = -.11$	$\gamma yu.x_2 = .33$		$\gamma yu.x = .14$
8. $\gamma yu = .38$	$\gamma yu.z_1 = .50$	$\gamma yu.z_2 = .04$		$\gamma yu.z = .22$
9. $\gamma yu = .38$	$\gamma yu.w_1 = .03$	$\gamma yu.w_2 = .50$		$\gamma yu.w = .34$
Family Income on Political Efficacy controlling for Dogmatism, I.Q. and Grade				
10. $\gamma yw = .22$	$\gamma yw.x_1 = -.46$	$\gamma yw.x_2 = .31$		$\gamma yw.x = -.07$
11. $\gamma yw = .22$	$\gamma yw.z_1 = .22$	$\gamma yw.z_2 = -.44$		$\gamma yw.z = -.12$
12. $\gamma yw = .22$	$\gamma yw.u_1 = -.02$	$\gamma yw.u_2 = .64$	$\gamma yw.u_3 = -.53$	$\gamma yw.u = .06$

Family Income on Dogmatism controlling for Grade and I.Q.

13. $\gamma xw = .44$ $\gamma xw.u_1 = .39$ $\gamma xw.u_2 = .57$ $\gamma xw.u_3 = -.20$ $\gamma xw.u = .36$
14. $\gamma xw = .44$ $\gamma xw.z_1 = .58$ $\gamma xw.z_2 = .09$ $\gamma xw.z = .37$

Grade on Dogmatism controlling for Family Income and I.Q.

15. $\gamma xu = .70$ $\gamma xu.w_1 = .36$ $\gamma xu.w_2 = .70$ $\gamma xu.w = .59$
16. $\gamma xu = .70$ $\gamma xu.z_1 = .80$ $\gamma xu.z_2 = .68$ $\gamma xu.z = .68$

I.Q. on Dogmatism controlling for Family Income and Grade

17. $\gamma xz = .51$ $\gamma xz.w_1 = .76$ $\gamma xz.w_2 = .39$ $\gamma xz.w = .50$
18. $\gamma xz = .51$ $\gamma xz.u_1 = -.2$ $\gamma xz.u_2 = .14$ $\gamma xz.u_3 = .5$ $\gamma xz.u = .078$

Key to Table: $\gamma = $ Gamma
y = Political Efficacy
x = Dogmatism; $x_1 = $ Low Dogmatic; $x_2 = $ High Dogmatic
z = I.Q.; $z_1 = $ High I.Q.; $z_2 = $ Low I.Q.
u = Grade; $u_1 = $ Grade 11 (4); $u_2 = $ Grade 11 (5); $u_3 = $ Grade 13
w = Family Income; $w_1 = $ High Income; $w_2 = $ Low Income

efficacy within grade eleven (4), a much better predictor in grade eleven (5) and is unchanged in strength in grade thirteen.

Just as the relationship between dogmatism and political efficacy remains when controls are applied, so too, for the most part, do the relationships between dogmatism and the characteristics of family income, I.Q. and grade (lines 13–18). Although much more extensive analysis would be necessary for any definitive conclusion to be drawn, it is reasonable to suggest from the evidence presented here that the personality characteristic of dogmatism can be best conceptualized as a mediating force between social structural factors and political efficacy. The conditions under which personality will act as a mediator and under which it may act on its own are, however, suggested by the data presented here.

In a class which is low in status within the school system (grade eleven (4)) and which has a high number of low I.Q. students, low I.Q. will strongly reduce the effect of grade on efficacy (Table 4, line 8). We may extend this a little further. We noted above that the best predictor of political efficacy within the grade eleven (4) group was personality. This is not surprising, since I.Q. measures the availability of certain learned skills. Where these skills are not available—where certain role facilities are not available—personality plays a predominate part in determining one's personal-role definition as a political actor. High dogmatic personalities (who predominate in grade eleven (4)) become the best predictors of level of political efficacy.

Thus the "property" variables (grade, etc.) have a peculiar predictive relation to our personal role-definition variable—efficacy. These "property" variables are good predictors of efficacy only in two cases: the grade eleven (5) and grade thirteen group. In the case of the grade eleven (5) there is greater variation in I.Q. scores and we are not surprised to see here that the impact of I.Q. on efficacy is strong and "normal." Where the students have the learned skills (or role facilities) they are able to make use of them to choose a politically efficacious role. The same reasoning applies in the case of the grade thirteen group. Although here the variability of I.Q. is just as small as in the grade eleven (4) grouping, the actual high availability of role facilities (in the form of learned skills) within this group makes I.Q. a good predictor of the efficacious political role.

This complex set of relations can be made clearer by looking at the relation between grade and dogmatism, dogmatism and efficacy and grade and efficacy. If grade is *antecedent* to personality which then determines efficacy we would expect the following relationship:

1. $\gamma yx.u = 0$ (Dogmatism on Political Efficacy controlling for Grade)
2. $\gamma yu.x = 0$ (Grade on Political Efficacy controlling for Dogmatism)

This relationship, as can be seen from lines 1 and 7, does hold but only for the low dogmatic group. In the case of the high dogmatic group, many of whom come from grade eleven (4), the lack of the extra role facilities concomitant with grade means that the students have to fall back on personality determinants alone for personal role-definitions; and since they are in the main "close-minded," it is not surprising that they are low in feelings of political efficacy.

Family income was but a weak predictor of efficacy. We may note, however, that the relation between family income as a structural variable and political efficacy is strongly mediated by personality, I.Q. and grade (lines 10, 11 and 12, Table 4). Thus we see in line 10 that the relation between income and efficacy holds only for the high dogmatic group, many of whom are in the low-income category. Here again, a structural variable which limits role facilities has some effect within the high dogmatic group, reinforcing the tendency for high dogmatic respondents to have a low sense of political efficacy. The reverse relation occurs in the low dogmatic group. Here there is a tendency for low income to be associated with high political efficacy, suggesting that a combination of low dogmatism, high I.Q. and high status grades is sufficient to "overcome" the debilitating effects of low family income. This comes out clearly in line 12, Table 4. Here we see that the relation between family income and efficacy clearly reverses itself in the case of the large percentage of low dogmatics in grade thirteen ($\gamma yx.u_3 = -.53$), showing how the *combination* of positive reinforcements of efficacy mentioned previously reduces the dependence of efficacy on family income.

CONCLUSION

We have suggested that the relevance of personality to political behaviour merits the continued concern of political scientists, particularly during this period of great social and political change. In this study of the effects of personality on the potential future political behaviour of adolescent

citizens, we have found that a model which sees personality as an intervening variable that reconciles and adapts the conflicting expectations of
political structures for efficacious political behaviour to the personal
facilities available to the individual is most useful. In the course of this
adaptive process, personality determines the kind of personal role-definition an actor will adopt. Degree of dogmatism was found to be a powerful
predictor of individual political role definitions. While personality had a
powerful independent effect on such role definitions, this effect was most
pronounced in a structural sub-unit (grade eleven (4)), where political
role facilities (as measured by I.Q. and family income) were restricted,
and where, furthermore, the students were aware that their life chances
were in a sense restricted ("education for employment"). Personality was
found also to have high predictive power in a structural sub-unit (grade
thirteen) which was most prestigious within the school system ("education for the professions") and where the students had greater role facilities
(largely I.Q. in this case) to give themselves a highly efficacious personal
role definition.

These findings give some support to what Glidewell and his col-
laborators have called "the circular process." Their model suggests that
the following underlying process is involved in developing a competent
efficacious personal role-definition. If, due to factors like family income
(which reflects status and class differentials), family attitudes and personality syndromes of the parents, a child in adolescence is fortunate
enough to possess a high learning capacity and has well-developed interpersonal skills, ". . . he is likely to have a high self-esteem and a capacity
to perceive accurately the nature of the approaches and responses of
others to him." He will be able to perceive correctly positive and negative
responses to his approaches to others and this in turn will facilitate his
social acceptance, his power and his competence in the classroom. As his
further efforts at social interaction "turn out to be profitable, self-esteem
further increases and his position in the social system becomes more
satisfactory. A circular, self-perpetuating interaction pattern becomes
established—sometimes at the level of popular conformity in a stable
social structure and sometimes at the level of relative independence,
originality and creativity in a flexible social structure."[27]

At the other extreme we have the child who, because of other family
characteristics (primarily determined by social class), enters the class-

room with a more limited learning capacity and with less than adequate interpersonal skills; he is likely to have a low level of self-esteem and relatively high anxiety. His interactions with teachers and peers are likely to be awkward and to induce unsatisfying or belittling responses. He is likely to feel humiliated to some degree and to respond with either aggression or withdrawal. "Aggression promotes counteraggression—withdrawal promotes passive rejection or counter-withdrawal." The responses of both peers and teachers to this child's attempts at interaction are not likely to increase his self-esteem or interpersonal skills. "He is likely to distort his perception of the responses by denial or projection in order to protect whatever limited self-esteem he can marshall in the face of rejection by others. His utilization of his intelligence is likely to be reduced. Again, a self-sustaining circular process is established. Rejection breeds defensiveness, perceptual distortions, further aggression or withdrawal, and reduction in self-esteem."[28]

Clearly the *interaction* of social structure and personality in an unending chain of developmental sequences affects personal role definitions. In our research we were not able to get at the early developmental processes which provide the child with the kind of personality which will grow and develop into the "open-minded" personality type we have examined here. By cutting into the developmental sequence at the adolescent level we are able to show how these previous experiences are reinforced or retarded within a particular social structure—the school. The effect of "streaming" is, as many educators have pointed out, not conducive to the development of efficacious democratic citizens. In fact, the situation in the school studied here reminds one of McGuire's assertion that two of the social functions of the public school seem to be (1) to make certain that only a minimum number of middle-class children decline on status; and (2) to recruit a necessary proportion of lower-class children into middle-class life to meet the increasing need for the motives and skills typical of the middle class.[29]

NOTES

1. E. Barker, trans., *The Politics of Aristotle* (Oxford: Oxford University Press, 1946), p. 322. It should be noted that "constitution" as Aristotle used the term was not merely a particular structural arrangement for handling decisions within the polity. It was "a scheme of life, directed to attain a particular quality of life." Ibid., p. 180.

2. N. J. Smelser and W. T. Smelser, *Personality and Social Systems* (New York: Wiley, 1963), p. 1.

3. D. J. Levinson, "Role, Personality and Social Structure in the Organisational Setting," *Journal of Abnormal and Social Psychology*, vol. 58 (1959), pp. 170–80.

4. As Levinson points out (ibid., p. 173), the term "role" may have three distinct usages: 1) the norms and expectations associated with a social position; 2) the way an occupant of a social position defines what he is supposed to do or think in a role; 3) the way persons occupying a social position act in accord or non-accord with the norms attached to that position. Usually, it is assumed that there is a high degree of congruence between these three aspects of role, but such an assumption cannot be made *a priori*. In this paper we use the second definition unless otherwise stated.

5. For an example of the kind of citizen role demands made in Canadian schools see G. W. Brown, *Canadian Democracy in Action* (Toronto: Dent, 1952), chapters 2 and 4. For a comprehensive bibliography on Citizenship Education, especially in the U.S.A., see C. W. Harris, *Encylopedia of Educational Research* (New York: Macmillan, 1959), pp. 206–10.

6. For a useful review of the research literature and findings dealing with the question of efficacy see L. W. Milbrath, *Political Participation* (Chicago: Rand McNally, 1965), pp. 56–64. See also the extensive footnote 4 in D. Easton and J. Dennis, "The Child's Acquisition of Regime Norms: Political Efficacy," *The American Political Science Review*, vol. 61 (March 1967), p. 27.

7. Ibid., p. 26.

8. "Role, Personality and Social Structure," p. 176.

9. M. Rosenberg, "Some Determinants of Political Apathy," *Public Opinion Quarterly*, vol. 18, no. 4 (1954–55), pp. 349–66.

10. "Role, Personality and Social Structure," pp. 177–78.

11. For an excellent review of these differing approaches, see N. Sanford, "Personality: Its Place in Psychology," in S. Koch, ed., *Psychology: A Study of a Science* (New York: McGraw-Hill, 1963), vol. 5, pp. 489–579.

12. H. Lasswell, "Democratic Character" in *The Political Writings of Harold D. Lasswell* (Glencoe, Ill.: Free Press, 1951), pp. 465–525; F. I. Greenstein, "Personality and Political Socialization: The Theories of Authoritarian and Democratic Character," *The Annals of the American Academy of Political and Social Science*, vol. 361 (September 1965), pp. 81–95.

13. M. Rokeach, *The Open and Closed Mind* (New York: Basic Books, 1960), p. 6.

14. Ibid., p. 7.

15. For a good review of this literature, see A. R. Cohen, *Attitude Change and Social Influence* (New York: Basic Books, 1964); also B. M. Hennessy, *Public Opinion* (Belemont, Calif.: Duxbury, 1965), chapters 19–21.

16. Rokeach, *The Open and Closed Mind*, p. 67.

17. K. J. Hayes, "Genes, Drives and Intellect," *Psychological Report*, vol. 10 (1962), pp. 299–342. See also D. Byrne, *An Introduction to Personality* (Englewood Cliffs, N.J.: Prentice-Hall, 1966), chapter 11. For a study of the impact of I.Q. on children's political perceptions, see R. D. Hess and J. V. Torney, *The Development of Basic Attitudes and Values Toward Government and Citizenship During the Elementary School Years* (Part I) (Chicago, 1965), chapter 5.

18. A. Campbell et al., *The Voter Decides* (Evanston, Ill.: Row Peterson, 1954), p. 187.

19. "The Child's Acquisition of Regime Norms," pp. 29–30.

20. Ibid., p. 32.

21. The personality and child development literature is immense. For
useful reviews and surveys see:
P. H. Mussen, ed., *Handbook of
Research Methods in Child Development* (New York: Wiley, 1960),
particularly chapter 16, "The
Measurement of Children's Attitudes
and Values," and chapter 18, "The
Appraisal of Personality Characteristics in Children." Byrne, *Introduction to Personality*, has a useful
chapter on "Determining the Antecedents of Individual Differences."
F. I. Greenstein, *Children and
Politics* (New Haven: Yale University Press, 1965), chapter 5. See
also M. L. Kohn, "Social Class and
the Exercise of Parental Authority,"
American Sociological Review, Vol.
24 (1959), pp. 352–66.

22. See *Ontario Conference on Education, November 1961*, sponsored
by the Ontario Association for
Curriculum Development, especially
the reports by group 1, *Organization
of the School System* and group 12,
*The New Secondary School Pro-
gramme.*

23. The quotation is from an explanation of the system given by a school
inspector. Ibid., p. 68.

24. R. H. Turner, "Modes of Social
Ascent through Education: Spon-
sored and Contest Mobility," in
A. H. Halsey et al., eds., *Education,
Economy and Society* (Glencoe, Ill.:
Free Press, 1965), pp. 123–24.

25. See L. A. Goodman and W. H.
Kruskal, "Measures of Association
for Cross Classifications," *Journal of
the American Statistical Association*,
vol. 49 (1954), pp. 732–64.

26. For a detailed explanation of partial
gamma, see J. A. Davis, "A Partial
Coefficient for Goodman and
Kruskal's Gamma," *Journal of the
American Statistical Association*,
vol. 62, no. 317 (1967), pp. 189–93.

27. J. C. Glidewell et al., "Socialization
and Social Structure in the Classroom," in L. W. Hoffman, ed.,
*Review of Child Development Re-
search* (New York: Russell Sage,
1963), pp. 247–49.

28. Ibid.

29. C. McGuire, "Social Stratification
and Mobility Patterns," *American
Sociological Review*, vol. 15 (1950),
pp. 195–204.

Children, Television and Politics: 7

Is the Medium the Message?

STUART B. PROUDFOOT

JON H. PAMMETT

In the literature concerned with the political socialization of children very little attention has been paid to the role of the mass media. Yet studies now indicate that children spend as much time in front of the television screen during the first sixteen years of their lives as they do in school.[1] The purpose of this paper is to report the results of a study of certain characteristics of the television medium as it relates to political knowledge and identification with political figures. The respondents were a group of some three hundred Canadian school children.[2] The major conclusion drawn from the analysis is this: television and print media appear to affect political knowledge and job aspirations in different ways. Television seems to appeal to and enhance the emotive orientations of its users while the print medium is more closely associated with cognitive phenomena.

Two interrelated ideas provide the theoretical basis for the analysis and lead to two research hypotheses. The first notion concerns the uses to which different media are put. For instance, one might ask: What does a child use television for? Or, with what purpose in mind does he or she turn to a book? Or, more generally, does print satisfy different needs than television? If so, what are those needs?

The second major theme upon which the discussion is based involves what might be termed the "technical" characteristics of the medium itself. In this regard some of the theories advanced by Marshall McLuhan will be employed. An attempt will be made to answer questions such as: What is television "good" at doing? What is print an effective medium for? Are there special characteristics of different media which make them more proficient in the dissemination of certain kinds of information or in creating or complementing certain moods or personalities? Obviously, these two notions are closely related, for it follows that if one medium is more effective in meeting certain user needs, increased usage for that purpose will result. It is the corollary, though, which may be more important. Consider, for instance, the value of knowing that certain kinds of responses to political phenomena are more liable to be elicited by employing one medium in lieu of another.

What does a child use television for? In order to satisfactorily answer this question it is instructive to consider the more general question of the function of art in people's lives. As Brodbeck[3] has pointed out, in the classical theories of aesthetics there have always been two fundamentally opposed types of theory concerning the role of art at the individual level. On the one hand are the theories which see emotion as the key variable. In such theories art appears as "a producer of relief, pleasure and indulgence for frustrated human wish and desire."[4] On the other hand are the theories "which have stressed the cognitive functions of art, in which art appears as a producer of insight, knowledge and learning."[5] Schramm has noted that in modern writings on the mass media, theories of the former type take the "psycho-analytical and voluntaristic view that art is, like the dream, a form of wish-fulfillment under the sway of the pleasure principles."[6] He further points out that, in contrast, theories of the cognitive variety are likely to view art as "an agency of socialization and social learning—an agency which, in other words, inculcates values, reinforces habits, and creates expectations much as parents and other real-life socializers do."[7] These two theoretical approaches were discussed formerly in terms of emotion and cognition, but one is now more liable to employ the terms wish-fulfillment and socialization. Regardless of the terminology, the underlying premises are the same.

With respect to this analysis we will consider that art—specifically the media—satisfies both kinds of needs, emotive and cognitive. The key questions which then arise relate to the patterns of media usage and differences in appeal among media, due both to content and to what we above termed technical attributes. To a discussion of those technical attributes we now turn.

Marshall McLuhan contends that the "content" of media is unimportant compared to the medium itself, and hence that the medium is the message. Different media have different attributes and it is those attributes which are important in understanding effects on media users. For our purposes we will employ the less ambitious idea that the medium via which some information or images is communicated *can in itself be important*, apart from the content of the message. Indeed, we could coin our own working slogan: "the medium matters." The McLuhan theory is based on two related ideas: the concepts of "definition" and "user participation." Accordingly, the lower the degree of definition, the greater the degree of user participation. And, the greater the degree of user participation, the "cooler" the medium. Conversely, "hot" media are those which involve low user participation. The relevant explanatory paragraph from *Understanding Media* is as follows:

There is a basic principle that distinguishes a hot medium like radio from a cool one like the telephone, or a hot medium like the movie from a cool one like TV. A hot medium is one that extends one single sense in "high definition." High definition is the state of being well-filled with data. A photograph is visually, "high definition." A cartoon is "low definition," simply because very little visual information is provided. Telephone is a cool medium, or one of low definition, because the ear is given a meagre amount of information. And speech is a cool medium of low definition, because so little is given and so much has to be filled in by the listener. On the other hand, hot media do not leave so much to be filled in or completed by the audience. Hot media are, therefore, low in participation, and cool media are high in participation or completion by the audience. Naturally, therefore, a hot medium like radio has very different effects on the user from a cool medium like the telephone.[8]

He contends that it is these characteristics of definition and participation which allow the print medium to be the more effective transmitter of fact and information, television the more effective involver of the audience in the "process" of the visual/oral presentation. McLuhan points out that "the television image is of low intensity [and therefore] does not afford detailed information about objects."[9] He contrasts this with print which he says involves "intensity and uniform precision" instead of the "diffuse texture" of the television image.[10] It is print, he argues, that has been responsible for the emphasis on exact measurement and repeatability that we now associate with science and mathematics.

For the moment let us accept McLuhan's theses about television as a cool medium (i.e., one low in definition and thereby demanding a high degree of user participation), and of print as a medium of high definition and lower user involvement. It is worth emphasizing that McLuhan's use of the word participation with respect to television is different from its usual connotation, that is, the antithesis of passivity. In McLuhan's terminology, participation refers to the viewer's involvement in the completion of the TV image. As noted earlier, what would seem to follow from an acceptance of these notions is that television would be the more effective medium for the communication of ideas and images which invite or demand high user participation. Concomitantly, it would follow that print is the more effective imparter of hard facts and information involving little user involvement in the process of "closing" and filling in the data being presented.

We are now ready to move toward the formulation of our research hypotheses. To do so let us attempt to integrate the earlier discussion of the emotive and cognitive functions of art for the individual and the McLuhanesque notions of the relative effectiveness of the print and television media for certain purposes. Based on McLuhan, we have proposed television as the medium requiring more user participation (due to low definition) compared to print with its high definition. It would seem then, a reasonable premise that TV would be the more effective medium for reaching and affecting the "emotive properties" of the user. Similarly, print, while affording less opportunity for involvement on the part of the user, would appear to have relatively greater potential for meeting cognitive needs. This is not to argue that television cannot function as an effective medium for imparting "low participation" information or that print is incapable of reaching the emotions of its readers. We are arguing instead that, based on the theories of McLuhan, television should be the more effective medium for reaching emotional "nerve ends" and print the better agent for imparting "hard" facts. One should not lose sight of the fact that the *content* of the two media is not unrelated to what we are arguing are the inherent technical attributes thereof. The argument is somewhat circular in nature; because television is perhaps more effective than print in involving the user it should come as no surprise that the bulk of television programming is geared to that purpose. Further, one might expect that the bulk of the "hard" information needs of the individual would be gained via print. Indeed, it is conceivable that it is the involvement in the participation process itself, which is required when watching TV, which distracts the viewer from the hard facts and data which form a part of the program.

As a basis for our hypotheses let us consider the creation of two media-user types. We have argued that television better meets emotive needs while print is more effective as a cognitive medium. Maybe what we are getting around to saying is that people more or less tend to view television for entertainment while reading books and newspapers more for their informational content, that is, for learning. In the comprehensive study of Schramm, Lyle and Parker, the authors note that by far the major reason children watch television is for entertainment.

. . . the passive pleasure of being entertained, living a fantasy, taking part vicariously in thrill play, identifying with exciting and attractive people, getting away from real-life problems and escaping real-life boredom . . .[11]

Coming in a poor second is the information children get from television. The authors point out that much of this learning is incidental; the children don't seek it out.

. . . they [the children] prefer incidental learning from television to purposeful and intentional learning. This is the heart of their objection to educational television. They can't go to educational television primarily for entertainment and expect to derive an incidental benefit by learning something useful. Instead, they have to go to it with the main purpose of learning something useful, and any entertainment they derive is incidental.[12]

In addition, one should not overlook the fact that television can provide children with escape from the often harsh realities of institutionalized learning in which the use of print (textbooks) plays no small part. To summarize, let us consider television as primarily a medium for satisfying fantasy-oriented needs of the user and consider print as basically meeting reality-oriented needs.

It would seem reasonable in view of the foregoing discussion that one could create two "ideal type" media users. These types could apply equally to adults, but for the purposes at hand we are concerned with children. The first type we have designated fantasy-oriented. By fantasy-oriented,

we mean that the user exhibits the following characteristics: he
1) seeks to remove himself from the problems of the real world;
2) seeks surrender and relaxation;
3) seeks emotional involvement;
4) seeks to avoid, at least temporarily, threat and anxiety;
5) seeks wish-fulfillment and pleasure.

At the other end of an imaginary reality-fantasy continuum is our second type, the reality-oriented child. In contrast to the fantasy child, the reality-oriented child embodies the following attributes: he
1) seeks to immerse himself in the problems of the real world;
2) seeks activity;
3) seeks cognition;
4) seeks to confront threat and anxiety in an effort to get a better view of problems;
5) seeks enlightenment.

In order to formulate our research hypotheses it was necessary to operationalize the reality-fantasy typology. In the original study conducted by Pammett, the school children were asked certain questions concerning their reading and television-viewing habits. While these questions were not specifically designed to elicit information for an analysis such as the one under discussion, they were judged adequate for the purpose. The respondents were asked five questions which were in turn combined into two indices: one regarding television viewing and one concerning reading interest. From these indices were created the two operational "reality" and "fantasy" groups.

Simply, the fantasy group included those children who
1) watched a large amount of television; and
2) expressed little interest in reading books.

In contrast, the reality group included those children who
1) expressed a strong interest in reading books; and
2) watched little television.

The two research hypotheses can be stated as follows: (1) the reality group of children will score higher on factual questions of political knowledge than the fantasy-oriented group of children; but (2) the fantasy group of children will express a greater desire to be (to have the occupation of) two highly placed political figures (the mayor and the Prime Minister) than their reality-oriented peers.

The analysis is divided into two sections corresponding to the two research hypotheses. Essentially, our first hypothesis boils down to the question: Does it matter if one is in the reality or the fantasy group in terms of being able to answer questions of political knowledge? Or alternatively, is there a relationship between group and political knowledge? Our theoretical discussion would lead us to believe that there should be a relationship between political knowledge and group and the analysis would appear to support our hypothesis. Four of the first set of six questions ask the respondent to name certain highly placed political figures. In addition, the respondents were queried as to whether they had "heard of" two prominent political institutions. Table 1 depicts the percentage breakdown by group for each question.

It can be readily seen from Table 1 that a consistently greater percentage of the reality group is able to answer the questions correctly. In order to measure the degree of statistical association of these differences, the table also includes the value of Yule's Q, which is in fact the gamma measure applied to a 2 x 2 contingency table. In addition, the table also shows the value of chi-square, along with its level of significance. The values of Q shown in Table 1 range from moderately to substantially positive. Similarly, six of the eight relationships show chi-square measures significant at, or greater than, the .05 level, and the cumulative chi-square is significant beyond the .001 level.

A second set of questions in the data set referred to descriptions of the roles of various political officials and institutions. The results of these questions are presented in Table 2, which is arranged in the same format as Table 1.

Again, as in the first set of questions, the reality group scores considerably better than the fantasy group. The strength of the relationships is roughly of the same order of magnitude as in the first set of questions; in this case three relationships are significant at the .05 level. It is interesting that significance levels are much the same as in the "Names" questions in view of the much lower N's involved. It appears that many respondents chose not to answer these more difficult questions perhaps to avoid giving an incorrect answer. Employing the technique of accumulating the chi-square values for each separate question yields a total of 20.02. With 5 degrees of freedom this value is significant at the .001 level.

The second set of questions was segregated from the first because they

Table 1 Groups of Fantasy- and Reality-Oriented Children, and Their Degrees of Political Knowledge

Question	Percentage of Group Giving "Reasonably Accurate" Answer*		Q	χ^2	Sign. at	N
	Reality	Fantasy				
1. Can you name the Mayor of Kingston?	87	75	.36	5.35	.02	288
2. Have you ever heard of the City Council?	68	53	.31	6.15	.03	284
3. Can you name the Premier of Ontario?	38	19	.44	11.18	.001	277
4. Can you name the Prime Minister of Canada?	64	58	.18	5.57	.02	300
5. Have you ever heard of Parliament?	82	75	.20	1.48	.22	284
6. Can you name the President of the United States?	86	78	.26	2.39	.12	282
7. Identify correctly either of two national names*	22	5	.66	10.95	.001	214
8. Identify correctly any of five inter-national names†	34	12	.59	19.24	.001	292

cumulative χ^2 = 62.31 significant at < .001

*The names were: John Diefenbaker, Mitchell Sharp.
†The names were: U Thant, Ronald Reagan, Harold Wilson, Charles De Gaulle, Leonid Brezhnev.

were judged to be more difficult. It was reasoned that the reality group might score relatively better on more difficult questions. However, in order to obtain decent marginals (enough respondents with any acceptable answer) it was necessary to accept answers which, while not incorrect, under circumstances of higher N's might not have been acceptable. By so doing, perhaps our ability to differentiate the children's ability to answer the questions was lowered. In addition, it would seem that stronger relationships were not found due to another reason alluded to above. The

Table 2 Accuracy of Role-Perceptions of Fantasy- and Reality-Oriented Children

Question	Percentage of Group Giving "Reasonably Accurate" Answer*		Q	χ^2	Sign. at	N
	Reality	Fantasy				
1. What does the Mayor do?	52	38	.35	6.29	.01	217
2. What does the City Council do?	77	66	.27	1.24	.27	117
3. What does the Prime Minister do?	56	30	.50	7.65	.006	124
4. What does Parliament do?	79	68	.28	1.24	.27	114
5. What does the President do?	74	59	.33	3.6	.06	167

cumulative $\chi^2 = 20.02$ significant at .001

*Children giving no answer to the questions have been excluded from the table.

fantasy group chose not to answer, or were not able to answer, the questions in greater proportions than the reality group. In the second set of questions the average percentage of no answers in the reality and fantasy groups were 48 per cent and 59 per cent respectively. While unprovable, one might speculate that a significant proportion of the fantasy group no answers would really have been incorrect answers. Even if the fantasy group had had the same proportion of no answers as the reality group the relationships would have been stronger.

In summation, it would appear that our first hypothesis has been substantiated: the reality-oriented children do score consistently higher than their fantasy-oriented peers on questions of political knowledge. However, can we be certain that the ability to answer such knowledge questions has anything at all to do with our reality-fantasy conceptions; could not, say, intelligence or the kind of home from which the children come be the major factors? It is entirely possible that these considerations are relevant. Unfortunately, the data available from the study do not allow us to control for intelligence, but we can see if the socio-economic level of the children's

Table 3 Group and Political Knowledge, Controlling for Socio-Economic Status
Yule's Q, chi-square and levels of significance

Question	Q	x^2	Significant At	N
1. Can you name the Mayor of Kingston, Ontario?				
All classes	.36	5.35	0.02	288
High SES	.66	8.23	0.004	128
Low SES	.09	0.08	0.78	160
2. Have you ever heard of Kingston City Council?				
All classes	.31	6.15	0.01	284
High SES	.55	8.41	0.004	127
Low SES	.06	0.03	0.86	157
3. Can you name the Premier of Ontario?				
All classes	.44	11.18	0.001	277
High SES	.42	4.28	0.04	121
Low SES	.43	4.90	0.03	156
4. Can you name the Prime Minister of Canada?				
All classes	.18	5.57	0.02	300
High SES	.34	3.38	0.07	142
Low SES	.02	0.01	0.96	158
5. Have you ever heard of Parliament?				
All classes	.20	1.48	0.22	287
High SES	.74	11.77	0.001	127
Low SES	−.26	1.57	0.21	160
6. Can you name the President of the United States?				
All classes	.26	2.39	0.12	282
High SES	.37	1.56	0.21	125
Low SES	.15	0.29	0.59	157
7. National names*				
All classes	.66	10.95	0.001	167
High SES	.75	8.90	0.003	79
Low SES	.32	0.21	0.65	88
8. International names*				
All classes	.59	19.24	0.001	292
High SES	.67	13.17	0.001	129
Low SES	.40	2.90	0.09	163

*See Table 1.

Table 4 Group and Political Knowledge, Controlling for Socio-Economic Class

Yule's Q, chi-square, and levels of significance

Question	Q	χ^2	Significant At	N
1. What does the Mayor do?				
All classes	.35	6.29	0.01	217
High SES	.29	1.57	0.21	104
Low SES	.43	4.80	0.03	113
2. What does Kingston City Council do?				
All classes	.27	1.24	0.27	117
High SES	.34	0.81	0.38	65
Low SES	.11	0.01	0.95	52
3. What does the Prime Minister do?				
All classes	.50	7.65	0.001	124
High SES	.32	1.01	0.32	61
Low SES	.63	6.20	0.01	63
4. What does Parliament do?				
All classes	.28	1.24	0.27	114
High SES	.34	0.77	0.38	62
Low SES	.21	0.13	0.72	52
5. What does the President of the U.S. do?				
All classes	.33	3.60	0.06	167
High SES	.34	1.05	0.31	79
Low SES	.15	0.22	0.64	88

homes is a consideration. We do this by holding constant the occupation level of the family breadwinner and seeing what happens to the relationship between group and knowledge. The results are depicted in Tables 5 and 6.

The effects of controlling for socio-economic status appear to be mixed. As depicted in Table 3, with one exception, the eight relationships formed by the "names" questions are maintained and, indeed, are stronger within the high SES category. However, within the low SES group, again with the one same exception, the relationships weaken and/or disappear. If socio-economic class were the factor causing the relationship between group and knowledge, however, we would expect the relationship to disappear within both categories of class.

In Table 4, a somewhat different pattern emerges. The strengths of the relationships are maintained within the high SES category (no Q value changes by more than 8 points), and by and large, within the low SES division as well. In the low socio-economic group, the Q values deviate by as much as 23 points, but not always in the same direction.

It is difficult, given such results, to reach any definite conclusions regarding the effects of socio-economic class on the ability of our reality-fantasy groups to answer political knowledge questions. We can say that the relationships do hold up within the high SES group and that the results are mixed within the low SES group. Statisticians and data analysts might tentatively place such results in the category of specification; in other words, one has to specify what category of a third variable (in this case socio-economic status) one is talking about before one can say what relationship obtains. But our difficulties are further compounded by the low N values which in effect mean that not only is there difficulty in achieving significance within an SES category but it takes very big differences in the Q values of the two SES groups for those differences to be significant. Nevertheless, it does appear that while socio-economic background seems to be a factor in the children's level of knowledge, its exact effects are complicated and do not adequately explain the reality-fantasy group differences.

The second part of the analysis revolves around the hypothesis that:

[While the reality-oriented children score higher than the fantasy-oriented children on questions of specific political knowledge] the fantasy-oriented children will express a greater desire to be (to have the occupation of) two highly-placed political figures (the mayor and the Prime Minister) than their reality-oriented peers.[13]

Table 5 depicts the percentage of each group which answered affirmatively the questions, "Would you like to be the Mayor?" and "Would you like to be the Prime Minister?" The table also presents the strengths of association and levels of significance for these relationships.

The results presented in Table 5 appear to confirm our hypothesis that the fantasy-oriented children identify more closely with political figures whom they see on television than do the reality-oriented youngsters. As in the knowledge questions investigated previously, however, it is possible

Table 5 Groups of Reality- and Fantasy-Oriented Children, and Their Identification with Political Figures

Question	Percentage of Group Answering Affirmatively		Q	x^2	Significant At	N
	Reality	Fantasy				
1. Would you like to be the Mayor?	27	48	.43	13.17	.001	292
2. Would you like to be the Prime Minister?	32	43	.23	3.18	.07	291

that the social class background from which the children come could be a factor influencing their answers. We have controlled for social class in Table 6, even though it might be expected that the reality-oriented children would come from the higher socio-economic classes, since reading books is usually considered to be more common with higher social classes. As can be seen from Table 6, however, controlling for social class does not wash out the relationship between group and identification with political figures. The relationships controlled for social class look very similar to the uncontrolled results.

Table 6 Group and Identification with Political Figures, Controlling for Socio-Economic Class

Yule's Q, chi-square, and levels of significance

Question	Q	x^2	Significant At	N
1. Would you like to be Mayor?				
All classes	−.43	13.17	0.001	292
High SES	−.38	3.83	0.051	129
Low SES	−.46	7.83	0.005	163
2. Would you like to be Prime Minister?				
All classes	−.23	3.18	0.074	291
High SES	−.20	0.92	0.337	129
Low SES	−.29	2.55	0.111	162

We feel justified, therefore, in claiming that the data analysis in this paper has produced support for our hypotheses. The children who like to read but watch little television show greater degrees of political knowledge, but the children who watch a lot of television and do not care as much about reading are more likely to want to emulate politicians, in the sense of vicariously wishing they could do their jobs. This relationship holds, in general, when controlled for social class, but might be affected by a control for I.Q., a measure we do not have in the data-set.

The results, however tentative and preliminary they might be, lead to intriguing speculations about their import. Children who have much of their contact with the political world through television may be in danger of coming to regard political officials much as they do other "actors" seen on television, as players in a drama played out for their entertainment. Coupled with the lower levels of factual knowledge about the political roles, institutions and personalities which seem to be present in such children, this passive attitude could lead to reduced interest in political participation of an active kind in society and in lowered concern for the real political problems that occupy the politicians. It is worth remembering, however, that it is the "extreme" groups we have singled out for this analysis; by far the majority of the children in the total study had moderate levels of both television-watching and desires to read. Thus, while the medium which transfers political perceptions may indeed "matter," most children are exposed to enough different media that the "messages" of any particular one are diluted.

NOTES

1. Wilbur L. Schramm, Jack Lyle, Edwin B. Parker, *Television in the Lives of Our Children* (Stanford: Stanford University Press, 1961), p. 12.
2. The original study by Jon H. Pammett and Howat P. Noble was conducted in 1966 in Kingston, Ontario. Its purpose was to measure the development of political knowledge and attitudes of a group of Canadian school children. The study consisted of a sample survey of 1,985 children in ten schools. The sample was a large representative one with ethnic, religious and income groups included in appropriate proportions. The survey was conducted among grades four to eight. In cases where more than two classes existed per grade, two classes were randomly selected; or where the classes were "streamed" one top and one lower stream class was randomly selected.

While Noble and Pammett, and now Proudfoot and Pammett, do not claim that the sample of Kingston children is representative of Canada as a whole the results should be treated as suggestive of further research. The most complete description of the findings of the study are included in the M.A. thesis of Pammett, Queen's University, 1967. See also Pammett, "The Development of Political Orientations in Canadian School Children," *Canadian Journal of Political Science*, March 1971.

3. A. J. Brodbeck, "The Mass Media as a Socializing Agency" (mimeo, paper read to American Psychological Association Symposium on Children and the Mass Media, San Francisco, 1955. Cited in Schramm, Lyle, Parker).

4. Schramm, *Television in the Lives*, p. 60.

5. Ibid.

6. Ibid.

7. Ibid.

8. Marshall McLuhan, *Understanding Media* (New York: New American Library, 1964), p. 36.

9. Ibid., p. 276.

10. Ibid.

11. Schramm, *Television in the Lives*, p. 57.

12. Ibid., pp. 58–59. The phenomenal success of *Sesame Street* is interesting in this regard.

13. It is interesting to think of the differences in the reality and fantasy children in this way. While both groups may watch the Prime Minister giving a speech on television they seem to derive something different from the experience. The reality children tend to note the name of the person involved, what he is doing, etc. The fantasy child, in contrast, tends to identify with the person on the screen; he involves himself with the figure, he would like to *be* him. This identification, however, seems to take place without a firm understanding or a realistic appreciation of what, say, the Prime Minister's job involves. In this participation and identification process, hard information such as the Prime Minister's name seems almost irrelevant.

PART THREE

The Socialization of
Activists and Elites

Political Education,

8

Political Action and the Community

THELMA OLIVER

The apparent conservatism of the socialization process poses vexing conceptual problems for the political scientist working in the field of political culture. In this paper I offer a simple taxonomy which permits more careful specification of phenomena associated with political learning.[1] For this purpose, it is useful to view the process we normally identify as political socialization from a broader perspective, using the term "political education" to describe the process by which political learning takes place. This permits use of the term socialization to refer to one pole of a political education continuum, with politicization at the other pole. We reserve the term socialization for the process which transmits the dominant political culture from generation to generation, maintaining support for the political system as it is, allowing for incremental change in an overall context of order, obedience and preservation of the polity. By contrast, the term politicization is reserved for the process which induces active discontent with the system, urging reform and ultimate transformation of the polity through political action and, if necessary, disorder. Together, socialization and politicization create a continuum of political education which accounts for change as well as conservation of the polity.

Table 1 presents in schematic fashion the attributes of each pole of the political education process. The two types of political movement also included in Table 1, reaction and revolution, provide perspective on the place of education in relation to other political processes. The categories used to describe socialization and politicization are attributes common to many social and political processes: substance, referring to the content that is transmitted; purpose, or the goal of the process in relation to the political system; mode, or form of activity characteristic of the process; objective, the target of activity; support-type, referring to the nature of

150

Table 1   Attributes of Political Education Processes Contrasted with Two Types of Political Movement

	Political Education		Political Movements	
	Socialization	*Politicization*	*Reaction*	*Revolution*
Purpose	preservation, incremental change	trans- formation, reform	restoration, retribution	elimination of old, establishment of new
Mode	order, obedience	disorder, action	control	violence
Objective	regime, community	authorities	system	system
Substance	dominant culture	policy, sub-culture	former culture	counter- culture
Support- type	diffuse	specific	opposed	opposed
Agents	systemic institutions: family, school, mass media, peers	individuals, groups	political organizations	political organizations

support generated by the process; and agents, the organizational form or source of personnel engaged in the process.

The purpose of socialization is to ensure the preservation of the political system as it is, with only incremental change where essential for minimal adaptation to the system's environment. The purpose of politicization is to reform the political system in some major way, as rapidly as possible. Socialization maintains, politicization transforms. The characteristic mode in which these purposes are pursued differs radically between the two education processes. Whereas socialization teaches the importance of order and obedience, so that "participation" has institutionalized meanings which require conformity to established rituals and roles, politicization teaches the need, however regrettable, to challenge established order; this means the disruption of those behaviour patterns which socialization has led everyone to expect and respect. That is not to say that politicization necessarily involves disregard for legal norms; as we will see this is seldom the case.

What politicization does that socialization does not is require, absolutely, the direct, personal and consistent pursuit of goals through political action. The target, or objective, of each type of educational process may sometimes be the same, but in looking at their operation in Canada we find that socialization is usually directed toward the regime and the political community, while politicization is directed toward the authorities. The regime includes all the constitutional and institutional roles and structures of the political system such as Parliament, the federal system, the electoral system, and so on. The political community encompasses much of what we mean when we refer to the "nation," the "national identity," and the history of the people who are members of the political system. The authorities are those individuals who perform the rule-making, administering, and adjudicating functions normally associated with government. Politicization accepts regime and community norms transmitted through the socialization process, but challenges the legitimacy and authority of those who claim to be implementing the will of the community through proper use of the regime.

Redefinition and reinterpretation of the meaning of regime norms and the nature of the community are also within the scope of politicization, as we note when the substance, or content, of the two processes are contrasted: socialization transmits the dominant culture, which is necessarily imprecise and compromising; politicization transmits sub-cultural beliefs and values, with an emphasis on more specific questions of public policy. Politicization urges people to act on some substantive political issue according to an articulate analysis of the public interest; socialization merely transmits norms which bind people together in a basic orientation to the polity without implications for specific action.

When these attributes are viewed in terms of their consequences for system support, they coincide with Easton's distinction between diffuse and specific support:[2] in a general way, socialization maintains diffuse support while politicization involves questions of specific support. While politicization does not necessarily set out to generate positive specific support for the authorities, we leave this possibility open because it is conceivable that responsive authorities will adapt to politicization, with the consequence that the process will generate positive support for specific policies and, ultimately, for the authorities making the decisions. However, since politicization occurs because authorities are at least initially unresponsive to the substantive demands that sub-cultural groups or individuals make upon the political system it is more likely that politicization will create "negative" support or alienation. On the other hand, while socialization will not normally be concerned with specific policy questions or with support for particular authorities, there are ambiguous situations, such as socialization to the "two nations" thesis of the Canadian political community, which impinge upon specific public policies, in this case language legislation. On the whole, however, the distinction between objectives of the two processes is reasonably sound, and the contrast in type of support affected by each process holds up well enough.

Finally, there is the difference between socialization and politicization agents. The established institutions of the political system, the family, the school, the mass media, and peers (in the form of voluntary associations and co-workers) do the work of socialization. Politicization is undertaken by individuals and sub-cultural groups. There are situations in which established institutions engage in politicization; for example, in Quebec society we might expect a high level of politicization to occur in many families, where the authority of the federal government and the legitimacy of the Canadian constitution for the people of Quebec are rejected. Similarly, it is widely believed that school teachers, technical instructors, university professors, journalists, broadcasters and artists in Quebec are more Séparatiste than not. In this example, not only the distinction between agents of socialization and politicization breaks down: the purpose, mode, objective, substance and support-type associated with politicization in Quebec often look more like those of a revolutionary movement than a political education process.

This draws our attention to two important generalizations which serve as caveats to Table 1: first, where agents of socialization begin to politicize their listeners, fundamental change and some measure of disorder, even violence, are inevitable; secondly, political education is closely related to political organization. This important point needs elaboration.

Political organization can be conceived, very simply, in terms of two types: political movements and political parties.[3] Organized political action will take either of these forms. In Canada, political parties compete for control of the institutional structure, engaging in political education to the extent that the articulation and aggregation of demands on the political system require communication of ideas about public policy and institutional reform. A movement seeks to increase its membership of convinced adherents, a goal quite different from that of the political party, which seeks only votes; the movement's primary goal is the achievement of an ideal, while the political party's primary goal is to obtain power, to manage the system. Since elections are the route to power, the political party is mindful of majority opinion; whether in or out of power, the political party will not challenge the status quo sufficiently to lose the potential support of the majority of people who have been socialized to accept the regime and community as they are. Some politicization on matters of public policy is essential for parties because they attempt to offer alternatives to the public, but parties will not present themselves as movements of reaction or revolution; if they do they cannot properly be described as political parties.

Students of electoral behaviour in Canada, along with students of other liberal democratic systems, find that participation in political parties and elections increases as socio-economic status (SES) increases, while alienation increases as SES decreases. That is, the poorer you are the less likely you are to participate in political life, and the more likely you are to be alienated from the political process.[4] One reason for this feature in countries like Canada is the shorter length of time poor people are exposed to agents of socialization, particularly the school; knowledge of the system induces a sense of competence and a tendency to participate in political life, while lack of knowledge and skill induces a sense of helplessness and apathy. Thus, the failure of socialization among poor people is, in an important way, responsible for the failure of the poor to organize or in some other way pursue their interest through the political system. It is an irony of the liberal democratic system that participation in public decision systems is effectively limited to those who are already in control of the allocation of resources. That is, those who control resources also control the decision systems able to reallocate resources. Thus the poor, those without resources, are unable to affect decisions which would reallocate resources in their favour. Only the beneficence of the powerful can effect reallocation. Politicization of the poor—an old idea recently revived—is undertaken in the hope that poor people can gain a voice in the political process sufficient to enable them to make their demands heard and to obtain favourable changes in public policy.

Until the 1960s, various political movements attempted to politicize the poor: Social Credit, the CCF, and a variety of more radical political groups. Social Credit identified the "fifty big shots" as the exploiters of the people, and offered financial reform as the solution to unjust distribution of wealth. The CCF presented a democratic socialist analysis of the source of Canada's inequitable distribution of resources. Groups such as Stevens' Reconstruction Party and the Communist Party of Canada had other solutions. But these were political movements only so long as their objective was to politicize the people; both Social Credit and the CCF became political parties with an electoral emphasis, and the other groups became ineffective.

By 1965 no group was seriously engaged in politicization of the poor. About that time the federal Liberal party began to respond to changes that were taking place in the United States under Lyndon Johnson's leadership: the American War on Poverty (the Economic Opportunity Act of 1964) introduced two important new concepts, community action, and government grants for the employment of youth.[5] At the same time, professionals in various social service fields in Canada were in the process of organizing communities to provide opportunities for local participation in decisions affecting the allocation of resources, both public and private, and the term "community development," which had referred to missionary work in the Third World (for example, Canadian University Students Overseas, CUSO), was adopted to describe the intervention of professionals and volunteers in low-income urban communities at home.[6] Thus, both federal politicians and public servants developed an interest in the political education process among the poor.

It was not long before unemployed young people, and university students in particular, also became involved in community development or community action funded by the federal government. Energy that had been directed toward international poverty through CUSO was now being directed toward domestic poverty through the Company of Young Canadians (CYC), and later the Local Initiatives Programme (LIP) and Opportunities for Youth (OFY).[7] Private charitable organizations, especially United Community Services (UCS), organized local area councils in most cities, and attempted to introduce the concept of citizen participation into decision-making. Citizen participation became the keynote of community development efforts, and cooperation between private organizations and federally funded community workers in their efforts to politicize the poor created the basis of a movement organized both through the institutional links among the people involved and through the growth of a common perspective on the importance of citizen participation. Their purpose was to transform decision systems in Canada so that the interests of the poor could be articulated and served by the poor themselves. The beneficent ruler was to be replaced by the articulate, competent, self-interested citizen. And this community action movement was conceived, by the participants, as the basis for fundamental change in the distribution of both power and resources in the polity. Through education and action the poor were to achieve personal development as well as policy goals; alienation was to be replaced by participation and achievement, and a permanent reorientation of the political life of Canada was to take place.

Social animation, community development, community action, advocacy planning, and citizen participation—these and other terms which are used to describe what we have called politicization have three characteristics that are especially interesting. First, those engaged in community work of this kind are employed by government or public agencies for the purpose of politicization; that is, governments in Canada employ people to create disorder. Secondly, politicization in this particular form frequently functions as co-optation. The community worker, a potential source of disruption, is co-opted to the established order through financial dependence, a sense of importance, the illusion of power to effect change, and the satisfaction derived from successful adaptation of people to the established order. Where real change is accomplished, it is more appropriate to think in terms of reform or, in some cases, transformation; clearly, co-optation does not take place where politicization has such consequences. The citizen who participates in community action as a result of politicization may develop skills and knowledge that are effective only because they conform to the structural and behavioural norms of the established order; where politicization amounts to nothing more than teaching people how to make the political system work for them, co-optation is virtually certain. It is probable that government sponsors politicization as a comprehensive adaptive strategy, defusing potential sources of disruption through co-optation of community workers and citizen participants.

These two characteristics of politicization through community development—government sponsorship and co-optation—are complemented by a third feature: the theory of community development requires withdrawal of persons engaged in politicization when there is evidence that the group has developed sufficient knowledge and skill to articulate its own interest.[8] This dictum, which follows logically from the self-reliance objective of community development, prevents organization along conventional lines. Thus, the community development movement, insofar as it exists at all, has no permanent locus, no durable identity, and no continuity of personnel. It remains an underground ideology rather than an organizational link among those whose work involves the education of others to political action.

Our taxonomy is useful to summarize these observations about community development as a type of politicization process. Its purpose is the reform of decision systems to include the participation of those affected by policy but unable to influence decisions because they are inarticulate and powerless. The mode varies from confrontation to more conciliatory petitioning or other forms of local action involving the concentration of energy and resources on specific issues defined by the people affected and designed to develop political skill. The objective is almost always municipal or provincial government, although action such as agitation for women's advocates at Manpower centres may indicate that the physical presence of any public agency in a neighbourhood creates a natural target for community action, whatever the actual substance of the policy area. Regarding substance, the sub-culture of poverty determines that social service policies (for example, child care, social assistance and housing) constitute the immediate policy problems upon which politicization is commonly focused. But the goal of self-control, as manifested in participation, is frequently viewed by the agent of politicization as the fundamental substantial element to be transmitted through the education process. Thus the community worker, who is the agent of this type of politicization, may have a different view of the substance, even of the purpose of the process; this accounts for the necessity of withdrawal when the community members are sufficiently skillful that their own primary interest, the policy area itself, begins to take precedence over the goal of developing skill and knowledge. Finally, there is a serious potential for the generation of specific positive support through co-optation and satisfaction with the results of participation, although community development may also result in the generation of serious disorder and ultimate transformation or violence, should large numbers of people be politicized without appropriate response from government.

This perspective on political education, political action and community development may be especially useful to those who hope to describe and assess changes in Canadian public policy and public administration, as well as political culture, over the past ten years. The politics of this decade have been extremely creative, to use Porter's term,[9] and creative politics present a challenge to the political scientist, who must find ways to model and evaluate change as it takes place. Perhaps this taxonomy, modest as it is, will provide an alternative to our concentration on the political party as a primary agent of political articulation, aggregation and education, directing our attention to other forms of political participation and other levels of organization as we seek to expand our understanding of informal political processes.

NOTES

1. The technique used in this paper to specify meaning owes much to Abraham Kaplan, The Conduct of Inquiry (San Francisco: Chandler, 1964), especially pp. 71–78, "Specification of Meaning."

2. David Easton, A Systems Analysis of Political Life (New York: Wiley, 1965), chapters 11, 12, 13.

3. See Walter D. Young, The Anatomy of a Party: The National CCF 1932–61 (Toronto: University of Toronto Press, 1969), Introduction.

4. David Schwartz, Political Alienation and Political Behavior (Chicago: Aldine, 1973). Chapters 1, 3 and 14 discuss SES, alienation and participation in an informative yet critical way.

5. For a detailed description and assessment of these events in the U.S. see John C. Donovan, The Politics

of Poverty (New York: Pegasus, 1973).

6. See James A. Draper, ed., Citizen Participation: Canada, A Book of Readings (Toronto: New Press, 1971).

7. See especially Robert S. Best, "Youth Policy," in G. Bruce Doern and V. Seymour Wilson, eds., Issues in Canadian Public Policy (Toronto: Macmillan, 1974), pp. 137–65; also Draper, Citizen Participation.

8. W. and L. Biddle, The Community Development Process (New York: Holt, Rinehart & Winston, 1965). See also Margaret Mitchell, Organize, Canadian Neighbourhood Services Association, 1975.

9. "Creative politics is politics which has the capacity to change the social structure in the direction of some major social goals or values. By

mobilizing human resources for new purposes, it has the initiative in the struggle against the physical environment and against dysfunctional historical arrangements. Creative politics requires a highly developed political leadership to challenge entrenched power within other institutional orders. It succeeds in getting large segments of the population identified with the goals of the political system and in recruiting their energies and skills to political ends." John Porter, *The Vertical Mosaic* (Toronto: University of Toronto Press, 1965), p. 369.

Adolescent Political Activity

as a Learning Experience:

The Action-Trudeau Campaign of 1968

JON H. PAMMETT

Pierre Elliott Trudeau won the leadership of the Liberal party of Canada on April 6, 1968, after a campaign that left observers convinced he was no ordinary politician. In Parliament only since November of 1965 and a cabinet minister since April of 1967, Mr. Trudeau was a newcomer to electoral politics (and the Liberal party). He was by no means the heir apparent to the prime-ministership when Lester Pearson announced in December 1967 that, having seen the country through its centennial year, he would be stepping down. But by the time of the leadership convention, Trudeau was the clear choice of the party. Shortly after assuming the leadership, Trudeau dissolved Parliament and called a general election for June 25, at which the Liberals won a total of 155 seats. The election campaign, like Mr. Trudeau's campaign for the leadership, was a whirl-wind affair, full of an enthusiasm rare in Canadian electoral history. Per-haps the most distinctive feature, however, of this first general election of Canada's second century was the extent of youth involvement in the campaign.

Thousands of young people flocked to campaign for Mr. Trudeau and the Liberals once the date of the election was announced. For some high school and university students, the timing of the campaign was opportune; they had just finished their school terms. For others, the timing was awk-ward, coming just as examinations necessitated a great deal of time spent on their studies; but they came anyway. This outpouring of youth all but overwhelmed Liberal organizers. In order to marshal this support, and take some of the pressure off local constituency executives, early in May the national office set up an organization named Action-Trudeau.

This paper is in part a study of a large number of young people who were members of Action-Trudeau during the 1968 campaign.* It does not, however, attempt to describe the activities of Action-Trudeau, or to measure the impact of the organization's campaign effort on the election outcome. Rather, I have chosen to study adolescent political participation from the standpoint of the individual motivations for this participation, and of the effects of campaign activity upon the personal development of those engaged in it. Participation in this campaign was, for many young people, a learning experience, both with regard to politics and themselves, and many quite deliberately engaged in it for those reasons. I hope to show in this paper why it was particularly appropriate for adolescents to engage in this activity, and some of the personal effects of these experiences.

ADOLESCENCE

Adolescence, the period of life which extends, in general, from puberty to the early twenties, is an important formative phase of an individual's life. It is at this time that many of the orientations that an individual will use to view the world and its events are formed. It is, above all else, a period of search for the roles to be undertaken and the loyalties to be given in the wider world of adulthood. The adolescent has a heightened self-awareness and self-consciousness. "At adolescence the self is, perhaps for the first time, felt to be tractible";[1] the individual can succeed in changing himself and try wholly different postures of regarding the world and acting in it.

It is often remarked that the adolescent is a "marginal man," no longer suitable for the dependent world of childhood yet not acceptable for the more structured adult society. In making this shift from a known but out-grown position to a more or less unknown, cognitively unstructured one,[2] the adolescent often experiences considerable emotional instability and stress. In his almost poetic style, Erik Erikson pictures the adolescent at this period of uprootedness:

Like a trapeze artist, the young person in the middle of vigorous motion must let go of his safe hold on childhood and reach out for a firm grasp on adult-

---

*A fuller account of this study may be found in Jon H. Pammett, "Personal Identity and Political Activity," unpublished PHD dissertation, University of Michigan, 1971.

hood, depending for a breathless interval on a relatedness between the past and the future, and on the reliability of those he must let go of, and those who will "receive" him. Whatever combination of drives and defenses, of sublimation and capacities has emerged from the young individual's childhood must now make sense in view of his concrete opportunities in work and in love; what the individual has learned to see in himself must now coincide with the expectations and recognitions which others bestow on him; whatever values have become meaningful to him must now match some universal significance.[3]

The adolescent may be seen as qualifying for adulthood.[4] This means that he must acquire some specific degree of competence in performing roles which another person (the adult, already qualified) recognizes as having reached a certain standard. If such a standard is certified, then youth is admitted to adult status and granted the right to assume new and wider privileges and obligations. But youth's claim to such status is always mediated by the adult occupants, who may choose to withhold it for any reason, even a reason (like age) which has little to do with the actual performance of many roles.

Somewhat paradoxically, this seeking to qualify for adult society involves a striving for emancipation from those adults who have been the principal figures in his personal development up to this stage. The parents (as seen by the adolescent, at least) become figures who strive to hold him back, to keep him protected, and in a subordinate position. The adolescent has a basic need for self-assertion, and this drive is a prime motivating force in development. Self-assertion is seen by one author as a generalized power drive, the desire of the adolescent to assert himself over the environment by making it conform with the self-concept he is building.[5] One anchor in youth society for the adolescent to grasp in the course of so much unstable activity is the peer group. Group relations become of major importance in this period. The conformity of youth to the norms of peer groups has often been noted, and not often sympathetically, but the fact is that such groups provide a very important "culture stop" on the passage to adult society. Peer groups provide acceptance, in a complete way, to a culture between that of childhood and that of adulthood.[6]

A major element in adolescent growth is the physical maturity brought on by puberty and the efforts that must be made to cope with sexual development. It seems to the adolescent that everything is happening at once, as Anna Freud points out:

It has struck me always as unfortunate that the period of adolescent upheaval and inner rearrangement of forces coincides with such major demands on the individual as those for academic achievements in school and college, for a choice of career, for increased social and financial responsibility in general. Many failures, often with tragic consequences in these respects, are due not to the individual's incapacity as such but merely to the fact that such demands are made on him at a time of life when all his energies are engaged otherwise, namely, in trying to solve the major problems created for him by normal sexual growth and development.[7]

The degree to which sexual growth will dominate all other phases will obviously vary with the individual (and also with the writer, depending on how closely he sticks to pure Freudian doctrine). Adolescence is also a period of great intellectual expansion and development, which could, at least in some individuals, complement other forms of development. The establishment of a sexual identity is only a part of the general development of identity which we will be speaking of shortly.

Since theorists and observers have seen adolescence as a time of change and growth, many have come to regard it as a period of great stress and turmoil (*Sturm und Drang*). Robert White states that this view only became prevalent when the Industrial Revolution and expanded educational opportunities greatly increased the period of time spent by many between puberty and entrance into adult work and marriage roles.[8] From this grew the custom of treating adolescents as not yet adult, and thus the period became a stressful one. Psychiatrists will often categorically render such a judgment: "Adolescence is a period where defensive mechanisms utilized in earlier stages become inadequate. As previous techniques fail, there is emotional turmoil."[9]

Other psychiatrists claim that the conception of adolescence as a period of turmoil comes from a concentration on disturbed patients. Those who study disturbed adolescents favour the turmoil theory, it is said, because that is all they see. In a long-range study of "normal" adolescents in two American high schools, psychiatrist Daniel Offer writes:

Adolescent turmoil represents a significant disruption in the psychic organization of the adolescent that leads to psychological disequilibrium and tumult, resulting in fluctuant and unpredictable behavior. Given this definition, we have not found turmoil to be prevalent in our normal adolescent population.[10]

Kenneth Keniston, in his study of young radicals, finds that the model of turmoil in adolescence seems to fit them, whereas many of the more "typical" adolescents do not show this degree of stressfulness.[11] It is probable that theorists will become more restrained in their description of the modal characteristics: turmoil seems to be simply too strong a word to describe the normal strivings of adolescents as they proceed toward maturity. Only in severely disturbed cases, one would think, does the stress reach critical levels. Certainly, there are few indications in our questionnaires that the respondents are (or were) in mental turmoil. As Erikson puts it: "Adolescence is not an affliction but a *normative crisis*, i.e., a normal phase of increased conflict characterized by a seeming fluctuation in ego strength, and yet also by a high growth potential."[12]

THE DEVELOPMENT OF EGO IDENTITY

In Freud's personality theories, the ego is represented as a relatively weak guidance system for the strong instinctual drives of the id. The id is really the aggregate of the individual's primitive emotional strivings, and involves a number of "primary processes," the most famous of which is the pleasure principle.[13] The id, having biologically determined instinctual drives which surge toward release, has a great deal of energy of its own. It requires a guiding and directing mechanism which will satisfy it yet keep it within some bounds.

This guiding mechanism is the ego, which in Freudian theory is distinctly subordinate to the id, often presented imaginatively as the rider on an unruly horse. It is in fact a part of the id, derives its energies from the id, and employs certain *learned* "secondary processes" to do its job. It basically tries to bring about the reduction of tension, tolerating it until some object on which to release it can be found. Conflicts arise over what instinctual needs to satisfy, and the ego, as the "executive of the personality," must seek to resolve them.[14]

Freud was less certain about the workings of the ego than he was about the id. Evaluators of Freud's work have found that the conception of the ego changed over the course of his life in a number of ways.[15] Yankelovich and Barrett see in Freud's arguments about the ego an attempt to define it in reaction to the id, as everything the id is not.

[Freud's theories of the ego] have an almost deductive flavor—as if the reasoning were, "Well, if the id behaves one way, then logically the ego must behave the opposite way." Thus, if the primary processes describe how id energies press toward discharge, then the secondary processes (associated with the ego) describe how they are channeled and controlled.[16]

Psychoanalysis has been concerned to a large extent since Freud's death with theories of the ego. The conception of the ego as a weak entity spending its derived energies almost solely on placating the demands of the id was unacceptable to many theorists. They saw the ego as a more important factor in personality development, doing more than simply maintaining defences. Increasingly, it has been seen as having many adaptive functions for the individual, allowing him to master his environment and adapt to reality. Many of the "ego-psychologists" have consequently revised the Freudian theory by proposing the concept of a more autonomous ego, not dependent to nearly so great an extent on the instinctual drives of the id. One of the most influential of these theorists, Heinz Hartmann, has said that the ego itself has certain inborn processes of development, follows its own timetable, and thus did not grow out of the id. It grows partly in its own predestined sequence (developing ego-functions like perception, memory and motor-skills) and partly from experience and learning.[17]

Robert W. White has also been influential in developing a revised psychology of the ego. In a highly regarded monograph, he produced a conception of "independent ego energies" which do not need to rely on the basic instinctual drives of the id for their existence.[18] White proposes to refer to the energy behind ego behaviour as "effectance," and the affect that attends it as a "feeling of efficacy."

Effectance thus refers to the active tendency to put forth effort to influence the environment, while feeling of efficacy refers to the satisfaction that comes with producing effects.[19]

The purpose of effectance in exploring the environment, according to White, is to develop competence, or more formally a "sense of interpersonal competence" in dealing with the persons and events found in the external world. The ego thus performs the function of reality-testing, for each person must construct his own world of "reality." This process is most intense over the formative years of childhood and adolescence, but does not end there, continuing at a slower pace for much of the individual's life.

What exactly is the ego seeking to do in this process of seeking competence and testing reality? For the most persuasive answer to this question (an answer favoured by White also) we must turn to the concept of ego identity, formulated by Erik Erikson, a man who has been called the most influential theorist of psychoanalysis since Freud.

Although the concept of ego identity is widely used inside and outside of psychoanalysis, Erikson offers no simple definition of its exact meaning. This, it seems, has been deliberate, and it is part of the fascination of Erikson's writing that he often seems to be experimenting with the concept even as he is writing about it.

So far I have tried out the term identity almost deliberately—I like to think—in many different connotations. At one time it seemed to refer to a conscious sense of individual uniqueness, at another to an unconscious striving for a continuity of experience, and at a third, as a solidarity with a group's ideals. In some respects the term appeared to be colloquial and naïve, a mere manner of speaking, while in others it was related to existing concepts in psychoanalysis and sociology.[20]

In another place, Erikson is quoted by his biographer, Robert Coles, as complaining that the term has received such wide usage by so many people in so many ways that it seems useless to attempt now to pin it down.[21]

It really is untrue, however, to say that Erikson has not made explicit attempts to explain the term. The most commonly used short definition is the following, taken from the influential monograph, *Identity and the Life Cycle*:

The sense of ego identity, then, is the accrued confidence that one's ability to maintain inner sameness and continuity (one's ego in the psychological sense) is matched by the sameness and continuity of one's meaning for others.[22]

The ego, the instrument for reality-testing and guidance of one's relations with the environment, develops a particular definition of itself, a sense of "the style of one's individuality"[23] and a realization that this style is the same one that others recognize one for.

Ego identity is partially conscious and largely unconscious. It is a psychological process reflecting social processes; but with sociological means it can be seen as a social process reflecting psychological processes; it meets its crisis in adolescence, but has grown throughout childhood and continues to re-emerge in the crises of later years. The overall meaning of it, then, is the creation of a sense of sameness, a unity of personality now felt by the individual and recognized by others as having consistency in time—of being, as it were, an irreversible historical fact.[24]

Erikson sees the development of ego identity as one step, but the crucial step, in an individual's total lifelong ego growth. It is the fifth step in the famous "eight ages of man," introduced in Erikson's first book.[25] Erikson posits a dichotomy of ego qualities at each definable psychosexual stage in an individual's life, from the earliest oral sensory, muscular and locomotor genital stages of childhood, through latency and adolescence to young adulthood, adulthood and maturity.[26] These ego qualities corresponding to the eight stages first mentioned, are basic trust *vs.* mistrust, autonomy *vs.* shame and doubt, initiative *vs.* guilt, industry *vs.* inferiority, identity *vs.* role confusion, intimacy *vs.* isolation, generativity *vs.* stagnation and ego integrity *vs.* despair. By placing a "vs." between the dichotomous qualities at each stage, Erikson means that the individual must develop more of the first quality than the second in order to maintain the growth of a healthy personality, but he does not mean that the second, or negative, quality is not instilled in the individual to some extent. We develop some of each quality at each stage; for "normal" growth the positive quality must prevail.[27]

The adolescent stage of development involves the ego qualities of identity *vs.* role confusion. Extreme role confusion would be the failure of the person to be able to define his individuality. He may be confused about many roles, though Erikson finds most role confusion in the area of occupation.[28] It is interesting to see the introduction of the sociological concept of role into psychoanalytic theory at this point. It emphasizes the way the individual is engaging in the testing of possible places he might occupy in society in various relationships with others. In late adolescence the young person, if ego identity and not role confusion is to predominate, undergoes an identity crisis, defined by Erikson as "a necessary turning point, a crucial moment, when development must move one way or another, marshalling resources of growth, recovery and further differentiation."[29] The resolution of this identity crisis marks the end of adolescence and the passage of the individual into the stages of adulthood.

The concept of the identity crisis was developed by Erikson in the course of his clinical work and its main value has been in this setting, although it has been used in a great many ways.[30] The concept has been used in the political sphere by Kenneth Keniston in his study of young radicals. Keniston finds that his subjects, whom he interacted with personally for an entire summer, had gone through *two* of these adolescent crises, the first in early adolescence leading to a pattern of success-striving, and the second, which is more like the Eriksonian identity crisis, in late adolescence involving the rejection of "conventional" activity and the adoption of a commitment to changing society via the Peace Movement.

Adolescence, according to Erikson's theory, is a stage of life when searching behaviour is culturally sanctioned. The ego development process is given a moratorium in which to try different roles and establish its identity. The moratorium is a culturally sanctioned period of delay, in which the adolescent is given the time to search for the roles that will be proper for him, to test the truth, in a way, and to do so without an undue number of pressures being put upon him to make quick decisions. Very often he must test the extremes of a certain type of behaviour before settling on a considered course, and consequently, his actions while in the moratorium are easily misunderstood as being ill-considered, meaningless and rebellious. This moratorium, which coincides with a young person's high school years and often extends into college years as well, provides a legitimate way for him to engage in the testing process.[31]

It was mentioned previously that Erikson considers the process of identity formation to be partially a conscious process on the part of the individual and largely an unconscious one. We are most aware of our identity, he says, when we are about to gain it and are "somewhat surprised to make its acquaintance."[32] What an adolescent may well be conscious of, however, is the restlessness and the searching behaviour in which he is engaging.

During the adolescent years, the search for identity becomes predominant in his strivings. Restlessly and self-consciously, he tries on mask after mask in an attempt to discover just who he shall be. His problem is to hit upon a unique set of social roles with which he can live comfortably for the rest of his life. He tries them on for size, imagining himself in these various social roles and positions, constructing role-identities that are now more, now less important in his thinking about himself. Because he is not yet a fully autonomous and equal citizen, the issue is not so much who he actually *is* but whom he shall *become*.[33]

An important process by which one's ego identity is established is that of identification. There has been a great deal of dispute in the literature about the proper meaning of this term. Indeed, Nevitt Sanford seriously proposes dropping the term altogether. Sanford says identification has been used to refer to the copying of another individual, adherence of an individual to any group of which he feels himself a part, the acceptance by any individual of a cause, empathy and vicarious living, closeness or conformity.[34] He proposes to reserve the term only for attempts to imitate exactly the behaviour of another as a defence mechanism employed to cope with serious threats to self-esteem.

Robert W. White sees value in a wider use of the term. Identification is not just imitative behaviour, and can be distinguished from it as the two phrases "wanting to do something that someone else has done" and "wanting to be like someone else" are different.

Wanting to be like another person implies something more. We speak of identification when the model *does* have personal importance, when we want to be like someone in a way that transcends any single act. . . . Identification is a particular form of imitation in which copying a model is generalized beyond specific acts and has the character of wanting to be and trying to be, competent like the model.[35]

Identification goes on throughout adolescence as the young person is engaging in the process of ego identity formation. For Erikson, identity is more than the sum of these identifications, however; it transcends them. Identity formation, he says, begins where the usefulness of identification ends. The individual selects from among his past identifications those things he wishes to maintain and assimilate into his identity, and those he wishes to repudiate. Out of this assimilation process, old identifications become part of the new configuration which is to be the person's identity. Thus, identification is a useful mechanism only up to a certain point and identity is conceived as a *Gestalt* which is more than the sum of its component parts.

If we regard identification, as White does, as a desire to be competent like a model, it becomes a term we can apply to the feeling of many young people for Pierre Trudeau during the 1968 campaign. They did not so much want to copy his actual behaviour as they were captured by his style, his competence and his sureness. In this sense we may speak of him as a model for the generalized copying that White proposes. The feelings that we will see expressed for Trudeau in the data can reasonably be termed identification and it may be hypothesized that they served for many adolescents as building-blocks in their development of ego identity.

The theoretical development given here suggests that we should find several co-ordinated motives among adolescents for engaging in the Action-Trudeau campaign, and several reported effects of such activity. The desire for role experimentation and learning should be present, and we should see many indications of the "search behaviour" so important to adolescence. Assertions of independence from parental authority, and the consequent influence of the peer group should be apparent. Identification with Trudeau, as defined above, will be an important motivating factor. Similarly, reported effects of the campaign should emphasize evaluation of the possible roles that were tested in the experience as well as the personal development to which the experience contributed. Observation of responses which suggest that these processes may have been at work will allow us to reason that campaign activity by adolescents may well have contributed to the formation of their ego identity.

ACTION-TRUDEAU

By mid-May of 1968, a little more than a month before the election, four national co-ordinators of Action-Trudeau had been appointed: Fred MacDonald, Raymond Décarie, Michael Ignatieff and Ruth Gilis. They in turn created the "Action-Trudeau Program," a program having no policy or issue basis whatsoever, but a good many methods of organization. It was a way, as one of the organizers put it, "to get twenty thousand kids organized in a hurry."[36]

The organizational structure of Action-Trudeau was basically a simple one. There was to be an Action-Trudeau group in each constituency, with a leader appointed by the riding campaign chairman. The local Action-Trudeau leader was to have three basic functions: he was to recruit, train and lead young workers in canvassing, phone and car-pool work, as directed by the riding campaign manager; he was to serve on riding campaign committees to co-ordinate the Action-Trudeau program with the local campaign; and he was to organize demonstrations and local entertainment. In addition to the local leaders, there were to be ten provincial Action-Trudeau co-ordinators, chosen by the provincial campaign chairmen. Their functions were: to serve on the provincial campaign committee to co-ordinate supply of Action-Trudeau promotion, kits and ideas to the ridings; and to co-ordinate the selection of the riding Action-Trudeau leaders with the riding campaign chairman.

The national co-ordinators were in charge of designing and supplying much of the Action-Trudeau promotion material, which consisted of buttons, folders, posters and dress-patterns. They shipped this material out by air freight to all the ridings where viable Action-Trudeau organizations had been set up. They also produced a series of memoranda giving instructions to canvassers working for the first time and suggestions on how best to use the Action-Trudeau team in concert with the rest of the constituency campaign effort. Not counting the shipments of buttons, pamphlets and posters, the organizers estimate they sent out at least eight mailings of instructions, "Instructions about how to canvass, how to get into apartment buildings, how to organize meetings, how to make Action-Trudeau dresses, how to run crowd control, how to run the P.M.'s visit, how to set up coffee houses, how to get out the youth vote. We just shovelled this stuff out by the ton."

The basic unit of the movement was the constituency Action-Trudeau group, separate from the regular constituency campaign organization, led by young people themselves (though many of the leaders had prior campaigning experience). The distinction of Action-Trudeau from the regular constituency organization and the fact that its leaders were also young had the effect of creating what one national co-ordinator terms "massive party hostility" towards Action-Trudeau. During the entire campaign, he recalls, one of the biggest selling jobs that had to be done was to convince regular constituency organizations of the necessity of a youth-led youth campaign. In some cases this convincing only took place with the realization on the part of the regular constituency organizations that they were incapable of dealing with the extraordinarily large number of young people who came to the party headquarters and wanted to join the campaign. It is difficult to gauge the exact scope of the movement. Although all but about twenty constituencies officially chose Action-Trudeau leaders, the movement was most prominent in the cities and in the provinces of British Columbia, Ontario and Quebec, where, in recent times at least, the Liberals have had their greatest electoral success. In New Brunswick and Newfoundland the provincial party heads refused to have anything whatever to do with the national Action-Trudeau group, and the promotional material was simply sent to the provincial party offices for them to use as they wished.

THE STUDY

The most basic problem in mounting a study of Action-Trudeau was the securing of lists of names of the actual campaigners. Although the national staff of the organization had asked for lists of those who participated from each constituency, only about seven hundred names existed in the organization's files in 1970, when this study was mounted. Two hundred of these names were of Action-Trudeau leaders in the constituencies, whose only addresses were committee rooms long defunct. Another 150 persons proved to be untraceable. In order to obtain more respondents, letters were written to scores of former Action-Trudeau leaders across the country, and copies of their membership lists obtained. In the end, 1,055 usable names with what were thought to be current addresses were forthcoming. To each of these persons was sent an introductory letter; a packet containing another letter, a questionnaire, and a stamped return envelope; and two follow-up letters urging return of the questionnaire. Of this total of 1,055, a group of 91 sets of materials was returned, marked "address unknown," and 17 people wrote asserting that they had never had anything to do with Action-Trudeau. Of the reduced total of 947 possible respondents, 509 (53.7 per cent) returned completed questionnaires.

The questionnaires utilized in the study were eleven pages in length, and contained 76 questions, of which 33 were open-ended. The respondents came from all provinces of Canada except three Atlantic provinces, New Brunswick, Newfoundland and Prince Edward Island, where Action-Trudeau was virtually nonexistent. The three provinces where Action-Trudeau was most active, Quebec, Ontario and British Columbia, comprise 75 per cent of the group to be studied here, although 52 separate constituencies are in some way represented. There is no way of knowing if those who did not return the questionnaire differed significantly in opinions or other characteristics from those who did. There was, however, no difference between the sexes on response rate, and no evidence that there was any urban-rural difference. It is also impossible to say whether young workers whose names were unobtainable were any different from those who formed this study. These points should not affect the significance of the results, however, since the object is not to draw a picture of the operation of the Action-Trudeau campaign from coast to coast but rather to see if certain processes of personal development seem to have been at work in a large number of the people studied. Even if it were true (and there is no evidence one way or the other) that the group of respondents studied here contains a disproportionately high number of people who found the campaign valuable in this connection, my conclusions would not be significantly altered, since a large number of participants would still have been affected.

REASONS FOR JOINING THE CAMPAIGN

According to Erik Erikson, identity-formation is a partly conscious but largely unconscious process. Its conscious element consists of a realization on the part of the individual that he wants to explore a good many of the different roles society offers. By asking our respondents simple and direct open-ended questions, and classifying the responses, it will be possible to detect many of the manifestations of the identity-building process. We will not, of course, be able to observe the formative process in each individual, but only certain patterns of thinking which accompany it.

Placed at the beginning of the questionnaire was the open-ended question, "Why did you join the Action-Trudeau campaign?" Table 1 is a summary of the percentages of people giving each of the major types of response. These general classifications are then broken down into sub-categories and further discussed in the remainder of this section.

Table 1   Reasons For Joining Campaign

I Direct Influence (family; friends; teacher)	22.4% *
II Trudeau (what he stood for; the Trudeau appeal)	38.7
III Personal Development (learning about politics; desires for involvement; interest in politics)	38.7
IV Party Orientation (prior participation; support of party, policy or local candidate)	28.6
V Other (for fun; other; no answer)	12.3

*Some persons gave two responses. The percentages in this table represent persons who gave a response in each category, and have been corrected to remove the effect of both responses being in the same category.

I *Direct Influence*

A. Family	5.9%
B. Friends	14.9
C. Teacher or School	3.6
	22.4*

Examples of Responses

A. (Family)
  – I come from a political family.
  – Mother was a Trudeau worker. I got in too.
  – My sister had already started working in the campaign and after hearing about it from her, I was interested.
  – Because my parents were Liberal.

B. (Friends)
  – I joined mainly because a group of friends did.
  – Because a friend of mine was working for it and asked if I would help.
  – Peer group pressure. At that time I had a desire to identify with

*The total percentage has been corrected to remove the effect of the few people who gave two responses in this category of direct influence.

young political-intellectual interests.
- I had friends who were members and they told me about the movement.

C. (Teacher or School)
- A teacher recommended it at school.
- A teacher almost forced it upon my class—the only choice we had was which party to work for.
- I joined because my teacher explained what fun it would be and how it would keep us busy on weekends.

In looking at the direct influence of others on the respondents' participation, friends played an important role. It is, of course, natural that a mass movement of this sort would attract people in groups and that the personal influence of friends would be important in getting young people, in particular the shyer ones, into the organization. It is also true that the influence of peer groups in adolescence is particularly strong. Adolescents are breaking away from their parents and asserting independence. Family influence is reported by only 6 per cent of the sample, and of this total some is influence by brothers and sisters who were also taking part in Action-Trudeau. The interesting thing about the influence of family and friends reported here, it seems to me, is not that the influence of friends so far outstrips that of family, but that it is itself so low. Allowing for some non-reporting of such influence because of the open-ended nature of the question, only a small minority report that their friends influenced them to participate. When specifically asked about friends' influence elsewhere in the questionnaire, many more people report it. The fact that it did not spring spontaneously to mind, however, indicates that for many respondents other things are more associated with their participation.

II *Trudeau*

D. What Trudeau stood for	7.2%
E. The Trudeau appeal (personal)	34.7
	38.7*

Examples of Responses

D. (What Trudeau stood for)
- I believed in what Trudeau stood for, a change.

*Total corrected for people giving both responses.

- I joined A-T because I believed Trudeau felt he could bring about a just society.
- To elect Trudeau, as I believed and still believe that he is the man to save Canada from the problems of language and foreign domination.
- Il me semblait de Trudeau seul possédait les qualités nécessaires afin d'amener nos deux grandes races ensemble, et c'est ce problème que je considerais majeur.
- I did so in order to get a good leader who would do things for all Canadians fairly.
- C'est dans le but très précis de donner au Canada un gouvernement majoritaire et seul Trudeau pouvait accomplir cette tâche.

E. (The Trudeau appeal)
- Mr. Trudeau was the most capable man to present himself in politics during my era (born 1946).
- I believed in Trudeau.
- Parce que pour la première fois un politicien offrait un aspect de jeunesse et de nouveauté.
- I watched Trudeau's election to party leader on T.V.—I became so enthusiastic that I went out and joined the Liberal Party.
- I felt Trudeau would be a good and honorable P.M. for Canada.
- Solely to get Trudeau elected.
- I found Trudeau very appealing and felt it was time for Canada to have such a P.M.—I felt he could put Canada in the limelight.
- It was one way of supporting Trudeau.

The two aspects of the Trudeau appeal embodied in the categories above were quite prevalent in the campaign, with the sheer personal appeal of the man predominating. The Trudeau appeal ran all the way from some of the giddier manifestations of "Trudeaumania" to the soberest evaluations of him as being the most capable man for the job. He was important to fewer because of what he stood for, change and reform, or the possibility of forging a national unity.

During the 1968 campaign, Trudeau was the dominant figure. He received publicity of tremendous magnitude, a barrage of coverage that was probably unprecedented in Canadian electoral history. He was a very appealing figure to youth, with his candid and honest manner, his startlingly fast rise to prominence, his reformist views and his modern modes of dress. He was an attractive model for the mechanism of identification. Young people wanted to be like Trudeau, not in the sense of imitation but in the sense of competence. Trudeau was "cool," he was witty, he understated his debating points, and he bypassed "hot" issues with the rhetoric of commitment. The young campaigners were linked with him, probably through the mechanism of identification, and he was an important reason in their deciding to join the campaign.

Yet fewer than half of the respondents spontaneously picked Trudeau as a reason for their participation. To anyone who followed the campaign and its publicity (which revolved around Trudeau) this surely is an extraordinary finding! As we shall shortly see, Trudeau seems to have been no more important than the desire to participate itself. It may be argued that Trudeau was more influential than he appears here, and this is probably true. No one who took part in the campaign was unaffected by Trudeau. But in the motivations for getting involved in the campaign, other factors assume at least equal importance, factors which are related to the process of personal growth in as direct a way as is the process of identification with a popular figure.

III *Personal Development*

F. Learn about politics, elections	14.9%
G. General desires for involvement	16.5
H. Interested in politics	8.0
I. Thought might be interested in politics	3.0
	38.7*

Examples of Responses

F. (Learn about politics, elections)
   – To learn how elections worked.
   – To learn more about politics.
   – I wanted to find out more about our government and see how interested I was in politics.
   – I thought if I went it would help me understand politics a little bit.
   – Pour voir comment s'organisait la propagande politique d'un parti.
   – Pour premier but c'était pour moi une chance de connaître la politique d'un parti un peu plus approfondi.
   – Curiosity.

G. (General desires for involvement)
   – I wanted to participate in some way.
   – Primarily to aid in some way.

*Total corrected for people giving two responses in this category.

    – I wanted to become involved in Canada and its government in my own small way.
    – I thought the experience would be worthwhile.
    – I wanted to do something for Canada.
    – I wanted an experience.
    – They say we are too young to vote and I wanted to do what I could.
    – Première occasion donnée aux jeunes de participer à une campagne électorale.

H. (Interested in politics)
    – I joined the campaign because I am interested in politics.
    – At that time I had just become really interested in politics and I wanted to find out all about it.
    – I joined mainly because I had a deep interest in politics.

I. (Thought might be interested in politics)
    – I thought it might be interesting as I had never done anything of the sort before.
    – I thought I would be interested in politics.

The four categories described above give substantial indications that motivations consistent with identity-seeking and identity-building were present in the group of young campaigners we are studying. It was proposed earlier that the searching out and trying on of different roles was an integral part of the process. We can see in the substantial numbers of young people who give responses involving learning of what politics, elections and campaigns are all about evidences of such a search. We can see in the desires to become involved, to participate in a movement and to support a good cause, a testing of the self and the person's desires to be committed. It is only by becoming involved in such a movement that one knows whether or not such participatory action is going to be a part of oneself for the future, a role one has tested and now knows about.

It is interesting indeed that responses indicating a desire for personal development are just as frequently cited as those involving Mr. Trudeau as reasons for becoming involved in the Action-Trudeau campaign. Of course, these two types of response are quite consistent with one another (and, because two responses were allowed to the question, some were given by the same people). According to our theoretical position, peer group activity, identification with an ideal model and role-searching behaviour are all to be expected if the adolescent is really using this political campaign experience as part of his crystallization of ego identity.

Nevertheless, I find it impressive that so many of the respondents saw clearly that they were not simply following a leader or their friends, but were seeking to learn about and involve themselves with new roles and situations in the world around them.

IV *Party Orientation*

J.	Prior participation	3.8%
K.	Support Liberal party	15.5
L.	Support a policy	5.0
M.	Support local candidate	7.8
		28.6*

Examples of Responses

J. (Prior participation)
- I worked for the Liberal candidate in the 1967 provincial election.
- Had assisted in previous Liberal campaigns and enjoyed it.
- I participate in every campaign.

K. (Support Liberal party)
- To support the party.
- I was interested in the Liberal party.
- I joined because there is little or no opposition to the Conservatives in this area (Nova Scotia).
- I always felt I was a Liberal.
- I was a member of the Young Liberals.
- I wished to do something to help the political party that I wished to be in office.
- Was a committed Liberal.

L. (Support a policy)
- I am a believer in the Liberal party policy.
- After examining all party policies I found that my own ideas and ideals were closest to the Liberal party.
- Je voulais politiser les jeunes en faveur du fédéralisme.

M. (Support local candidate)
- We had a candidate in our constituency that I thought would work for our area.
- Parce que le candidat local de mon comté était le père d'un de mes meilleurs amis.
- To help our local candidate.
- I knew the local candidate in our riding and supported him before I began.

*Total corrected for people giving two responses in this category.

The responses in this group are of a different order than those we have been discussing so far. They are what we might call the more "conventional" determinants of political campaign activity, and had the 1968 campaign been a more normal one there is no doubt that these reasons for participating would have been more important, if only because a lot of the young people with the other reasons described so far would not have been present. A few of the respondents cited their past participation as a reason for their 1968 activity; the 3.8 per cent who did so, however, do not approach the number who actually had prior campaign experience. Another question in the survey tells us that 22 per cent had participated before. It seems that many respondents who participated before were in Action-Trudeau for reasons other than habit. It is useful to think of the people giving responses in this classification as party regulars, people who would have been there even if the party had been running another campaign with Lester Pearson at its head. These people were oriented to the party itself, its policies, and the local candidate. This picture, however, would probably not be entirely accurate. In the first place, our sample is only of Action-Trudeau, the youth part of the total campaign organization in the constituencies; so, few of our respondents are long-time party regulars. Secondly, policy, local candidate, and party were important to some of the first-time campaigners as well.

---

v *Other*

N. Fun	8.6%
O. Other	1.6
P. No Answer	2.4
	12.3*

*Total corrected for people giving two responses in this category.

The social aspect of the campaign was much emphasized in the publicity which surrounded it at the time; young people were represented by some as being out for kicks, novelty and fun. The data in this study show that the social or fun aspect of the campaign was not a primary motivating factor. This is not to say that the experience was not a pleasurable one for most of the participants or that a lot of social activities did not occur—it was and they did. However, for most of the respondents the good times and social activities were by-products of the main campaign activities and not their main goal. Indeed, at another point in the questionnaire, the fun aspect of the campaign was rated last as a motive for joining it. The classification above shows that a few people gave responses which could not be classified into any of the categories, and also that a very few people declined to answer the question at all.

EFFECTS OF THE CAMPAIGN

The effects of the campaign experience of 1968 on the young people involved in it ranged from the negligible to the profound. Most felt, however, that the experience had been of benefit to them. Of the many types of evidence on this point produced by the questionnaire, only the most direct will be reported here. Placed as the final item in the survey, an open-ended question asked, "What were the main effects the experience of the campaign had on you?" Up to three responses per person were coded to this question, though by no means everyone gave that many answers. The answers are grouped into five classifications for presentation in Table 2, and the remainder of this section provides an elaboration of these results.

Table 2   Effects of the Campaign Experience*

I Identity-building effects	58.7%
II Specifically political effects	17.5
III Disillusionment	13.9
IV Other effects	22.8
V No effects	12.6

*Figures in the table are percentages of the total sample who gave a response in that classification. They have been corrected to remove the effect of those persons who gave two or three responses in the same classification.

I *Identity-Building Effects*

A. Enhanced political interest for future	19.6%
B. Learning about politics, campaigning	22.7
C. More aware of politics	8.9
D. Satisfaction in being involved	11.9
E. Personal development	15.3
	58.7*

*The component percentages indicate the percentage of the total sample giving each response. The total has been corrected to remove the effect of persons giving more than one response in classification I.

Examples of Responses

A. (Enhanced political interest for future)
   - The main effect of the campaign on me was that I became more interested in politics, and my interest has kept up.
   - It started me into the world of politics in which now I am very deeply involved.
   - It heightened my interest not only in that election but in politics in general. Even today I pay great attention to the political scene, not just in Canada but all over the world.
   - Stimulated further interest in politics. I took a political science course at university.
   - I now want to work in every election I can!

B. (Learning about politics, campaigning)
   - I learned to appreciate the complexities of politics and campaigning.
   - The campaign showed me a wealth of political scheming that I would have missed out on.
   - I managed to reach my goal of learning to a fair extent.
   - The election made me realize how someone can be swept to victory on merit of an image and made me feel that we were finally putting some life into Canadian politics and politicians.
   - Became more aware of the "inside workings" of a political campaign.
   - I learned a lot about politics.
   - It was a unique, educational, interesting activity with a sense of purpose.
   - Une connaissance plus approfondie du travail que demande une election.

C. (More aware of politics)
   - Made me more aware of politics.
   - Je suis maintenant plus réaliste en face de la politique et surtout des politiciens. Ils m'apparaissent maintenant comme des hommes ordinaires et loins de l'infaillibilité.
   - It opened up my political sensitivity and my awareness has been building on it.

D. (Satisfaction in being involved)
   - I felt I had worked for something I believed in.
   - It gave me a chance to be involved with people striving toward the same goal—a Liberal victory.
   - The inner satisfaction of a job well done.
   - La satisfaction de l'esprit d'avoir bien fait le bien.
   - It made me feel useful.
   - I began to perceive the complexity of the vast political structure of the country and to feel as if I had contributed a minute but nevertheless important part of myself to make it work.

- I had the satisfaction of helping to elect a man to Parliament when I couldn't vote.
- I felt involved in something. It was a good experience.

E. (Personal development)
- Made me less self-conscious and able to speak up a little more.
- It was a new and fascinating month. I learned more of people and politics and it was an opportunity to learn more of myself. It is now a pleasant memory and another experience to draw upon.
- The campaign taught me to fight for what I believe.
- Made me much more aware of others, confident working in groups and able to meet and talk with strangers.
- Got to know a lot more about human nature and how to accept disappointment after working hard to do something.
- I have more patience (listening to the same speech ten times a day).
- I gained confidence because Mr. ――― had confidence in all his campaigners.
- Plus de maturité.
- Generally has given direction to my life, since now I want to be a political reporter.
- The election was my first contact with the world outside my own small world. Broadened my outlook on life. I'll never forget it.

Responses in classification I are not the only ones that can be cited as evidence that the campaign experience was useful for the process of identity-building, but they are alike in that they all directly refer to benefit gained, and they are all positive in nature. Responses which are negative in nature have been separated for convenience, and form classification III. Similarly, responses which are specifically political in nature will be presented in classification II. Especially when comparison is made with the number of people giving other types of responses (such as those in categories IV and V), it is clear that most of the reported effects of the Action-Trudeau campaign are consistent with the theory that the experience was a step for many in the formation of ego identity. Let us take categories A to E in turn.

From the profusion of positive effects of the campaign which abound in this first classification of responses, we know that most of the young campaigners felt the experience to be a pleasurable one. Many of them knew little or nothing about politics before they came in contact with Action-Trudeau, and found that the experience attracted them very much to politics. We can see in category A an indication of a substantial awakening of interest in politics, a desire to remain closer to the world of politics than in the past and a desire to take part in future political campaigns. For some, the interest that was pricked at the time has now worn off to some extent. Many feel they would have different reasons for joining a future campaign. But a heightened interest in things political which has remained with them has definitely been a prime effect of campaign experiences for the participants.

Going hand-in-hand with enhanced interest for the future is the second effect listed in this first classification. Many, as we saw earlier, joined the campaign for investigative reasons, and learning about various aspects of politics and campaigning was definitely an important result of the activity. The learning took different forms; some people refer to the "political machine and the way it operates," while others took a more gentle view of campaigning and still others found the dynamics of the appeal of a leader or a candidate to the public a fascinating study. The fact that learning, as well as enhanced interest for the future, should be an important effect of the campaign tells us that a testing of the various roles in political life has taken place, and this role-testing is a process central to the formation of ego identity. Young people were finding out what politics was like and many of them liked what they found.

Category c, labelled "more aware of politics," is really differentiated from the first two categories only because it includes those people who specified heightened awareness as a result of their campaign activity.[37] People in this category, by using the word "aware," signified that politics had not been a subject of much concern for them in the period prior to the campaign. This campaign brought political activity into focus for them. Also, many in this category mentioned that their campaign experience made politics more realistic for them, implying that they had held a rather fanciful impression of what went on in politics prior to this time. Category c can be considered, along with A and B, as an indication that the person has "tried out" political roles for himself.

When we come to those in Category D who expressed satisfaction in being involved, we are dealing in many cases with statements of personal feelings about the activity. This comes across much more strongly in the next category, called "personal development," but is important here as well. There were satisfactions for many in just being involved, in feeling they had done a good job, in being able to contribute part of themselves to a collective endeavour with a definable goal, and of having their contribution valued by others. As we have theorized, adolescence is a period in which the young person is striving to establish independence and looking for places to be able to place his trust on his own terms and by his own decision. He wants the responsibility of being able to decide what things to work for and has much energy to contribute. Once this decision is made, he will perform gladly under orders and do the most unimportant work and still be able to feel he is contributing because he has made the decision to commit himself.

Finally, answers have been reserved for category E which give direct indications that the young person has undergone some personal development as a direct result of his campaign activity. For all those who specifically recognized this, of course, there are many more who experienced these benefits and do not directly say so; many of the other categories of responses show the benefits. Answers here speak of the growth of patience, self-confidence, maturity, respect for others and further personal characteristics. Some people were so strongly affected as to change prospective career goals and university majors to those having a political aspect. A surprising number (surprising because realism dictates that only a few will actually have these opportunities) stated a desire to run for political office themselves at a future date.

II *Specifically political effects*

F.	More interested in Liberal party	2.1%
G.	More concerned with issues	3.9
H.	Other political effects	10.7
I.	Lost faith in Liberal party	1.6
		17.5*

F. (More interested in Liberal party)
  – I became interested in working for the Liberals.
  – Became a Liberal.

G. (More concerned with issues)
  – More concerned with issues facing Canadians.
  – I began to see that Canada is what we make it and I wanted to be involved in making it. I became aware of the various political

*Total corrected to remove the effect of people who gave more than one response in this classification.

ideologies, their purposes and aims.

- Began to see politics more in terms of party policies and the issues between parties, rather than just a popularity contest between the leaders.

H. (Other political effects)
- That one has to study politics to know the background. Political groups should hold meetings to teach interested individuals.
- It showed me how important it is to have a good leader in our government.
- It taught me that young people, if they are cohesive, can have a great effect on the political system.
- How important it is for everyone to take part in our civic duties. How lucky we are to live in a country where everyone has a free vote and that you should never waste it.
- What people can accomplish if they work together.
- Fighting for demands is often the real answer to success in politics.
- The effect image-promotion has on the vote-getting abilities of a political party.

I. (Lost faith in Liberal party)
- The main effect was that I will never believe in the Liberal party.

These comments were differentiated from the previous classification because they were specifically political in nature. There are grounds for believing that these responses were somewhat more likely to have been given by the older respondents and those who had campaigned before. However, they can be interpreted, in some cases at any rate, as responses consistent with the identity-building theory. That is, for some young people their contacts with the political world enabled them to establish certain political principles within themselves—take up certain party affiliations or perhaps change them. More common were the reports in category H, of assorted "other political effects." It is difficult to put a more specific label on this category because it involved a great variety of answers. Some answers took the form of a statement of the importance of participation in order to achieve political goals, while others saw the importance of having good leaders or candidates.

Whatever their form, the campaign effects in classification II were more explicitly "political" than an awakening or strengthening of "interest in politics." They showed the respondent was thinking less in terms of his personal development than we noted before. However, we must not overlook the political connotations of many of the responses in classification I, showing as they do "learning about politics," "enhanced political interest for the future" and more "awareness of politics." In the case of these earlier categories, the remarks were placed explicitly in the context of personal learning about political things or of the development of interest or awareness. The remarks in category H, or indeed in all of classification II, are not the only ones dealing with the context of political roles and principles—just those dealing more with the political world than the personal.

III *Disillusionment*

J. The ignorance of the voters	1.9%
K. Disgust for politics	10.3
L. Tried it, and found not interested	2.7
	13.9*

J. (The ignorance of the voters)
  – Became aware of the vast amount of political ignorance.
  – I couldn't believe how narrow-minded the people here are.

K. (Disgust for politics)
  – A continuing feeling of the phoniness of the average politician.
  – Made me rather cynical about party politics.
  – Que trop de facteurs sont concentrés sur la discretion et les caprices de trop peu de chefs politiques qui en abusent trop souvent.
  – La méfiance et le dégoût.
  – Soon all the commercialism turned me off.
  – Realized finally the futility of that kind of politics.
  – I am disappointed in people and politics. The group never stayed together and as a result I feel we were used and then dropped. The older Liberals were delighted with us for showing an interest but as soon as the election was over, they disappeared.

L. (Tried it, and found not interested)
  – Actually I realized that politics is a game only experienced people can play. It takes intelligence and a high ability to talk your way into or out of a situation. I really don't think I'll ever work for a campaign again.
  – It was an experience but I found out a lot about politics that scared me. It was a dog-eat-dog life and not for me.
  – It turned me away from political activity.

*Total corrected to remove the effect of people giving more than one response in this classification.

Negative experiences, classified here, are evidence that some young people who joined the campaign found themselves very disenchanted with politics. When we consider, however, that 22 per cent of those who had contact with the voters during the campaign reported that the main effect on them was that the public was ignorant or disinterested, it becomes significant that only 2 per cent mentioned this as a major effect of the campaign experience as a whole. For many people, then, the reaction of the public was not important. More important was the personal development, learning, involvement and enhanced interest noted previously.

In categories K and L, I have distinguished between those whose responses indicated that a good deal of real disgust for politics developed as a result of campaign experience and those who tried political campaigning and simply decided that they did not find it very interesting or worth pursuing again. In connection with the experimentation with different roles which takes place in adolescence, I had expected more young people to indicate that they had, in effect, experimented with politics and discarded it as not being a role they were interested in adopting. Very few in fact did so and this, as well as indications elsewhere in the questionnaire that most would like to work in a political campaign again soon, shows the overwhelmingly positive nature of the effects of the campaign. Most young people were interested, involved and found the experience such a stimulating one that they are prepared to repeat it in the future, though with different purposes in mind.

The bulk of the negative responses falls in the "disgust" category; those who have turned away from active politics because of their campaign experience seem to have done so with rancour. Some of these people were disgusted only by "party" politics and now style themselves "radical." Others were turned off completely, whether from bad experiences in dealing with the public, uninteresting jobs, or a dislike of the way politicians and their organizers try to win votes at election time. Whatever the cause, these negative reactions were not widely prevalent among the campaigners, and even some of those who did give responses of this type indicate a fascination with the process at the same time and a willingness to work again.

As befits any "other" classification, this one collects all the odds and ends which cannot be consistently fitted into one of the others. In some cases, responses in category M, dealing with the inherent satisfaction in

---

IV *Other Effects*

M. Satisfaction in group activity; meeting people	10.7%
N. Expressions of personal exhilaration	6.4
O. Other	6.8
	22.8*

M. (Satisfaction in group activity)
- I met a lot of people—this I enjoyed immensely.
- Met some great people.
- I found myself to be very much at home in a group and in communicating with people.
- Le travail de groupe.
- Met new faces.
- J'ai bien aimé travailler en groupe avec des gens qui avaient à coeur de remporter cette élection.

N. (Personal exhilaration)
- Wonderful. I cannot wait to work again.
- Excitement, exhaustion and exhilaration.
- Personally exhilarating.

O. (Other)
- One man can't change everything.
- We took a greater interest in the results.
- The adults did not consider us capable enough to do any really useful jobs.

*Total corrected to remove the effect of people giving more than one response in this classification.

---

meeting others and in working in a group, can be considered to have much in common with responses labelled indications of identity-building and classified earlier. The desire to interact with members of the peer-group is important in adolescence and can be seen in some of the answers in category M. However, some of the responses listed here are not much more than expressions of delight at meeting some new friends (or "new faces," as one person put it). Similarly "expressions of personal exhilaration" were not considered to necessarily be indications of personal or political development. After all, an enjoyable time does not necessarily indicate that the experience had any lasting value for the participant. Thus answers which were not detailed enough to allow a judgment to be made on the actual meaning of the campaign activity for the person were placed in classification IV.

v *Unaffected*	
P. Campaign had no effects	3.5%
Q. No answer	9.1
	12.6

Three and a half per cent of the sample declared that the experience of the campaign had no effect on them, and another 9 per cent did not answer the question. Those who did not answer the question are considered "unaffected" here because most of them scored very low on indexes designed to measure by a consideration of the total questionnaire how important the campaign experience had been to the person in helping to form his sense of ego identity. Neither of these categories was employed as one of a multiple response on this variable so the figure of 12.6 per cent can stand as a reasonable indication of the proportion of young people who were completely unaffected by their activity with Action-Trudeau.

In taking an overall look at all the categories of responses it is striking that so many of them are consistent with the theoretical formulation that the campaign activity, by teaching young people about political roles and about themselves, helped many of them along the road to the crystallization of their sense of ego identity. We have seen that almost 60 per cent (58.7 per cent) of the sample gave at least one answer classified explicitly as "identity-building." In addition, over 30 per cent (31.4 per cent) gave responses in classifications II or III, which denote gains in personal political perspectives. The evidence is overwhelming that most of the participants in Action-Trudeau were personally affected by their experience, and that most of those affected gave responses fully consistent with the theory that their experience helped in the creation of ego identity.

CONCLUSION

Participation in a political movement can have quite a pronounced effect on personal development. Being political, such a movement has an intrinsic importance; in the case of Action-Trudeau, the government was being chosen and the country's leadership was at stake. The fact that the movement was a scheduled political event which built to a climax sustained the interest of the participants and ensured that they took the activity seriously. The atmosphere of importance which surrounds a political campaign makes it unlikely that sustained activity within it will be on a frivolous basis, and thus participation in such a movement may well be regarded as a significant experience by adolescents.

Evidence from the study of Action-Trudeau members shows that desires for such an experience were present in the motivations for joining the campaign. Identification with Trudeau as an ego ideal was a way for adolescents to try to imitate his valued characteristics, to be mentally allied with him and to thereby derive some of the competence seen in the idealized figure. By identifying with Trudeau, and translating this identification into action by means of participation in the political movement formed to support him in the election, young people were seeking for themselves Trudeau's valued characteristics and were trying on the active political roles that went with Trudeau's world. Expressions of desires for personal development, learning about politics, and involvement, form an impressively large part of the rationale for joining the campaign. The hallmark of adolescence as the stage of life leading to the formation of ego identity is a searching for the roles and the personal characteristics that the young person will call his for the rest of his life. This realization that he is searching for and experimenting with a great many possible roles is the conscious manifestation of the largely unconscious process of ego identity formation in the adolescent.

The learning process that many of the participants underwent took place on two levels. The first was the overtly political level. The campaigners learned how a campaign was run, the techniques for canvassing voters, assessing their intentions and planning to get the favourable ones to the polls. They learned how demonstrations, speaking tours and rallies were engineered to provide the impression that their candidate's strength was building. They came to grips with the often-sobering realization that many people held views completely different to their own, and that particular issues which meant a great deal to them meant little to many voters. They learned of the compromises necessary in political life and the way issue positions must be softened to attract to the same party those of differing viewpoints. All these experiences were part of the process, inherent in building the sense of ego identity, of familiarization with and evaluation of a set of roles, in this case political roles. Especially once the participants realized the scope of a political campaign, some degree of judgment inevitably took place. Was this going to be a once-in-a-lifetime activity for them, or were they attracted to the world of politics more generally? Although decisions of this sort about future political roles were likely not made on the spot, information was being gathered to allow such decisions to be made at the time of the crystallization of their ego identity.

The second level at which the learning process worked was that of development of the personality. Contact with voters and relations with other members of the campaign group caused some participants to report that these experiences allowed them to gain patience and self-confidence. In addition, some reported that their outlook on others had been significantly broadened and that they were now much more tolerant of other people and their opinions. These are, needless to say, important acquisitions on the road to maturity. It is reasonable to assume that the range of personal development effects of the campaign experience was much wider than it appeared from the answers reported in the previous section to the open-ended question asking for effects of the campaign. For one thing, the acquisition of personality characteristics is often an unconscious process—it is not always apparent to oneself that a set of experiences is giving one the quality of self-confidence, for example. Also, even if one did come to realize this, there may have been some tendency to answer a questionnaire item asking about effects of the campaign in terms of more specifically political learning, because such a response might be thought to be more appropriate to a questionnaire dealing with political activity. In any case, both the political and personal types of learning relate to the same process of developing a stable conception of the self.

I have been dealing in this study with one particular political movement at one point in time. The findings, however, are open to a more general interpretation. It would seem reasonable to hypothesize that all mass movements which attract adolescents are serving the same sorts of functions for their participants in terms of helping their development of ego identity. Movements centred less around an individual leader and more around the promotion of an issue or set of issues may well do this to a greater degree. It would be interesting to compare the present findings regarding Action-Trudeau with samples of young campaigners for Eugene McCarthy in the 1968 American presidential primaries and George McGovern in the 1972 campaign, for example. It seems probable that the same basic pattern found here would exist in these and other comparative cases.

It is difficult, in these more quiescent political times, to recapture effectively the excitement and spirit of the Action-Trudeau campaign. The 1968 campaign injected into the political sphere numerous young people who under more normal circumstances would never have dreamed of becoming politically active. The questionnaire responses indicate that many would like to recapture the treasured feelings of the campaign experience. But an irreplaceable part of the particular mix of factors that made the Action-Trudeau campaign the exhilarating experience it was for so many was the time in their lives at which it came, a time when they were more open than they ever would be again to learning new roles, and trying new things. Action-Trudeau involved in politics a group of young people at the point in their lives when they were most likely to be seeking the truth about themselves. For the participants in the 1968 campaign this characteristic of adolescence will never come again, and those who remain politically active will do so for reasons connected more with parties and issues. For new adolescents, however, it seems likely that in the future there will be new political movements, and new personal challenges to be worked out within them.

NOTES

1. Edith Douvan and Joseph Adelson, *The Adolescent Experience* (New York: Wiley, 1966), p. 14.
2. Kurt Lewin, "The Field Theory Approach to Adolescence" in J. M. Seidman, ed., *The Adolescent* (New York: Holt, Rinehart and Winston, 1960), pp. 32–42.
3. Erik H. Erikson, "Identity and Uprootedness in Our Time," in his *Insight and Responsibility* (London: Faber, 1964), p. 90.
4. A good discussion of this is found in Kaspar D. Naegele, "Youth and Society: Some Observations," in Erik H. Erikson, ed., *Youth: Change and Challenge* (New York: Basic Books, 1963), p. 46.
5. James E. Horrocks, "Adolescent Attitudes and Goals" in Mustafer Sherif and Carolyn W. Sherif, eds., *Problems of Youth* (Chicago: Aldine, 1965), p. 17.
6. For an argument that youth culture is a separate entity, see James S. Coleman, *The Adolescent Society* (New York: Free Press, 1961). This view is disputed by, among others, Daniel Offer, *The Psychological World of the Teenager* (New York: Basic Books, 1969), who sees much more basic value continuity in adult and youth cultures. The relation of peer groups and adolescent development to student political activism of a radical nature is discussed by E. W. Bakke, "Roots and Soil of Student Activism" in Seymour M. Lipset, ed., *Student Politics* (New York: Basic Books, 1967), pp. 54–73.
7. Anna Freud, "Adolescence as a Development Disturbance" in G. Caplan and S. Lebovici, eds., *Adolescence: Psychological Perspectives* (New York: Basic Books, 1969), pp. 5–10.
8. Robert W. White, *Lives in Progress*, 2nd ed. (New York: Holt, Rinehart and Winston, 1966), p. 21.

9. P. L. Giovacchini, "Compulsory Happiness; Adolescent Despair," *Archives of General Psychiatry*, vol. 18 (1968), p. 657.
10. Daniel Offer, *The Psychological World of the Teenager*, p. 179.
11. Kenneth Keniston, *Young Radicals: Notes on Committed Youth* (New York: Harcourt, Brace and World, 1968), p. 102.
12. Erik H. Erikson, "Identity and the Life Cycle," *Psychological Issues*, vol. I, no. 1 (New York: International Universities Press, 1959), p. 11.
13. An inventory of the primary processes is given in Daniel Yankelovich and William Barrett, *Ego and Instinct* (New York: Random House, 1970), pp. 68–73.
14. Nevitt Sanford, *Self and Society* (New York: Atherton, 1966), pp. 78–82.
15. Yankelovich and Barrett, *Ego and Instinct*, pp. 23–24, 31–33, 73–87.
16. Ibid., p. 73.
17. Ibid., pp. 102–9.
18. Robert W. White, "Ego and Reality in Psychoanalytic Theory," *Psychological Issues*, vol. III, no. 3, 1963. See also the discussion in Robert W. White, *Lives in Progress*, pp. 357–63.
19. White, "Ego and Reality in Psychoanalytic Theory," p. 185.
20. Erik H. Erikson, *Identity: Youth and Crisis* (New York: Norton, 1968), p. 208.
21. Robert Coles, *Erik H. Erikson: The Growth of His Work* (Boston: Little, Brown, 1970), p. 264.
22. Erik H. Erikson, "Identity and the Life Cycle," p. 89.
23. Erikson, *Identity: Youth and Crisis*, p. 50.
24. Erik H. Erikson, "Youth: Fidelity and Diversity" in Erik H. Erikson, ed., *Youth: Change and Challenge*, p. 11.
25. Erik H. Erikson, *Childhood and Society*, 2nd ed. (New York: Norton, 1963), pp. 247–74. (Originally published in 1950.)
26. An "epigenetic" chart is presented in ibid., p. 273.
27. Richard I. Evans, *Dialogue with Erik Erikson* (New York: Dutton, 1969), pp. 11–58.
28. Erikson, *Childhood and Society*, p. 262.
29. Erikson, *Identity: Youth and Crisis*, p. 16.
30. "To pick a few items from the top of my desk, the papers discuss the 'Identity Crisis of Africa' or of the Pittsburgh Glass Industry; . . . the American Psychoanalytic Association is addressed by its president on the 'Identity Crisis of Psychoanalysis'; . . . the Catholic Students at Harvard announce that they will hold an 'Identity Crisis' on Thursday night at 8 sharp." Quoted in Robert Coles, *Erik Erikson*, p. 264.
31. Erikson, "Youth; Fidelity and Diversity," p. 3.
32. Erikson, "The Problem of Ego Identity," p. 118.
33. G. J. McCall and J. L. Simmons, *Identities and Interactions* (Glencoe: Free Press, 1966), p. 209. See also Gordon W. Allport, *Pattern and Growth in Personality* (New York: Holt, Rinehart and Winston, 1961), p. 125.
34. Nevitt Sanford, "The Dynamics of Identification," *Psychological Review*, vol. 62, no. 2 (1955), p. 106.
35. Robert W. White, "Ego and Reality in Psychoanalytic Theory," pp. 111–12.
36. Much of the information in this section comes to me from personal communications with the Action-Trudeau organizers, and an examination of the national files of the organization. I have pledged to maintain the anonymity of all respondents, and not to quote explicitly from confidential documents.
37. The same response was not coded both C and either A or B.

Parliamentary Experience and Legislative Behaviour

10

JACK S. CRAMER

An examination of the literature dealing with the behaviour of members of legislative bodies reveals that, for the most part, the entire area of post-incumbency political socialization has been analysed *en passant* at best. This apparent neglect is surprising when one observes the significance several researchers have attached to the variable, "legislative experience or tenure" in their theoretical writings. For example, Wahlke, Eulau, *et al.*, have emphasized that:

Day to day involvement in the legislative system plays an equally important part. . . . The legislative experience (both quantity and quality) is an important variable in shaping the legislative role.[1]

While Allan Kornberg's study of Canadian members of Parliament has focused primarily on the influence of pre-incumbency variables such as social background and motives for candidacy, it was also suggested that legislative behaviour is a product of both initial expectations, and "attitudes and perspectives *subsequently* developed in response to expectations and requirements of significant others interacting with him in the legislative system."[2] Other empirical investigations of political socialization of legislators have touched on such diverse areas as the age at which first political identifications occur, recruitment patterns and the early or primary agents of socialization.[3] While these analyses do make significant contributions toward a total understanding of the political socialization process, in some instances they tend to imply that these are the only components that need be studied. Clearly, a great deal of pioneering research will have to be undertaken to fill the void.

We shall view post-incumbency socialization, as opposed to pre-incumbency socialization, as the process by which new or freshmen members of Parliament internalize the attitudes, behaviour patterns and group norms that are operative within the legislative setting. Pre-incumbency socialization refers to the processes that occur prior to election to office and/or exposure to the parliamentary arena. Post-incumbency socialization is mostly secondary: the legislator learns specific behaviour patterns and organization norms associated with the role(s) he is playing. In other words, it is the learning that results from direct political experience: this is "probably the most important form of learning for most adults."[4]

Researchers have acquired some empirical evidence of the existence and nature of the group norms and legislative behaviour patterns to which we have alluded. Allan Kornberg's survey of members of Parliament revealed that about 84 per cent of those interviewed perceived the existence of specific "rules of the game," or norms and sanctions that were functioning within the legislative setting.[5] For example, members listed rules to decrease conflict (no personal attacks on a member, never bring personalities into debate, don't be overly or stupidly partisan); rules to expedite legislative business (do not speak without proper knowledge of the subject); and rules which reinforce respect for formal rules (know and observe the proper rules of debate, know the correct forms of address). A significant percentage of the sample in the Kornberg investigation perceived the existence of legislative sanctions, "actions deemed punitive or detrimental to the incumbent of the legislative position."[6] Sanctions, such as social ostracism, which are employed by colleagues, could be perceived as being personally embarrassing. Such sanctions must certainly be considered as potentially important socializing pressures impinging upon the individual's awareness. In another exploratory study, Kornberg demonstrated the functional importance members of Parliament attach to the need for parties to act cohesively at all times.[7] Further evidence of the existence and nature of group norms has been demonstrated by Donald Matthews. Matthews' interviews reveal that the American senator is obliged to serve an apprenticeship period during which time his subordinate status is impressed upon him. He may receive thankless or unwanted committee assignments and is expected to keep his eyes open, his mouth shut, and follow his party leader.[8] These findings suggest the desirability of conducting further analyses of the functioning of legislative norms as prerequisite to a complete understanding of the "learning" dimension of the socialization process.

The objectives of the current investigation are extremely modest, since at this time there are significant limitations to an attempt to systematically analyse the entire socialization process. The paucity of empirical data available on political socialization in legislative bodies requires the researcher to conduct some basic, pioneering studies. In addition, the data for the study to follow were obtained from a comprehensive survey of legislative role behaviour—a survey which was only tangentially concerned with political socialization.

This paper explores some of the relationships between length of parliamentary experience or tenure, and legislative behaviour. More specifically, it is thought that there will be observable perceptual and behavioural differences between inexperienced or freshmen members of Parliament and their more experienced colleagues. As new members come more and more into contact with the legislative environment, they become increasingly socialized into its roles. We would anticipate that the lag in extent of socialization between inexperienced and experienced members, and the psychological adjustment process associated particularly with the socialization of new members, will be manifested in observable differences. It is most probable that new legislators internalize some aspects of the group ideology more quickly than other aspects. For example, during the course of the interviews it was noted that members had organized their parliamentary offices in a very similar fashion: photographs of party leaders were placed on the walls, evidences of past achievements were exhibited, and so on. Further, Kornberg has found no appreciable differences between freshmen and experienced members in their awareness of the informal rules of the game that operate in the House.[9] However, complex roles, such as orientation to party and constituency, may develop and crystallize only after considerable interpersonal contact and after continued occupancy of the roles (that is, at an advanced stage in the learning process). It can therefore be predicted that role perceptions and behaviour would vary with the length of tenure. To further illustrate, Wahlke and Eulau have reported a significant association between tenure and orientation vis-à-vis interest groups. Legislators with more experience evidenced a greater propensity to be "facilitators" (had receptive attitudes toward interest groups) than experienced members.[10] Evidence of perceptual changes over time is documented in the Hoffman, Ward study of the 26th Parliament. When asked if there were any differences between current and initial expectations about the legislative environment, fully 23 per cent of the M.P.'s felt that their first expectations of what they could accomplish as individuals were overly optimistic.[11]

THE STUDY

Ideally, for studies of the political socialization process in legislative bodies, longitudinal techniques should be employed. Through an examination of perceptions and behaviour over time, it could be determined if differences can, in fact, be attributed to the lag in socialization, or are due to new modes of thought and behaviour prevalent in the freshman group of legislators. Unfortunately, because of the nature of the available data and the tremendous effort that would have to be devoted to such an investigation, we are forced to adopt a "quasi-longitudinal" approach. In brief, this method suggests that the "developmental nature of political socialization can be simulated by examining different groups of people," at successive experience levels. Variations in perceptions and behaviour between groups would be indicative of development.

Data for the project were obtained from a fourteen-page questionnaire administered by personal interview to 150 randomly selected members of Parliament in Ottawa during February and March 1970. The questionnaires were translated into French for distribution to francophone members. Legitimacy for the study was effectively established by obtaining prior authorization in writing from the Whips of the Liberal, Progressive Conservative and New Democratic parties. The Whips helped the researchers by distributing their letters of authorization to those party members who had been selected for the sample. The study's interviewers were carefully cautioned against making interpretive comments regarding the content of questions during the course of the interview, and there is, therefore, no reason to suspect differences resulting from variance in administration of the questionnaire. The researchers found that many respondents welcomed discussion after the questionnaires had been completed in writing. Completed questionnaires were sealed in unmarked envelopes in witness of the respondents. Members of the New Democratic Party served as respondents for purposes of the pre-test and the eleven completed questionnaires received have been included in this study. A total of 92 questionnaires were received from Liberal and Progressive Conservative respondents, representing a response rate of 61.4 per cent.

For purposes of this study, respondents have been grouped according to length of parliamentary experience in the following manner:

Freshmen (0–2 years)   N = 36
Middlemen (3–10 years)   N = 35
Veterans (over 10 years)   N = 32

Total   N = 103

The classification employed is convenient in that there are sufficient respondents in the cells for meaningful statistical analysis.[12]

It is of interest to note that, for the sample, length of tenure in the House of Commons was an important factor in determining which members occupied senior positions. Only three of the freshmen indicated that they were other than backbenchers ("other" included cabinet, front bench, shadow cabinet or parliamentary secretary). Twelve middlemen and a total of nineteen veterans were members of the more senior categories of House positions. These data confirm Allan Kornberg's findings that Canadian parliamentary leaders evidence a fairly long period of tenure relative to non-leaders.[13]

Variation across the House tenure categories for pre-parliamentary political experience was very slight. Almost 50 per cent of the respondents in each category had held municipal elected public office prior to incumbency and about 15 per cent had held provincial elected public office. Municipal office, therefore, appears to be a rather important stepping stone in the legislative political career. Approximately 40 per cent of the respondents in each category had prior experience in provincial, municipal or federal party office. As Kornberg has suggested, many Canadian members of Parliament have developed very distinct relationships with their parties years before incumbency, due to extensive involvement in party activities.[14] Party office is another important stepping stone in many political careers.

THE HYPOTHESES

A review of the literature together with subjective impressions gained through conversations with members of Parliament provided a rough indication of the nature of perceptual and behavioural differences which exist between tenure groups. Possible differences have been stated in the form of specific hypotheses.

Perception of Representative Role

Hypotheses: 1. Inexperienced or freshmen parliamentarians will evidence a greater propensity to indicate a "politico" pattern in their normative representational role expectations or will fail to exhibit any clear pattern than will experienced parliamentarians. 2. A greater proportion of experienced members will indicate a "trustee" or "delegate" normative pattern than will inexperienced or freshmen members.

The concept of legislative role as it has been used in our study has been largely adapted from Wahlke and Eulau.[15] Normative representational role expectation simply refers to the individual member's perception of his relationship with his constituents vis-à-vis decision-making. A representative may base his legislative decisions on his own judgment or he may take cues or follow instructions. The Burkean "trustee" is a free agent: he perceives that his decisions are based on his own convictions or judgment. The "delegate" feels obligated to always represent the wishes of his constituents in his decision-making. Finally, a third type—the "politico"—represents an overlap or combination of the trustee and delegate roles. He typically sees himself as a trustee in some decision situations, and a delegate in others. Assuming that the role concept becomes more fully developed as the individual gains more and more experience in a position, it is our contention that the freshman incumbent might adopt the politico role orientation very readily. The politico role can be viewed as a transitional state, halfway between trustee and delegate, and as such may represent a condition of non-commitment.[16] The position is less dogmatic than either trustee or delegate and may facilitate avoidance or reduction of dissonance associated with decision-making. The flexible nature of the politico orientation would easily permit the individual to change behavioural cognitive elements or add new cognitive elements when faced with perceptual or behavioural inconsistency. On the other hand, the extreme orientations, delegate and trustee, would require considerable behavioural adjustment and adaptation prior to their internalization, because they are much more rigid. Similarly, we would anticipate that freshmen legislators would fall disproportionately into the "no-trend" (mixed) category, again indicating non-commitment and maximum flexibility.

Table 1 Perception of Representative Role

	Trustee	Delegate	Politico	Mixed	(N)
Freshmen	25.0%	3.1	53.1	18.7	(32)
Middlemen	35.0	2.9	38.2	23.5	(34)
Veterans	61.3	6.5	25.8	6.5	(31)
Total	40.2	4.1	39.2	16.5	(97)

The data in Table 1 lend some support to our hypothesis. Clearly freshmen were overrepresented in the politico category and underrepresented in the trustee group. The variance in the trustee group is striking. Of the veterans, 61 per cent were trustees as opposed to only 25 per cent and 35 per cent of the freshmen and middlemen respectively. The trend observed in the trustee and politico categories may indicate that as experience increases, and the member is re-elected, he gains confidence in his own judgment and moves further away from feelings of obligation to his constituents. The data in the mixed category do not support our expectations. Controlling for pre-legislative elected public and for party did not alter any of the observed patterns.

Relationship to Party

Hypotheses: 1. Inexperienced members will *perceive* greater independence from party ties than experienced members.

2. Experienced members will *demonstrate* greater independence from party ties in their voting behaviour than inexperienced members.

The extreme stringency of party discipline in the British-model parliamentary system has been discussed by Richard Rose, Allan Kornberg and Leo Epstein.[17] Since the government requires consistent support from a substantial number of its party members to remain in office, and since the opposition parties also require member support to maintain a reputation for being *capable* of supporting a government, party cohesion norms are probably quickly internalized by members of Parliament. Kornberg's study of cohesion in Canadian parliamentary parties has noted that fully 89 per cent of the respondents interviewed indicated that party cohesion was both necessary and advantageous. Such behaviour is required to "maintain their parties as viable, organized, effective groups."[18] It is also possible that the party solidarity norm has been encouraged by public pressures.

It is our contention that perceptions of party loyalty and allegiance become more acute with increasing legislative experience. The veteran member of Parliament owes his political good fortune in large part to his party. We would therefore expect experienced members to indicate, in their perceptions, closer ties with their respective parties than freshmen legislators. At the same time, the long-standing tradition of party discipline would mitigate strongly against any behaviour suggesting public defiance of party positions, either in voting behaviour or overt discussion in the House of Commons. As Epstein has suggested: "Deviation has to be justified as exceptional, as infrequent, and most telling of all, as undamaging to the maintenance of a government by the party leaders."[19]

It might be expected, however, that veteran members, because of their status, could deviate, on occasion, from the party ranks and that such behaviour would be tolerated. Veterans should be psychologically secure since the internalization of roles and the behavioural adjustment processes would be at an advanced, and therefore relatively stable, state of development. Freshmen, on the other hand, could be expected to exercise more caution. The indicator of members' perceptions of relationship to party was an evaluation of the strength of caucus decisions. Actual party relationship was measured by examining number of votes against party and number of abstentions.

The data in Table 2 very weakly support hypothesis 1. A slightly smaller proportion of freshman respondents than middlemen or veterans indicated that caucus decisions are always binding. In view of the theory

Table 2   Frequency Caucus Decisions Are Binding

	Always	*Sometimes*	*Never*	*(N)*
Freshmen	24.2%	54.5	21.2	(33)
Middlemen	34.3	45.7	20.0	(35)
Veterans	30.0	56.7	13.3	(30)
Total	29.6	52.0	18.4	(98)

just discussed, such a relationship indicates that inexperienced members perceive greater independence from party ties than experienced members. Since pre-parliamentary experience in parties may psychologically prepare members for acceptance of party prescriptions, a control for previous party office held was introduced.

Table 3   Frequency Caucus Decisions Are Binding: No Previous Party Office

	Always	*Sometimes*	*Never*	*(N)*
Freshmen	0.0%	70.0	30.0	(10)
Middlemen	31.2	37.5	31.2	(16)
Veterans	42.9	50.0	7.1	(14)
Total	27.5	50.0	22.5	(40)

Table 3, showing legislators with no previous experience in party office supports this interpretation, and lends additional support to hypothesis 1. There was no change when controlled for party.

Turning to hypothesis 2, we note that the data in both Tables 4 and 5 support our expectations. Clearly, new members were more hesitant than

Table 4   Abstentions Against Party (since the election)

	None	*Some*	*(N)*
Freshmen	93.1%	6.9	(29)
Middlemen	80.8	19.2	(26)
Veterans	75.0	25.0	(20)
Total	84.0	16.0	(75)

Table 5   Votes Against Party (since the election)

	None	*Some*	*(N)*
Freshmen	88.6%	11.4	(35)
Middlemen	81.2	18.7	(32)
Veterans	46.2	53.8	(26)
Total	74.2	25.8	(93)

their more experienced counterparts in demonstrating overt disagreement with the party position. The differences become more acute for votes against party. It is significant that both of the freshmen indicating abstentions had prior party experience and that three of the four voting against the party position had pre-parliamentary party experience. Controlling for party did not change the pattern.

Relationship to Constituents

Hypothesis: Inexperienced parliamentarians will demonstrate closer ties with their constituents than will experienced parliamentarians.

It was thought that the new member, having been recently elected by his constituents, would perceive a greater responsibility for constituency affairs than would the experienced legislator who has been re-elected frequently. Then, too, close and continued contact with constituents would facilitate information-flow to the new member, thus permitting development of the representational legislative role.

An examination was undertaken of both the frequency of member-initiated constituency contacts and the significance members attached to their contacts with constituents.

Table 6   Number of Constituency Visits Per Session

	1 per wk.	*Every 2 wks.*	*Less Often*	*(N)*
Freshmen	55.6%	16.7	27.8	(36)
Middlemen	58.8	17.6	23.5	(34)
Veterans	37.5	28.1	34.4	(32)
Total	51.0	20.6	28.4	(102)

Table 7 Number of Constituency Visits (Controlled for Time to Reach Constituency)

| | Up to 3 Hours | | | |
	1 per wk.	*2 weeks*	*Less*	*(N)*
Freshmen	100.0%	0.0	0.0	(15)
Middlemen	73.3	13.3	13.3	(15)
Veterans	81.8	0.0	18.2	(11)
Total	85.4	4.9	9.8	(41)
	More than 3 Hours			
	1 per wk.	*2 weeks*	*Less*	*(N)*
Freshmen	23.8%	28.6	47.6	(21)
Middlemen	47.4	21.1	31.6	(19)
Veterans	14.3	42.9	42.9	(21)
Total	27.9	31.1	41.0	(61)

The data in Table 6 only weakly support our hypothesis. Both freshmen and middlemen visited their constituencies more frequently during the parliamentary session than did veterans. A slight pattern emerged when the number of constituency visits per legislative session was controlled for time to reach constituency. All freshmen who were within three hours travelling time from their constituency made visits once per week as compared with 73.3 per cent for middlemen and 81.1 per cent for veterans.

Turning now to an examination of respondents' evaluations of the importance of constituent contacts, we would again anticipate that freshmen members, in their efforts to seek out information to develop roles, would attach greater significance to such contacts than experienced members.

The data in Table 8 only weakly support our expectations. A slightly greater proportion of freshmen indicated that visits to constituency were important as a means of discovering constituents' views than middlemen or veterans. Controlling for pre-legislative experience, the differences become more acute. "Inexperienced" freshmen were overrepresented (66.7 per cent as compared with 57.1 per cent and 50 per cent for middlemen and veterans respectively) in the "very important" category.

Table 8   Visits to Constituency Evaluation

	V. Important	Fairly Important No Opinion	F. Unimp. V. Unimport.	(N)
Freshmen	61.1%	33.3	5.6	(36)
Middlemen	54.3	40.0	5.7	(35)
Veterans	54.8	41.9	3.2	(31)
Total	56.9	38.2	4.9	(102)

Examining types of communication on an individual basis, freshmen with no pre-legislative experience (elected public office) were disproportionately represented in the "very effective" category for visits from constituents (Table 9).

Table 9   Visits Ratings (From Constituents)

	Previous Experience					No Previous Experience				
	VE	NE	D	DR	(N)	VE	NE	D	DR	(N)
Freshmen	38.5%	7.7	23.1	30.8	(13)	52.9%	23.5	5.9	17.6	(17)
Middlemen	60.0	40.0	0.0	0.0	(10)	30.0	30.0	30.0	20.0	(20)
Veterans	66.7	20.0	0.0	13.3	(15)	33.3	50.0	8.3	8.3	(12)
Total	55.3	21.1	7.9	15.8	(38)	38.8	28.6	16.3	16.3	(49)

VE = Very Effective   NE = Not Effective   D = Difficult to Say
DR = Don't Receive

Freshmen also attached slightly greater importance to letters from constituents than did middlemen or veterans, although the difference in evaluation of telephone calls was not appreciable. In addition, freshmen were more likely to list constituents as an important factor in influencing their voting decisions than middlemen and veterans.

In summary, while the data presented do not reverse the hypothesis that inexperienced members will demonstrate closer ties with their constituents, they support it tenuously at best. Relationships with constituents may very well become established rather early in the legislative career; more significant differences might be exhibited if the study had been conducted just after the general election.

Participation in the Legislative Process

Hypothesis: Experienced parliamentarians will participate to a greater extent in the legislative process than will inexperienced parliamentarians.

Freshmen legislators' potential uncertainties or lack of complete knowledge about both the informal and formal rules of the House of Commons may discourage frequent participation in legislative debates and discussions. It is possible that early participation may be prevented by the new members' uncertainty about group expectations. Donald Matthews, for example, has shown that legislative norms require the freshman to defer to senior colleagues. There is, in fact, a direct relationship between seniority and the frequency of activity in floor debates.[20] Then, too, there are extensive empirical data which support the hypothesis that the more stimuli about politics an individual receives, the greater the likelihood he will participate in politics, and the greater will be his depth of participation.[21]

The method used to test the hypothesis was to examine the frequency of member acts in the House of Commons during the debates on the Criminal Code amendments of 1969.

Some differences in the behaviour of experienced and inexperienced members emerge from Table 10. Proportionately fewer freshmen spoke in the House, in caucus and with the party leader than did middlemen or veterans. Our hypothesis is confirmed, although the differences are large only with respect to speaking in the House. Freshmen were slightly overrepresented in "discussions with members of other parties" relative to middlemen or veterans. Private discussions probably fall outside the jurisdiction of most informal norms in the House of Commons and there would therefore be less pressure on the freshman member to defer to his/ her seniors. It would have been desirable to examine the actual number of communication acts for the three experience groups; however, the questionnaire utilized a simple "yes—no" choice for each type of act, rather than requesting a quantitative response.

CONCLUSION

This study has examined one small segment of the total post-incumbency socialization process. We have speculated that perceptual and behavioural

Table 10   Frequency of Participation

	Spoke in House			Spoke in Caucus		
	Yes	No	(N)	Yes	No	(N)
Freshmen	21.9%	78.1	(32)	80.0%	20.0	(35)
Middlemen	38.7	61.3	(31)	86.2	13.8	(29)
Veterans	56.0	44.0	(25)	100.0	0.0	(28)
Total	37.5	62.5	(88)	88.0	12.0	(92)

	Discussion with Party Leader			Discussion with Party Members		
	Yes	No	(N)	Yes	No	(N)
Freshmen	80.6%	19.4	(31)	100.0%	0.0	(35)
Middlemen	85.7	14.3	(28)	90.6	9.4	(32)
Veterans	84.0	16.0	(25)	100.0	0.0	(29)
Total	83.3	16.7	(84)	96.9	3.1	(96)

	Discussion with Members of Other Parties		
	Yes	No	(N)
Freshmen	73.3%	26.7	(30)
Middlemen	59.3	40.7	(27)
Veterans	65.2	34.8	(23)
Total	66.2	33.7	(80)

differences between inexperienced or freshmen members of Parliament and more seasoned members could be observed, since there would be a socialization gap between the two groups. The general hypothesis was supported, to some extent, by the available data for the four areas of possible difference that were investigated: perception of representative role, relationship to party, relationship to constituents and participation in the legislative process. Freshmen legislators were over-represented in the politico category of perception of representational role and slightly under-represented in the trustee group relative to middlemen and veterans. It has also been shown that inexperienced members had some tendency to perceive greater independence from party ties and that experienced members demonstrated more independence from their parties in their actual behaviour. The hypothesis that inexperienced members would demonstrate closer ties with their constituents was weakly supported by the available data; and, finally, it was observed that in a number of cases, senior parliamentarians participated to a greater extent in the legislative process than did new members.

The fact that some perceptual and behavioural differences were observed, even though the freshmen members had almost two years of parliamentary experience at the time of our study, suggests that it may be useful to conduct a similar inquiry just after a general election. It is clear that the entire area of socialization in legislative bodies requires extensive treatment in the future. As was suggested earlier, longitudinal analyses may be able to determine whether behaviour differences can, in fact, be attributed to the lag in socialization mentioned earlier, or if such differences are due to new modes of behaviour prevalent in the freshman group of legislators. Since new party leaders may have significant impact on the nature of existing legislative norms, it would be necessary to examine this area in detail as well. In addition, the party caucus is probably an important agency in the socialization process and should be explored systematically, though the confidential nature of its proceedings will present certain research difficulties. Psychologists might also be interested in study of the nature of the adjustment process operating during the socialization of legislators. Finally, case studies of "deviant" members of Parliament might also be pursued. For example, it would be of interest to examine the characteristics of members involved in back-bench revolts. If this study has established the potential for further investigation of socialization in legislatures, then its purpose has been achieved.

NOTES

1. John C. Wahlke et al., *The Legislative System* (New York: John Wiley, 1962), p. 23.
2. Allan Kornberg, *Canadian Legislative Behavior* (New York: Holt, Rinehart and Winston, 1967), p. 10.
3. See, for example, Allan Kornberg and Hal H. Winsborough, "The Recruitment of Candidates for the Canadian House of Commons," *The American Political Science Review*, vol. LXIII (Dec. 1968), pp. 1,242–57. Allan Kornberg, Joel Smith and David Bromley, "Some Differences in the Political Socialization of Canadian and American Party

Officials," *Canadian Journal of Political Science*, vol. II (March 1969), p. 64.
4. Richard E. Dawson and Kenneth Prewitt, *Political Socialization* (Boston: Little, Brown, 1969), p. 58.
5. Allan Kornberg, "Rules of the Game in Legislative Politics—A Comparative Study," in Heinz Eulau, ed., *Political Behavior in America* (New York: Random House, 1966), p. 235.
6. Ibid., p. 238.
7. Allan Kornberg, "Caucus and Cohesion in Canadian Parliamentary Parties," *American Political Science*

Review (March 1966), pp. 83–93.

8. Donald Matthews, *United States Senators and Their World* (New York: Vintage, 1960), pp. 92–93.

9. Allan Kornberg, "Rules of the Game," p. 235.

10. Wahlke, *Legislative System*, p. 341.

11. David Hoffman and Norman Ward, *Bilingualism and Biculturalism in the Canadian House of Commons*, Documents of the Royal Commission on Bilingualism and Biculturalism (Ottawa: Queen's Printer, 1970), p. 89.

12. It would have been interesting, if not desirable, to group respondents also according to the dates of changes in party leadership. However, the manner of coding for parliamentary experience did not permit such analysis. The expanded distribution is as follows:

Years as M.P.		
	%	(N)
2 or less	35.0	(36)
3–5	16.5	(17)
6–10	17.5	(18)
11–15	23.3	(24)
16–20	6.8	(7)
21–25	1.0	(1)
26–30	0.0	(0)
over 30	0.0	(0)
Total	100	103

13. Allan Kornberg, *Canadian Legislative Behavior*, p. 21.

14. Ibid., p. 55.

15. Wahlke, *Legislative System*, pp. 267–86.

16. See John C. Wahlke and Heinz Eulau, "Role as a Basic Unit of Analysis," in Eulau, ed., *Political Behavior*, pp. 24–48.

17. Richard Rose, "Parties, Factions and Tendencies in Britain" in Henry S. Albinski and Lawrence K. Pettit, eds., *European Political Process* (Boston: Allyn and Bacon, 1968), pp. 190–203; Allan Kornberg, "Caucus and Cohesion in Canadian Parliamentary Parties," *American Political Science Review* (March 1966), pp. 83–93; and Leon Epstein, *Political Parties in Western Democracies* (New York: Praeger, 1967), p. 319.

18. Allan Kornberg, "Caucus and Cohesion," pp. 83–93.

19. Leon Epstein, *Political Parties*, p. 319.

20. Donald Matthews, *U.S. Senators and Their World*, p. 184.

21. Lester W. Milbrath, *Political Participation* (Chicago: Rand McNally, 1965), p. 39.

The Socialization of

11

Freshman Legislators:

The Case of Canadian M.P.'s

RICHARD G. PRICE

HAROLD D. CLARKE

ROBERT M. KRAUSE

The political recruitment function consists of the special political socializations which occur in a society "on top of" the general political socialization. They include orientations to the special role and the political system of which it is a part, and to political inputs and outputs.[1]

Despite the prominence accorded this definition in an essay responsible for introducing Gabriel Almond's influential "structural-functional" conceptual framework to political scientists,[2] the subsequent effort devoted to studying political recruitment in the last decade,[3] and the significance generally accorded elite attitudes and behaviour for understanding the operation and stability of contemporary democratic political systems,[4] only a few rigorous empirical studies of the socialization of political elites are available.[5] Even more importantly, however, only a handful of the existing elite socialization studies have dealt explicitly with the question of role socialization *per se* as a dimension of political recruitment.[6] In brief, relatively little is known about how, when, and what political elites learn about their respective roles both prior to and subsequent to incumbency. That literature which does focus on role socialization tends to deal with relationships between a variety of pre- and post-incumbency experiences and particular legislative role orientations. Largely neglected as an influence or phase of the role socialization process is the political campaign,[7] in spite of the presumed importance of elections in democratic politics. In an effort to fill this lacuna in our understanding of elite political behaviour, the present analysis focuses on the role socialization experiences of forty-seven of the fifty freshmen members of the 30th Parliament. It consists of four parts: a description of how legislators define the basic features of the job of a member of Parliament; what they consider the favourable and unfavourable aspects of the position; identification of the various agents and experiences involved in the process of role socialization; and, whether or not their ideas about the job have changed over time. Three specific phases of the role socialization process were isolated in order to assess their effects, if any, on the role socialization process. These periods consist of: the entire period of a legislator's life prior to nomination by his party; the period between the nomination meeting and the election of July 8, 1974, that is, the period of the election campaign; and the abbreviated post-incumbency period between July 8 and the opening session of Parliament on September 30, 1974.

The data for this analysis were gathered through personal interviews with freshman members of Canada's 30th Parliament conducted in the first two weeks of October 1974. Freshmen were defined as members who were elected to Parliament on July 8, 1974, and who had never served previously in the House of Commons. As a consequence, the freshman population consisted of fifty M.P.'s, forty-seven of whom (94 per cent) were interviewed. The survey instrument was divided into two parts. Part I consisted of an eight-page questionnaire containing items dealing with general background information, general political socialization, and prior political experiences. Members were asked to complete the questionnaire after the interview, or at their leisure. Part II, the interview schedule itself, was composed of items dealing with role socialization, role orientations, the nomination process, and questions probing short-term and long-term political ambitions.

PRE-NOMINATION ROLE SOCIALIZATION

Extent

In order to ascertain how much members believed they knew about the job of being an M.P. prior to their nomination, they were asked the following question:

Before your nomination as a candidate in this year's election, how much did
you know about what the job of being a member of Parliament would involve?

The data suggest that, contrary to what might be assumed given the
specialized nature of the legislative job, considerable pre-nomination
political learning does occur. Very few (14.9 per cent) of the M.P.'s
believed that they knew virtually nothing about what being a member
involved. On the other hand, approximately 85 per cent reported knowing
either "a few things" (38.3 per cent) or "a great deal" (46.8 per cent)
about the job. The distribution of these data is almost identical to that
obtained in an earlier study of Canadian provincial backbenchers where,
allowing for some differences in research strategy,[8] 36.5 per cent of all
MLA's reported knowing a great deal, 50.2 per cent a few things, and 13.3
per cent virtually nothing about the job prior to their election as an MLA.
The obvious conclusion with regard to both freshman M.P.'s and provincial MLA's is that considerable role socialization, at least from the perspective of the incumbent, does indeed occur prior to incumbency.

Subjective reports regarding the extent of pre-incumbency knowledge
do not permit one to establish, with a high degree of confidence, the scope
of pre-incumbency job learning, or to determine the content of the freshman M.P.'s concept of the job of being a federal legislator. Thus, those
forty freshmen who said they knew either a few things or a great deal
about the job prior to nomination were asked a subsequent open-ended
question concerning their pre-nomination concept of the job of being a
member of Parliament.

The richness of freshman M.P.s' pre-nomination job concepts is indicated by the fact that 12.8 per cent of the M.P.'s answering the open-
ended question mentioned only one feature of the job, and 72.3 per cent
gave two or more responses. While the modal category was two mentions
(34.2 per cent), three mentions were volunteered by 23.4 per cent of the
M.P.'s, 8.5 per cent mentioned four features, and 6.4 per cent offered five
responses. Another, and perhaps better, strategy for estimating the richness of legislators' images of the job involves ascertaining not simply the
"number of mentions" but the number of different features of the job
identified by legislators. If responses are divided into three types—
constituency and representation, policy, and general parliamentary
responsibilities associated with being a member—the data reveal that, for

the pre-nomination period, 14.9 per cent said they knew virtually nothing about the job, 29.8 per cent mentioned one basic feature of the job, 46.8 per cent two different features, and 8.5 per cent three different aspects of the job. That only slightly over half (55.3 per cent) of the freshman M.P.'s identified more than one feature of their future legislative position suggests that pre-nomination role concepts were not particularly well developed.

Content

Table 1   Freshman M.P.'s Identification of the Major Features of the Job Prior to Nomination

Job Feature	Mention				
	First	*Second*	*Third*	*Fourth*	*Fifth*
Constituency work	68.1%	34.1%	12.8%	2.1%	0.0%
Ombudsman	(36.2)	(6.4)	(8.5)	(2.1)	(0.0)
Communicating with constituents	(4.3)	(12.8)	(0.0)	(0.0)	(0.0)
Constituency contact	(2.1)	(6.4)	(0.0)	(0.0)	(0.0)
Representing constituents	(25.5)	(8.5)	(4.3)	(0.0)	(0.0)
Involvement in policy	8.5%	25.4%	12.7%	6.4%	0.0%
General activities	8.5	12.7	12.7	6.4	6.4
No mention	14.9	27.7	61.7	85.1	93.6
	(47)	(47)	(47)	(47)	(47)

Regarding the content of pre-nomination role socialization, the data in Table 1 reveal, almost without qualification, that freshman M.P.'s recall defining the job principally in terms of their constituency. This emphasis on constituency work and representation overshadows matters of public policy and such required activities as attending House debates, committee work, and caucus responsibilities. Whenever freshmen did discuss the job in terms of public policy, party, or House activities, these things were generally mentioned only after making a reference to the constituency-service or representational features of the job. The following comments provide a more concrete appreciation of how M.P.'s viewed their future jobs in the pre-nomination period:

I'm an ombudsman. It involves representing constituents to government and the government to your constituency. Day-to-day correspondence with ministers can get things changed.

To take the concerns or problems of my constituents and direct them to the proper departments for solution. I know how to get around such customs problems as fees on farm implements because of my previous experiences.

The riding of —— has traditionally been a rather visible constituency—a highly politicized constituency. We should have a great deal to say about grain, transportation, and the general approach of government in Canada.

Writing and establishing policy and doing it in light of my perspective and that of my constituents.

To solicit cabinet ministers for projects in my riding, represent the riding generally, and legislate.

Overall, the data in Table 1 are striking in two respects. First, the pre-nomination emphasis on constituency work and the representation of constituents generally is consistent with how the Canadian mass public views the job of a member of Parliament. According to a 1972 Gallup report, Canadians have a very clear-cut opinion on what a member should do if he finds his own view on an issue at odds with that of a majority of his constituents.[9] In such a circumstance, people suggested that an M.P. should vote according to the majority viewpoint in his riding. Second, while the open-ended question on pre-nomination legislative role socialization was not intended to yield data compatible with the concepts of representational role focus or style as they have been conventionally measured by political scientists, the emphasis on constituency in the data in this study are congruent with Kornberg's earlier observation that the predominant representational role style among members of Parliament is that of delegate-servant.[10] On the other hand, in terms of representational role focus, the present data do not confirm Kornberg's observation that many legislators conceptualize their constituency in national as opposed to local terms.[11]

Evaluations

How prospective M.P.'s evaluate their future job is important in the sense that such evaluations may subsequently affect their political style, how they adapt to legislative life, their desire (or lack thereof) for institutional reforms and eventual political career patterns. Thus, an exploration of freshman M.P.S' perceptions of both the positive and negative aspects of their future job is in order.

The data on pre-nomination job evaluations indicate that freshmen varied considerably in the absolute number of favourable aspects of the job they identified prior to nomination. At one end of the continuum, 14.9 per cent mentioned nothing favourable about the job, and, at the other, 19.1 per cent mentioned three or more favourable things about the job. Most freshman M.P.'s, however, mentioned either one (36.2 per cent) or two (29.8 per cent) aspects of the job which they personally found appealing. Basically freshmen perceived the job favourably for two reasons. On the one hand, 46 per cent of the M.P.'s assessed the job favourably because they believed it would provide them with an opportunity to help constituents, get personally involved in national issues, and to some extent help to improve Canadian society generally. These statements by two members are reasonably typical of those dealing with society.

I wanted to do some good for Canada and the people in my riding.

Getting answers back to people. There is a lot of satisfaction in helping people with their problems.

On the other hand, 54 per cent of the legislators evaluated the job positively because they appraised the position primarily in personal-instrumental terms. They wanted to be a member of Parliament because the job involved opportunities for self-development, the wielding of political power, and an increase in material gain and social prestige.

I love politics and wanted to expand my own knowledge.

I would be in a position to telephone a federal or provincial authority and get action. My name would carry weight. I would help people get jobs and help in court cases for fishermen. I would be in a power position.

Freshman M.P.'s are not political neophytes and, hence, one would not expect them to take a "Panglossian" view of the political world. A substantial proportion of those elected to Parliament for the first time in 1974 had been active in party politics (78.7 per cent) or had actually held local or provincial public elective office (21.3 per cent) prior to their nomination. Such experiences would, one might think, partially condition how potential candidates evaluate the job in negative as well as in positive terms.

When members of Parliament formally sought their party's nomination they did so recognizing that the job of an M.P. had some unfavourable aspects to it. With regard simply to how many negative aspects were identified by M.P.'s, 10.6 per cent mentioned no unfavourable aspects and 23.4 per cent mentioned three things about being an M.P. which they considered unfavourable. Most members, however, mentioned one (25.5 per cent) or two (40.4 per cent) unfavourable things they perceived prior to the nomination.

How potential freshmen assessed the negative aspects of being an M.P. prior to their nomination is interesting in several respects. First, some hint of occupational role strain is evident since 21.3 per cent of the responses dealt specifically with the fact that M.P.'s believed their constituents entertained an unfavourable view of politics. Parenthetically, it might be noted that a variety of public opinion data indicate that those members who discussed the job of legislator in relation to this dimension of Canadian political culture are correct in their assessments that many Canadians visualize politics in Ottawa and elsewhere in at least a partially negative fashion.[12]

Secondly, freshman M.P.'s did not respond to the question on unfavourable aspects of the job by underlining job insecurity. This lack of emphasis on job insecurity is particularly striking given three facets of recent political competition in Canada. First, minority governments, with their attendant inherent instability, have occurred with sufficient frequency in the past decade or so (1962, 1963, 1965, and 1972) that aspirants for federal office might well have entertained the possibility of being elected to Parliament in 1974, yet have foreseen the necessity of seeking re-election within two years. Secondly, the political climate was extremely volatile in the spring of 1974. Many political analysts were either unwilling to predict the outcome of the 1974 federal election, or they emphasized the likelihood of a minority government, without predicting whether the Liberals or Conservatives would assume office. Thirdly, election data show that many freshmen eventually faced intense inter-party competition within their own constituencies.[13] In light of the above, it is mildly perplexing to discover that job insecurity was mentioned by so few members (three) when the political environment was highly uncertain.

Thirdly, most students of Canadian politics take it for granted that backbenchers generally lack influence due to the lack of suitable institutional mechanisms facilitating meaningful backbench inputs into the public policy process and, hence, turn their attention to constituency work. The data reveal, however, that only 14.9 per cent of the legislators referred specifically to lack of influence as an unfavourable characteristic of the job. To some extent, the low salience associated with the perceived lack of influence is understandable in light of reforms undertaken by the Trudeau government since 1968. This is true, in particular, with regard to changes made in the committee system allowing for the existence of twenty standing committees which meet regularly every week. Aspiring M.P.'s may well have presumed that committee work would provide them with an opportunity to influence policy outside of party caucus. Another possible explanation is that many freshman M.P.'s simply took their relative lack of influence as given, a "necessary" feature of the Canadian form of parliamentary government to which they had long been reconciled.

Fourthly, complaints about career sacrifice were surprisingly rare. To the extent that career sacrifice involves a loss of income, the small proportion of members pinpointing career sacrifice as an unfavourable dimension of becoming an M.P. (4.3 per cent) is surprising given that 48.9 per cent enjoyed a total family income exceeding that which they could hope to have as an M.P. Obviously, then, whatever career sacrifices had to be made by freshmen were presumably outweighed by other more favourable intangible perquisites.

Finally, it should be noted that many responses (46.8 per cent of the "first mentions") concerned those aspects of being an M.P. which involved "personal inconveniences"; for example, necessarily neglecting one's family, travelling, and the loss of privacy which results from becoming a member of Parliament.

In conclusion, the following comments are representative of responses volunteered by freshman M.P.'s about unfavourable aspects of the job:

Dealing with the public's perception that the backbencher is an ineffectual "desk thumper."

I had only a little idea of the degree of responsibility of an M.P. M.P.s *do a lot of work!* [respondent's emphasis], "bust their —— for the people," yet people are unsympathetic and cruel about it when a member gets clobbered at the polls. People don't know what is involved.

The political aspect of the job. There is no permanence in it—no security in the long run. You also have to neglect your usual work or career.

The isolation of the job, especially for someone 1,800 miles from the constituency. Besides, travelling is a pain in the neck.

Agents

Over the past decade, a substantial effort has been devoted to analysing the recruitment of political party workers and public office-holders in North America, the usual concern involving an attempt to resolve the problem of why some men and women are politically active and others are not. One set of variables receiving considerable attention is that associated with the process of political socialization. Scholars have discerned that a multitude of agents may be involved in this process, including, for example, such diverse agents and influences as the family, peer groups, school, mass media, political parties, and the general socio-political environment. The assumption underlying the following analysis is best explicated, perhaps, in *The Legislative System,* where Wahlke and his colleagues discuss the development of role orientations:

Legislators do not begin to acquire and form their legislative role concepts and orientations only at the official dawn of their legislative careers. Before that moment they have probably heard and thought about legislative work more than has the average citizen and, in many cases, even before it occurred to them that they might some day hold such office.[14]

While specific role orientations are not the subject of analysis here, how legislators defined and evaluated their job prior to nomination is, and, as a consequence, it is important to assess the contributions of different agents of socialization to freshman members' conceptions of the position of an M.P. The results of the investigation of the agents of role socialization in the pre-nomination period are displayed Table 2.

Those agents receiving the greatest attention simply in terms of frequency of mention are the mass media (81 per cent), discussions with public office-holders (66 per cent), working for a political party (67 per cent), materials learned in university (50 per cent), and participation in community organizations (38 per cent). Previous analyses of mass publics

Table 2   Pre-Nomination Agents Providing M.P.'s with Information About the Job of M.P.

Agents and Experiences	Agent Mentioned*	Agent Mentioned As Most Important
Discussions with family or other relatives	35.7%	7.1%
Discussions with friends not active in politics	19.0	0.0
Materials learned in public or high school	26.2	2.4
Materials learned in college or university	50.0	9.5
From discussions with public office-holders	66.2	23.8
Following political affairs in the mass media	80.9	4.8
Working for a political party	66.6	21.4
By holding public elective office	19.0	16.6
Participating in community organizations, professional organizations, or trade unions	38.0	2.4
Participating in fraternal organizations	12.0	0.0
Other:		
Government experience	7.1	4.8
Political friends	9.5	4.8
Miscellaneous	2.4	2.4

*Percentages exceed 100 because more than one agent could be cited.

have confirmed the importance of the family as an agent of general political socialization. Research generally has discovered, for example, that the family plays a significant role in the development of an initial interest in politics, the acquisition of a party identification, and development of a sense of political efficacy. This sample of elites suggests that the family is also involved in the more specific process of role socialization. At the same time, however, the family appears to be a less important agent of role socialization than several others in the sense that the family was mentioned less often (35.7 per cent) than the previously mentioned agents. Additionally, agents which do emerge as widely recognized influences of job learning are those potentially involved in the legislative recruitment process itself. For example, working for a political party and discussing politics with public office-holders may all occur shortly before the nomination. Thus, the data in column one of Table 2 suggest, but do not document conclusively, that what learning about the job of an M.P.

does occur in the pre-nomination period may, indeed, take place shortly before the nominating meeting. The probability that considerable pre-nomination learning occurs around nomination time is strengthened by Kornberg's observation that Canadian political parties are active partici-pants in the recruitment process, particularly in competitive constituencies where the outcome is in doubt.[15] In this regard, nearly two-thirds of these freshman legislators were elected in what, by any reasonable criterion, would be judged to be competitive ridings.

When M.P.'s were asked to single out the most important agent of pre-nomination job learning, political experiences that probably occur in adulthood assume even greater prominence. While discussions with office-holders (23.8 per cent) and working for a party (21.4 per cent) remain the most salient agents of learning, the value of previous public elective office-holding is recognized by an additional 16.6 per cent of the M.P.'s. In summary, then, the data suggest that freshman members tended to consider experiences closely associated with the nomination or adult political experience more generally as the primary agents of legislative role socialization in the pre-nomination period.

ROLE SOCIALIZATION IN THE CAMPAIGN PERIOD

Analyses of political campaigns have seldom focused on what Froman refers to as the latent functions of campaigns, that is, on the extent to which "campaigns influence the agenda of political issues to be discussed and acted upon by the elected candidates."[16] Furthermore, suggests Froman:

This, perhaps, is one of the most important functions of campaigns: the inclusion, exclusion, and crystallization of issues and problems on the agenda of office holders. Campaigns are also likely to be instrumental in creating, rein-forcing, and perhaps even changing attitudes about issues and problems. . . .[17]

To the extent that scholars have focused their attention on the latent effects of political campaigns in Canada and the United States, it appears that statistically significant relationships do occasionally exist between inter-party constituency competition and the development and/or change of representational role orientations. In Canada, for example, Kornberg discovered a modest correlation between subjective competition and representational role style (Gamma = .24) but not representational role focus.[18] As one might expect, members of Parliament, perceiving their districts as very competitive, tended to adopt a delegate-servant orientation.[19] On the other hand, no statistically significant relationship existed between objective constituency competition and representational role-taking.[20] Similarly, according to the analysis of Clarke, Price, and Krause, provincial legislators in Canada were not more inclined to spend a higher proportion of their time attending to constituency work as a consequence of either objective competition (both within their constituency and province) or subjective perceptions of competition.[21] In the United States, however, state legislators and congressmen tended to adopt a district orientation with increases in political competition, and the representational role style of congressmen (that is, being a constituency delegate) was similarly affected by district competition.[22]

The present analysis of campaigns as one agent or experience in the role socialization process does not focus directly upon the development of specific representational role orientations but rather upon the extent to which freshman members changed their ideas about the job of an M.P. as a consequence of the campaign; how job concepts changed as a consequence of campaigning; and what kinds of campaign experience contributed to members' altered concepts of their job.

When queried concerning alterations in job concept as a result of campaign experiences, 4.3 per cent of the M.P.'s reported their job concept changed "a great deal," and a further 34.0 per cent said their job concept changed "somewhat." Fully 61.7 per cent reported no change whatsoever as a result of campaign experiences. As one would expect, campaign learning occurred most frequently among those members who reported knowing "virtually nothing" prior to the nomination. To a considerably lesser extent, candidates stating that they knew "a great deal" about the job in the pre-nomination period reported learning something about the job of being an M.P. during the campaign for parliamentary office. Overall, although the statistical relationship between how much legislators knew about the job before being nominated and how much they subsequently learned about it during the campaign is relatively modest (Gamma = −.15), the tendencies in the data are, nonetheless, plausible.

Table 3   The Effects of the Political Campaign on Learning About the
Job of a Member of Parliament

Amount of Campaign Learning	Extent of Pre-Nomination Knowledge		
	A Great Deal	A Few Things	Virtually Nothing
Learned somewhat or a great deal in the campaign period	36.4%	33.3%	57.1%
No campaign learning	63.6	66.7	42.9
	(22)	(18)	(7)

Gamma = −.15

At first blush, it is perhaps surprising that so few freshmen changed
their concept of the job as a direct consequence of campaigning. Yet it
should be recalled that many freshman members of the 30th Parliament
were by no means lacking in political experience at the time of this
particular campaign. Over three-quarters (78.7 per cent) had been party
activists, and had, in all likelihood, been through the rigours of campaigning before on behalf of other candidates. Furthermore, the fact that 21.3
per cent previously held local or provincial office means that some M.P.'s
had previous campaign experience as a candidate. In addition, 23.4 per
cent of the freshmen had sought a party nomination prior to 1974. All in
all, then, the fact that extensive changes in how freshmen perceived their
job did not occur is, perhaps, partially explained by their extensive pre-
1974 political experience.

Nonetheless, that 38.3 per cent of the members reported some changes
in their basic ideas about the job requires some elaboration. Hence, those
legislators reporting some change in their ideas about the job were asked
to specify the nature of these changes. The data on change in job concept
as a result of the campaign are summarized in Table 4. These data are
instructive in several respects.

First, although slightly in excess of one-third of the members reported
some change in their image or concept of the job as a consequence of
campaigning, the extent to which opinions changed evidently was not
substantial. In this regard, the above mentioned tendency for legislators
to place themselves in the "somewhat" rather than the "a great deal"

Table 4   Basic Dimension of the Job of an M.P. Changed as a Result of Campaigning

Dimension of Job Changed	Number of Mentions		
	One	Two	Three
Opinions about constituents and the constituency	33.3%	11.1%	5.6%
Attitudes towards national policy	5.6	5.6	5.6
Opinions about general responsibilities of the job	61.1	27.8	0.0
No mention	0.0	55.6	88.9
	(18)	(18)	(18)

category of change is the finding that less than 50 per cent of the freshmen mentioning a change in job concept cited at least two features of the job which changed, and only two M.P.'s cited three changes. Thus, while changing one's perception about even one aspect of the job may, indeed, be important for that person, it seems likely that for most members, only modest changes in job concept occurred. Secondly, as the data in Table 4 document, almost no changes took place in legislators' attitudes toward policy or the policy process as a direct consequence of political campaigning. Thirdly, changes about the job accruing from the campaign tended to involve the significance of constituency work (33.3 per cent of first mentions), or an increased realization of how complex and time-consuming an M.P.'s responsibilities are (61.1 per cent of first mentions). Overall, then, to the extent that the campaign changed M.P.'s ideas about the job, the areas affected were often rather pedestrian: for example, learning that you can't please everyone, that the job involves heavy responsibilities, that travelling is seldom fun, that some loss of privacy occurs, and that campaigning is hard work. In effect, the influence of the campaign was succinctly summed up by one member:

It [the campaign] made me more aware that political involvement might be "more than I could chew." The job was more important than I imagined. It requires a total commitment. I began to feel sorry for M.P.'s.

Finally, an attempt was made to identify those particular campaign experiences contributing to changes in job image. In this regard, the data reveal that the types of experiences ostensibly responsible for contributing to changing perceptions of the job are exactly the kinds of activities candidates generally are expected to engage in—for example, attending all-candidates meetings, canvassing, and talking with voters about local or national matters (72 per cent of the first mentions)—or might voluntarily pursue under special circumstances—for example, discussing the campaign with former members or other members of Parliament. Additionally, the data suggest that most freshmen who reported changing their ideas about the job recalled one campaign experience, or at most two, as being involved in changing their perceptions—and usually those experiences involved constituents.

POST-ELECTION PERIOD

Extent

Even though the period between the election of July 8 and the opening of the first session of Parliament on September 30 was only slightly over two and a half months long, it was not assumed that this period was inconsequential for the process of legislative role socialization. Rather, the post-election period involved, for many M.P.'s, a considerable and unavoidable shift in their life-styles and exposure to hitherto unexperienced contacts with the political world. Furthermore, since political socialization experiences do not necessarily involve passive acceptance of available stimuli,[23] it was assumed that at least some of the freshmen, especially those eager to be successful, would avail themselves of the hiatus between the election and the opening of Parliament to actively seek out information about their new positions. Leaving aside questions regarding the content or agents of role socialization for the moment and focusing on the extent of socialization, the data confirm the assumption that the post-election period can be of significance for legislative role socialization. Over two-thirds of the freshmen (71.1 per cent) changed their conception of the job "somewhat" (11.1 per cent) or "a great deal" (60.0 per cent) after the election. That these changes tended to be matters of degree rather than wholesale shifts is indicated by the datum that twenty-seven of the thirty-two M.P.'s (84.4 per cent) reporting a change place themselves in the "somewhat" category.

Not unexpectedly, the significance of the post-election period for role socialization varies inversely with the amount of knowledge freshmen

Table 5   Subjective Assessment of Knowledge of Job in Pre-Nomination Period by Subjective Assessment of Extent of Change in Conception of Job in Post-Election Period*

Post-Election Change in Job Conception	Pre-Nomination Knowledge of Job		
	A Great Deal	A Few Things	Virtually Nothing
A Great Deal or Somewhat	59.1%	76.5%	100.0%
None	40.9	23.5	0.0
	(22)	(17)	(6)

Gamma = −.58
*Missing data (N = 2) eliminated from the analysis.

report possessing about the job in the pre-nomination period. Whereas 59.1 per cent of the M.P.'s reporting "a great deal" of pre-nomination knowledge indicated post-election socialization, all those stating they knew "virtually nothing" prior to nomination mentioned a change in job concept after the election (see Table 5). The strength of this relationship is indicated by a Gamma of −.58. Some freshmen then, recognizing their naïveté about what being a member of Parliament actually involves, evidently use the post-election period to acquaint themselves with their new position, or at the very least, find themselves quickly placed in situations where learning about the job of an M.P. is unavoidable.

Content

M.P.'s reporting a change in job conception during the post-election period were asked about the content of this change. Analysis of the responses to this question indicates that only 40.1 per cent of the eligible M.P.'s (N = 32) gave more than one response and a mere 15.6 per cent gave three responses. These data provide further evidence that the scope of change in job conception, as a consequence of post-election influences and activities, tends to be rather modest.

As the data in Table 6 document, post-election changes in job concept were predominantly of two types: first, those dealing with relationships between an M.P. and his or her constituents, primarily in the area of so-called constituency "case-load";[24] and secondly, changes involving learning about the job in a more general sense, its possibilities, its limitations,

Table 6   Content of Change in Job in Post-Election Period

Job Feature	Number of Mentions		
	One	Two	Three
Constituency work	31.2%	6.2%	3.1%
Partisan norms	6.2	3.1	0.0
General activities	59.4	28.1	12.5
Other	0.0	3.1	0.0
N.A.	2.1	0.0	0.0
No mention	0.0	59.5	84.4
	(32)	(32)	(32)

and its demands. Not surprisingly, given previous research which indicates that the norm of party discipline is acquired through more general political socialization processes,[25] only a few legislators mentioned the party or norms of partisanship.

The types of changes mentioned by freshmen can perhaps best be appreciated by a perusal of the following sample comments. The largest single category of responses (59.4 per cent of the first mentions) dealt with various miscellaneous features of the job. Several M.P.'s, for example, mentioned a growing recognition of their relative lack of influence in the legislative process:

I became more realistic and less "euphoric." I learned where the legislative machinery fits *vis-à-vis* cabinet. In a sense, I came to Ottawa believing an M.P. is more potent than he actually is.

I have more doubts about how efficiently M.P.'s can play the legislative role because of their lack of expertise compared to the bureaucrats. The legislative role is much less direct than I thought.

I learned not to be in a hurry. Every new M.P. wants quick change. Forget it. You will only wear yourself out. Go through channels.

Others were impressed by the amount of work the job entailed, especially in the area of responding to inquiries and pleas for help from constituents:

My volume of mail is heavy and I need to tend to this, that, and every other thing. Sitting in the House has provided a learning experience, that is, finding out how to speak, what to say in order to have an impact. In short, I may have to learn a new style.

On July 12th, I came to Ottawa and spent two weeks here learning about the job, and hired a good staff. Then I got right into the ombudsman role. I had a lot of success in this regard in setting things right. I learned to work quietly and not to try and accomplish things by being rough. I set up an efficient riding organization.

On the other hand, some M.P.'s expressed the view that constituency service work or the job, generally, was actually less onerous than they had anticipated:[26]

I tended to exaggerate the impact of constituents—good secretaries take care of their problems.

I learned that if you hire two top-notch secretaries, 90 per cent of your work is done. So, I hired two from —— staff.

Less pressure than I had thought.

The effects of post-election role socialization, then, would seem to be conditioned by legislators' pre-election expectations about the job. Since these pre-election images of what being an M.P. involves vary from one legislator to another, the post-election stage of the role socialization process ostensibly has no uniform impact on M.P.'s.

Evaluations

Freshmen, in addition, were asked explicitly whether or not their evaluation of the favourable and unfavourable aspects of the job altered during the post-election period. Given the variance in the data on changing job conceptions analysed above, and the differing job conceptions held by M.P.'s when they entered the post-election period, one might anticipate that M.P.'s would mention favourable and unfavourable features of the job with approximately equal frequency. This expectation is borne out by the data. Fifty per cent of the M.P.'s stating that their conception of the job changed in the post-election period denied that these changes involved favourable or unfavourable evaluations. Of the remaining 50 per cent, the number of favourable comments on "first mention" is slightly greater than the number of unfavourable responses. Furthermore, the number of favourable and unfavourable comments is equally balanced for the second and third mentions; however, the smaller number of members making more than one mention suggests that incremental rather than comprehensive job re-evaluations are the norm.

When asked specifically how their evaluation of the position had changed, M.P.'s mentioned a variety of job features. Constituency service tasks, the influence (or lack thereof) of the position, and the realities of being separated from one's family were the most popular themes. Interestingly enough, not a single member spoke of constituency service work in a negative way. The following two responses are typical of how freshmen evaluate constituency service work:

I am pleased with the settlement of problems for individuals, the little things that matter to people.

Handling of constituency problems and breaking up bureaucratic problems provide some satisfaction.

Several members did mention a change in their personal evaluation of the influence potential of the job. Some believed they could exercise more influence than they previously assumed. For others, who may perhaps have had an unrealistically high initial estimation of how much influence could be exercised by backbenchers,[27] the post-election period provided their first confrontation with the realities of the situation confronting a freshman M.P. and, hence, they found themselves less influential than they had previously estimated. Moreover, as the following examples indicate, some members were quite explicit regarding *how* they could (or could not) exercise influence, whereas others were much less specific. Legislators with a favourable view of their influence potential reported that:

. . . When you get into the nitty-gritty you *do* have power, for example, L.I.P grants regarding winter works. [Also] power in caucus if you want to use it. You can put a Minister on the spot, or play a game, hoping to become a Parliamentary Secretary, and so forth.

I assumed that an M.P. has more power than he does.

[There is an] opportunity of doing something more than the majority of citizens can: [I] can affect people's lives. [It is] sobering to realize the impact I can have on people's lives.

Finally, members referred to effects of the job on their personal lives or to the general pro's and con's of being a member of Parliament. Again, as the following statements illustrate, some of the comments involved positive evaluations, whereas others were negative:

[I'm] running all the time, various functions, constituency tasks. Things pile up dramatically. [It's] a traumatic situation moving to Ottawa, also a new home in ———. [I] need to find free time.

. . . less pressure was favourable. I like setting my own schedule. I control how pressured I will be.

I became very anxious, surprised by the degree of "strangeness." This is a game for loners. I was shocked to discover what the game of politics involved. I'm beginning to understand the attitudes needed to be a successful politician.

Agents

The data in Table 7 provide evidence that several agents played a part in the post-election role socialization of freshmen. For example, five of the agents were mentioned by more than 40 per cent of the M.P.'s. These agents included most of the actors who interact with M.P.'s on a fairly regular basis: talking with other M.P.'s (53.1 per cent), civil servants (40.6 per cent), and constituents (43.7 per cent). As one might expect, more freshmen (56.2 per cent) mentioned the party caucus than any other single agent, experience or institution of post-election learning. In this regard it might be noted that members of Parliament often attend more than one caucus within the same party. For example, Liberals from Toronto attended the Metro-Toronto caucus, and the Ontario Liberal caucus, in addition to regular meetings of the national party caucus. That the caucus is mentioned more often than any other agent at least suggests that caucus was one arena where freshmen were "learning the ropes" not only by conversing with other freshmen or backbenchers, but with party leaders as well. Noticeably absent from this inventory of role socializing agents is the legislative standing committee. This is not surprising in that although Mitchell Sharp (President of the Privy Council) had announced the membership of standing committees on October 3, 1974, most committees had not met at the time these interviews were conducted.

Somewhat surprising in light of previous research indicating that, contrary to the conventional wisdom, interest groups do interact with

M.P.'s and that M.P.'s value the information supplied by these groups,[28] are the findings that only 15.6 per cent of the freshmen cited interest groups as an agent of socialization and not one member judged interest groups as "most important." To explain these findings, one might speculate that interest group representatives had insufficient time to contact new members, many of whom had been in Ottawa only a short time. Another possibility which cannot be ruled out is that freshmen thought it would be inappropriate to admit that their conceptions of the job had been influenced in any way by interest groups. This possibility would not appear to be a strong one in that Presthus' research indicates that most M.P.'s view interest groups as legitimate actors in the legislative system. On the other hand, it may be that the legitimacy ascribed to interest groups develops over time as members come into contact with lobbyists.[29]

Finally, only slightly over one-quarter (28.1 per cent) of the freshmen mention explicit instruction as a mode of role socialization. This datum is not surprising in that, as far as the authors were able to determine, only the Progressive Conservatives established a program of instruction for incoming members. Availing themselves of the services of a doctoral candidate in political science specializing in parliamentary procedure, the Conservatives established a series of seminars to instruct new members on topics ranging from proper decorum in the House, to methods involved in performing constituency service tasks, to various facets of the legislative process. The Liberals, even though they had the largest proportion of the incoming freshmen, evidently did not feel the need to set up a formal program. The NDP and Social Credit parties, with one new member each, could hardly have been expected to establish such programs.

Turning now to the "most important" agents of post-election socialization, the data in Table 7 reveal that members do not agree upon any single significant agent of post-election learning. Rather, the picture is one of considerable heterogeneity, with no more than 25 per cent of the M.P.'s selecting any one agent, and only three of the thirteen possible agents (including the "other" category) mentioned by more than 7 per cent of the respondents. "Attendance and/or participation in party caucus" was the most frequently cited experience (25 per cent). Above, it was noted that caucus provides a forum where freshmen can interact with other M.P.'s (freshmen and non-freshmen) and with party leaders. There is also the possibility that the party leaders use caucus meetings (in

Table 7   Post-Election Agents of Legislative Role Socialization

Agents and Experiences	Agent Mentioned*	Agent Mentioned as Most Important
Talking informally with other M.P.'s	53.1%	15.6%
Attendance and/or participation in party caucus	56.2	25.0
Talking with interest group representatives	15.6	0.0
Talking with civil servants	40.6	3.1
Talking with constituents	43.7	21.9
Setting up a constituency office	21.9	0.0
Experiences associated with moving to Ottawa	46.9	6.3
Interview by mass media	15.6	0.0
Instruction by party leaders	28.1	6.3
Talking informally with party activists who are not public office-holders	18.7	3.1
Talking informally with former M.P.'s	25.0	6.3
Talking informally with other public elective office-holders (M.L.A.'s, local councilmen, etc.)	15.6	0.0
Other	9.4	3.1
N.A.	0.0	9.3
	(32)	(32)

*Percentages exceed 100 because more than one agent could be cited.

addition to a special ad hoc system of instruction for the freshmen) as opportunities to provide cues to freshmen regarding what the leadership considers "proper" behaviour. Or, it may simply be that freshmen learn in caucus meetings by observing the behaviour of more senior colleagues. In any event, the finding that caucus is the most frequently mentioned agency of post-election role socialization, taken in conjunction with the results of similar research at the provincial level where a plurality (34.2 per cent) of the MLA's cited caucus as the most important agent of post-incumbency role socialization, strongly suggests that caucus, in addition to its classic functions of maintaining party cohesion, devising strategies to deal with impending House business, formulating party policy, and providing a vehicle for backbenchers to vent their grievances and frustrations,[30] plays an important part in the legislative role socialization process.

Another post-election socialization experience considered the most important by a sizable group of M.P.'s (21.9 per cent) was "talking with constituents." That new members should cite such conversations is not unexpected, since many M.P.'s reported spending a considerable proportion of their working time in the post-election period setting up constituency offices and performing constituency service tasks. In this regard, several M.P.'s spontaneously mentioned being inundated by requests for aid immediately after their electoral victory and, in some cases, even prior to the election. It might be recalled that some M.P.s' evaluations of the job (both favourable and unfavourable) were influenced by experiences associated with trying to handle a perceived "floodtide" of constituent requests. Then, too, the relative frequency with which freshmen interacted with constituents may be due to the fact that many of the new M.P.'s remained in their constituencies until shortly before the opening of Parliament on September 30, and, hence, had only minimal opportunities to interact with possible socialization agents in Ottawa. Again, since Parliament was not yet in session and parliamentary committees had not yet met, socialization experiences which might have resulted from participation in these legislative arenas was not a possibility.

CONCLUSION

On September 30, 1974, fifty freshmen officially became members of Parliament. Based upon interviews with forty-seven of these freshman members, it was clearly confirmed that an abundance of experiences helped contribute to their perceptions of the job prior to the nomination; further, incremental adjustments occurred in their impressions and evaluations about the job as a consequence of the political campaign, and as a consequence of political activities occurring in the abbreviated post-election period. Hence, in this analysis at least, legislators either pursue or accept the nomination of their party with preconceived impressions about being a member, only to find that these same impressions change perceptibly in a relatively short period of time.

Despite the lengthy description of legislative role socialization presented in this paper, many relevant topics remain to be investigated. Most obvious is the need to examine role socialization during the post-incumbency period. The results of previous research with Canadian provincial MLA's[31] and the findings of Price and Bell's study of California freshman assembly-men[32] suggest that considerable change and development in legislative role orientations can occur "on the job." Suggestions about the potential importance of the post-incumbency period can be found in the present study, since many legislators reported changing their concept of the job in the truncated period between their election and opening of Parliament —that is, before having contact with many such prominent features of legislative politics as House debates and committee sessions. In order to provide an adequate description of the entire role socialization process, then, an investigation of M.P.s' post-incumbency learning is essential.

In addition to broadening the scope of inquiry by encompassing the post-incumbency period, future legislative role socialization research needs to focus on a number of topics, at least some of which should be investigated in both the pre- and post-incumbency periods. One potentially important set of explanatory variables not utilized in the present research concerns the personalities of the freshman M.P.'s. The extent to which pre- and post-incumbency role socialization is shaped by basic personality characteristics such as ego strength or the level of self-esteem is an important empirical question. Without entering into a complex discussion of the impact of personality on political behaviour[33] previous research, in particular Barber's analysis of Connecticut state legislators,[34] makes it reasonable to assume that the nature, extent, and outcome of the role socialization process will vary in accordance with individual personality differences.

Another promising avenue for future study focuses on the fashion in which inter-party (or even intra-party) differences in recruitment processes are linked to role socialization. In Canada, existing research suggests that the candidates nominated by the several political parties vary substantially in terms of their social background as well as in terms of ideologies or belief systems.[35] These variables may, in turn, affect the serial processes of pre- and post-incumbency role socialization. With regard to social background variables, M.P.'s with high status "brokerage" occupations presumably have been exposed to different stimuli in the pre-nomination period than individuals with lower status "non-brokerage" occupations. In turn, the skills and predispositions acquired by virtue of practising a particular type of occupation may influence an M.P.'s style of behaviour in the post-incumbency period with the end result being exposure to different stimuli and, hence, differences in post-incumbency role socialization.

Then, too, the tendencies of parties to recruit candidates with differing ideologies or belief systems may be significant for understanding legislative role socialization. First, ideological differences between M.P.'s in the four major parties may reflect specific differences in pre-nomination conceptions of the job of a member of Parliament, differences which have their origins in more general conceptions of the political world. Additionally, and similar to the argument made above about brokerage and non-brokerage occupations, M.P.s' ideologies may affect their behaviour as incumbents and thus influence which stimuli they are exposed to in the post-incumbency period. Differences in this regard will thereby affect the nature of post-incumbency role socialization.

Finally, there are additional reasons to believe that the content of post-incumbency role socialization will vary not only from one legislative system to the next, but between parties within a single legislature. Recent research at the provincial level in Canada indicates that variations between parties' competitive positions will lead, over time, to the development of distinctive styles of opposition, with members of parties in differing competitive positions emphasizing different aspects of their legislative role orientations.[36] It would seem plausible, then, that freshman members of different parties will be exposed to varying cues from more senior party colleagues; in this case, the content of post-incumbency role socialization will vary from one party to the next within a single system. Extending this line of reasoning, one can hypothesize that the degree of variance in cues to which freshmen are exposed will be a function of the degree to which patterns of inter-party competition are stable over relatively long periods. More generally, one can combine this argument with some of the previous suggestions regarding future research and propose that the net result of the interaction of system levels of inter-party competition, differential recruitment patterns between parties, and the results of post-incumbency role socialization will be the development of relatively distinct "legislative political cultures," which will vary not only at the system level, but also within systems by party. These legislative political cultures, as components of the more general elite political cultures of political systems, will in turn influence both directly and in a more indirect and subtle fashion, the role socialization of successive "classes" of freshman legislators.

NOTES

1. Gabriel A. Almond, "Introduction: A Functional Approach to Comparative Politics," *The Politics of the Developing Areas*, eds. G. A. Almond and J. S. Coleman (Princeton: Princeton University Press, 1960), p. 32.

2. In their analysis of "Competing Paradigms in Comparative Politics," Holt and Richardson state that "the most widely heralded and best known structural-functional paradigm in political science is that developed by Gabriel A. Almond. The extent to which Almond's framework has penetrated the discipline in just a few years is remarkable." Robert Holt and John M. Richardson, Jr., "Competing Paradigms in Comparative Politics" in R. Holt and J. Turner, eds., *The Methodology of Comparative Research* (New York: The Free Press, 1970), p. 33.

3. For a classification and brief summary of the literature on political recruitment, see Allan Kornberg, Harold D. Clarke and George L. Watson, "Toward a Model of Parliamentary Recruitment in Canada," in Allan Kornberg, ed., *Legislatures in Comparative Perspective* (New York: David McKay, 1973), pp. 250–81.

4. See, for example, G. Almond and S. Verba, *The Civic Culture* (Princeton: Princeton University Press, 1963), chapter 15.

5. Concerning the dearth of studies of elite socialization, see Jack Dennis, "Major Problems of Political Socialization Research," *Midwest Journal of Political Science*, vol. 12 (February 1968), pp. 85–114. On the socialization of legislative elites in Canada, see Allan Kornberg and Norman C. Thomas, "The Political Socialization of National Legislative Elites in the United States and Canada," *Journal of Politics*, vol. 27 (November 1965), pp. 761–75.

6. All of the published work refers to studies carried out in the United States. See Kenneth Prewitt, Heinz Eulau and Betty H. Zisk, "Political Socialization and Political Roles," *Public Opinion Quarterly*, vol. 30 (1966), pp. 569–82; Charles G. Bell and Charles M. Price, "Pre-Legislative Sources of Representational Roles," *Midwest Journal of Political Science*, vol. 13 (May 1969), pp. 254–70; C. G. Bell and C. M. Price, "Socializing California Freshman Assemblymen: The Role of Individuals and Legislative Sub-Groups," *Western Political Quarterly*, vol. 23 (March 1970), pp. 166–79; C. G. Bell and C. M. Price, "The Rules of the Game: Political Fact or Academic Fancy?", *Journal of Politics*, vol. 32 (November 1970), pp. 839–55; and Herbert B. Asher, "The Learning of Legislative Norms," *American Political Science Review*, vol. 67 (June 1973), pp. 499–513.

7. The effects of political campaigns on the attitudes and opinions of successful and unsuccessful candidates for public office has not been emphasized, although scholars have focused considerable attention on competition and its effects on various dimensions of legislative behaviour. Exceptions include Lewis A. Froman, Jr., "A Realistic Approach to Campaign Strategies and Tactics," in M. Kent Jennings and L. Harmon Zeigler, eds., *The Electoral Process* (Englewood Cliffs: Prentice-Hall, 1966), pp. 1–20; Charles O. Jones, "The Role of the Campaign in Congressional Politics," ibid., pp. 21–41; C. L. Kim, "Political Attitudes of Defeated Candidates in an American State Election," *American Political Science Review*, vol. 64 (September 1970), pp. 879–87; Roman March, *The Myth of Parliament* (Scarborough: Prentice-Hall, 1974), p. 68.

8. Harold D. Clarke, Richard G. Price and Robert Krause, "Timing and Agents of Legislative Role Socialization: The Case of Canadian Provin-

cial Legislators," unpublished paper, Department of Political Science, University of Windsor, 1975. This analysis was based on a mail survey of all provincial MLA's in Canada (excepting cabinet ministers) carried out in 1972.

9. Canadian Institute of Public Opinion Survey, December 27, 1972.

10. Allan Kornberg, *Canadian Legislative Behavior* (New York: Holt, Rinehart and Winston, 1967), p. 108.

11. Ibid., p. 108.

12. For public opinion data on this point see the following surveys by the Canadian Institute of Public Opinion: Nov. 6, 1968; Nov. 5, 1969; May 24, 1972; Nov. 24, 1973; May 8, 1974. That Canadians' images of politicians is not entirely negative, however, is suggested by Pineo and Porter's analysis of occupational prestige in Canada. In their study an M.P.'s prestige score (84.8) was exceeded only by those for senators, provincial premiers and physicians. See Peter C. Pineo and John Porter, "Occupational Prestige in Canada," *Canadian Review of Sociology and Anthropology*, vol. 4 (1967), pp. 24–40.

13. That many of the freshmen faced stiff inter-party competition in their own ridings is suggested by the fact that 64 per cent campaigned against incumbents, 34 per cent defeated their nearest rival by 5 per cent or less, and another 30 per cent defeated their nearest challenger by 10 per cent or less.

14. John Wahlke et al., *The Legislative System* (New York: Wiley, 1962), p. 23.

15. Kornberg, *Canadian Legislative Behavior*, p. 53.

16. Froman, "Campaign Strategies and Tactics," p. 3.

17. Ibid., p. 3.

18. Kornberg, *Canadian Legislative Behavior*, p. 109.

19. Ibid., p. 111.

20. Ibid.

21. Harold D. Clarke, Richard G. Price and Robert Krause, "Constituency Service Amongst Canadian Provincial Legislators," *Canadian Journal of Political Science*, vol. 8 (December 1975), pp. 520–42.

22. Wahlke et al., p. 292; Roger H. Davidson, *The Role of the Congressman* (New York: Pegasus, 1969), p. 128.

23. For a discussion of various possible models of the learning processes involved in political socialization, see Dennis, "Major Problems of Political Socialization Research," pp. 105–108.

24. On the importance of constituency service as a component of Canadian legislative behaviour see Clarke, Price and Krause, "Constituency Service Amongst Canadian Provincial Legislators," op. cit.

25. Kornberg, *Canadian Legislative Behavior*, pp. 54–55.

26. In Clarke et al.'s study of the constituency service behaviour of Canadian provincial legislators it was discovered that there is considerable variance in the amount of time spent on constituency service tasks. See Clarke et al., table 1.

27. That some M.P.'s may have unrealistically high estimations of their influence in the legislative process has been suggested by the findings of Kornberg's research. See Kornberg, *Canadian Legislative Behavior*, p. 81.

28. Robert Presthus, "Interest Groups and the Canadian Parliament: Activities, Interaction, Legitimacy, and Influence," *Canadian Journal of Political Science*, vol. 4 (December 1971), pp. 444–60.

29. It should be noted, however, that Presthus did not find a statistically significant relationship between frequency of interaction between M.P.'s and interest group representatives and the degree of legitimacy M.P.'s ascribed to interest groups. See Presthus, "Interest Groups and the Canadian Parliament," p. 456, table IX.

30. On the functions of caucus in the Canadian parliamentary system, see

Allan Kornberg, "Caucus and Cohesion in Canadian Parliamentary Parties," *American Political Science Review,* vol. 60 (March 1966), pp. 83–92.

31. Clarke et al. found that 75.8 per cent of the provincial MLA's reported a change in their legislative role concepts as a result of post-incumbency experiences. See Clarke et al., "Timing and Agents of Legislative Role Socialization," table 5.

32. Price and Bell, "The Rules of the Game," p. 855.

33. For a discussion of the importance of personality variables for understanding political behaviour see Fred I. Greenstein, *Personality and Politics* (Chicago: Markham, 1969). See also James David Barber, "Strategies for Understanding Politicians," *American Journal of Political Science,* vol. 18 (May 1974), pp. 443–67.

34. James David Barber, *The Lawmakers* (New Haven: Yale University Press, 1965).

35. For data documenting inter-party differences in the social backgrounds of candidates nominated by Canadian political parties, see Allan Kornberg and Hal H. Winsborough, "The Recruitment of Candidates for the Canadian House of Commons," *American Political Science Review,* vol. 62 (December 1968), pp. 1242–57. On the existence of ideological differences between candidates of different parties, see Allan Kornberg, *Canadian Legislative Behavior,* pp. 121–26.

36. Lawrence LeDuc, Jr., and Walter L. White, "The Role of Opposition in a One-Party Dominant System: The Case of Ontario," *Canadian Journal of Political Science,* vol. 7 (March 1974), pp. 52–69.

PART FOUR

Attitudes Toward Canada and the
Canadian Political System

Children and the Monarchy:

12

Canadian Perceptions of the Queen

MICHAEL S. WHITTINGTON

The persistence of any political system will depend upon its maintaining a minimal level of support from individuals in society. According to David Easton, there are three generalized objects of political support: the authorities, the regime and the political community.[1] The specific real world phenomena towards which our supportive attitudes can be directed are thus classifiable as being authorities-related, regime-related or political community-related. On another dimension,[2] these specific objects of support can be institutional (or structural), conceptual or symbolic.

Symbolic objects of support are different from either the structural or conceptual ones. These latter two categories for the most part include objects which can be related in some way to the policy process. The structures of the regime, for instance, provide the institutional mechanisms within which policy-making occurs and the conceptual objects provide the boundaries of legitimate governmental enterprise and the agenda for policy decision-making. This means that the positive or negative feelings people have for these objects may be related more to the policy decisions affected by the objects than to the objects themselves. Any support for the regime which is generated here is consequently more likely to be "specific" or related to allocative outputs.[3] Only in areas where support for the political system is unaffected by our satisfaction/dissatisfaction with the allocative outputs of the system is the object of support likely to be symbolic. Symbols of the regime and of the political community rarely have a demonstrable impact upon the outputs of the system and as such our attitudes towards them are perhaps reflective of more generalized or diffuse support for the system.[4] To put this distinction in other terms, diffuse support for the regime or the political community may be reflected

240

in our attitudes towards the symbols of the regime and the political community.

In Canada the monarchy would appear to be such a symbol and attitudes towards the personalized form of the symbol, the Queen, may be an indication of the level of diffuse support for the Canadian political system. That the monarchy in Canada has little impact on the policy process is not difficult to establish, for it is of the essence of our system of government that Parliament is supreme. While it has taken centuries to evolve, few today would question the fact that the head-of-state role is functionally subordinate to Parliament and the cabinet which is responsible to Parliament both in Canada and in the United Kingdom. Moreover, the residual prerogatives still exercised by Her Majesty in Britain are performed for the most part by the Governor General and Lieutenant-Governors in this country. Thus, if the monarchy is of any significance in Canada, it is as a symbol and not as an actor in the central processes of government.

But a secondary question must be answered if one is to justify the relevance of this paper, and that is whether the monarchy is significant to Canadians even as a symbol. Several surveys of the Canadian Institute of Public Opinion have investigated this and, while support for the monarchy is certainly not unanimous among Canadians, a lot more Canadians opt for its retention than for its abolition. As Table 1 illustrates, however, there are significant differences in the attitudes of English- and French-speaking Canadians to the monarchy, and in fact the difference is so striking that one might hypothesize that the monarchy is a negative symbol for non-English Canadians.

Having established at least the possibility that the monarchy is a symbol (perhaps positive and perhaps negative) we must ask the question "Of

Table 1 Preference of Monarchy over Republic by Language

	Language			Total Sample
	English	*French*	*Other*	
Monarchist	64.0%	24.0%	44.0%	50.5%
Republican	22.8	47.1	43.1	32.4
Can't Say	13.4	28.8	13.0	17.6

SOURCE: Canadian Institute of Public Opinion, Survey No. 331, 1968.

what is it a symbol: the authorities, the regime or the political community?" While there are no hard data to establish this one way or the other, it seems reasonable to presume that the monarchy could only become an important symbol of the authorities if a particular political party or political leader were able exclusively to identify with the monarchy or conversely if the Queen were to throw her support exclusively behind a particular set of authorities. This has not happened in Canada[5] and so we can fairly safely assume that the monarchy might be a symbol of either the political community or the regime (or both) but not of the authorities.

To establish whether the monarchy is more a symbol of the political community than of the regime, or vice versa, seems impossible with the data available. However, one might speculate that where the Queen is viewed as a reflection of the "Britishness" or the "Englishness" of our political community she is more likely to produce negative attitudes on the part of non-British ethnic groups, than where she is viewed as a symbol of the parliamentary regime and responsible government. It is in this latter sense, as a symbol of the regime, therefore, that the monarchy could prove most useful in maintaining and generating support for the system. For in a presidential system where head-of-state and chief executive or "policy-making" roles are combined in the same person, massive withdrawal of support for the authorities, such as happened with Watergate, may have a negative effect upon the support for the regime as well. By contrast, where the symbolic, head-of-state roles are separated from the governing or policy-making roles, even a total rejection of the government of the day should not cause our perceptions of the system to alter very much.[6]

MONARCHISM AMONG CANADIAN CHILDREN

The source of the data for this paper is a study of Canadian elementary school children's attitudes to various Canadian and American authority roles. The study is described in the introductory article of this volume.

The part of the study which is relevant to this paper was intended to elicit the children's relative attitudes to the nine political authority roles, including the Queen, Governor General, Prime Minister, Provincial Premier, Local Mayor, American President, Federal M.P., Federal Cabinet Minister, and American Congressman. These roles were presented to the respondents in pairs, and they were asked to indicate, first which in each pair they liked more, secondly which in each pair was more powerful, and thirdly, in which in each pair they had the most confidence ("who is more likely to be right?"). On the basis of these responses (the average response rate was over 80 per cent) we were able to derive each child's attitudes towards these authority figures in terms of a hierarchy of affection, perception of relative power, and a hierarchy of confidence. For this paper, our concern is restricted to the relative perceptions of the three Canadian head-of-state roles: Queen, Prime Minister, and Governor General. Where the children perceive these three roles in a hierarchical relationship, there are six possible combinations,[7] although in our tables we have reduced these to three, depending upon which role is placed first in the hierarchy.

Of the nine authority roles compared by our respondents, the Queen is the one viewed by far the most favourably, and while the Governor General and Prime Minister score second and third respectively they are a long way behind the Queen in the children's affection. Thus, the most common hierarchy of affection for the three head-of-state roles demonstrated by our respondents is one with the monarchy first (67.4 per cent); the second most common hierarchy of affection is one with the Governor General first (18.0 per cent); and the least common hierarchy of affection is one with the Prime Minister first (14.6 per cent). While it is difficult to come to any conclusions with such aggregated figures, the one point that can be made is that the two predominantly symbolic figures, the Queen and the Governor General, fare far better as objects of children's affection than does the one instrumental or policy-maker role, the Prime Minister.[8]

Male-female differences in the children's affection for the monarch are striking, but are what one might have predicted given the CIPO findings that 54.7 per cent of females sampled were monarchist as opposed to only 45.3 per cent of males.[9] As shown in Table 2, little girls are considerably more monarchist than their male schoolmates, and considerably less favourably impressed by the Governor General. The best explanation for this would seem to be the greater ease of identifying with a symbol with which one shares common characteristics. Presumably a male monarch or a female Governor General (Governess General?) could alter these results significantly.

Table 2 Relative Affection: Head of State by Sex

Hierarchy of Affection with:	Male	Female
Queen First	60.8%	74.1%
Governor General First	23.3	12.5
Prime Minister First	15.9	13.4
N =	(1905)	(1870)

The relationship between our dependent variable and grade in school is as we might expect; affection for the monarch is higher among the younger children and declines slightly but consistently with age. Table 3 shows the changing pattern of relative affection for the three head-of-state roles as the children advance in school. While the Queen declines in importance to the children as they mature, the table would indicate that they shift their affection to another, at least partly symbolic figure, the Governor General, and not to the top policy-maker, the Prime Minister, for whom affection seems actually to decline slightly.

One possible explanation for the decline in affection for the Queen in the later grades is that with age and maturity the children become less symbolically and more instrumentally oriented. They begin to perceive symbols as "merely symbols" and not "where it's at" in politics. Moreover, for many children, in the later grades new political objects, more closely related to the policy process than is the monarchy, become salient. The likelihood that the child will identify with a political party, for instance, increases with age, and children with a party loyalty are on the average less likely to be monarchist than are apartisan children. Again this might be explained in terms of an increasing instrumental as opposed

Table 3 Relative Affection: Head-of-State Roles by Grade

Hierarchy of Affection with:	4	5	6	7	8
Queen First	74.0%	73.3%	69.3%	65.9%	59.4%
Governor General First	9.2	12.8	16.3	20.4	29.3
Prime Minister First	16.8	13.9	14.4	13.7	11.3
N =	(596)	(619)	(655)	(583)	(505)

to symbolic orientation. The child begins to identify with objects such as political parties which are authorities-related and hence have an instrumental or policy relevance that the purer symbols such as the monarchy lack.

Another attitudinal variable which correlates both with grade in school and with partisanship is the level of knowledge the child possesses. On the basis of twelve cognitive questions about political authority figures the children were assigned a percentage score, and then placed in one of three groups: better than 75 per cent, 50–75 per cent, and less than 50 per cent. As expected, the better the children did on this "test," the less likely they were to place the Queen first in a hierarchy of affection (see Table 4).

This inverse relationship between level of awareness of political facts and the likelihood of positive affection towards the monarchy again could possibly reflect a growing concern with political objects which have a policy relevance. However, what is difficult to explain, if we are to view the declining affection for the Queen in later grades (among partisan children, and among the more informed children) as a reflection of emerging concern with instrumental or policy-related political objects, is the increased affection for the largely symbolic Governor General role and the mildly decreasing affection for the definitely policy-relevant Prime Minister role. Perhaps the declining affection for the Prime Minister could be explained in terms of a growing disaffection and cynicism with politicians generally. But the apparent shift in affection from the Queen to the Governor General, although consistent throughout our sample (except in Quebec), is puzzling. Perhaps the Governor General gains in relative affection in later grades because he is marginally a more "instrumental" figure than the monarch in the Canadian system, while at the

Table 4   Relative Affection: Head-of-State Roles by Level of Cognition

	Cognitive Score (% correct answers)		
Hierarchy of Affection with:	*Above 75%*	*50%–75%*	*Below 50%*
Queen First	55.6%	65.7%	71.8%
Governor General First	29.5	20.3	12.9
Prime Minister First	15.0	13.9	15.3
N =	(387)	(1721)	(1679)

same time his role in the system is insulated from the partisan associations which likely moderate the affection for the Prime Minister. On the other hand, the findings could be related to the increased awareness of the role of the Governor General in the higher grades. The simple fact that more students in the higher grades will recognize the role will increase the likelihood that the role be selected by our respondents.

Finally, it may be possible to explain the developmental decline in relative affection for the Queen in terms of non-political factors. It must be admitted that we have only *presumed* the monarchy to be symbolic of the political community and/or the regime when in fact such affection may be purely a reflection of childhood's fascination with fairy tales, fantasy and the pomp and ceremony that surrounds monarchy as a social phenomenon. As a child matures he or she will likely take some pride in being able to part company with "childish things" such as being "turned on" by monarchy. Older children, more partisan children, and more politically aware children may simply tend to make this break from childhood sooner than their younger and less conscious or less aware peers.

The place of residence of our respondents is perhaps one of the best predictors of a positive affect for the Queen. Rural respondents are much more likely to be monarchists than are their urban peers, although they do not show any great difference in the distribution of non-monarchist sentiments between the Governor General and the Prime Minister. The greater likelihood that rural children will place the Queen first in a hierarchy of affection is probably related to the higher commitment to traditional values which we usually attribute to rural communities. Such communities tend to be socially more conservative, perhaps more conscious of local history and old country roots, and with the exception of the prairies, more likely to be populated with British ethnic stock.

While socio-economic status might be expected to be a predictor of monarchism, the findings of the data being used here do not indicate any strong relationship at all. While the lowest SES category does seem to be slightly more monarchist than any of the higher ones, the relationship is not statistically significant. It is possible that the reason for this lies in the weakness of our measure of SES rather than in the real world. The researchers attempted to code the children's description of their parents' jobs in such a way as to give a rough indication of SES. As with most surveys of this type, we found that the children were often not capable of giving us any decipherable description of their parents' occupations and where an answer was forthcoming it was frequently difficult for us to reliably assign a code. In fact, of 5,842 respondents only 1,907 could be assigned an SES category. Thus we cannot conclude that SES is not a relevant predictor of monarchism but only that our study did not uncover such a relationship.

The most interesting and, in the Canadian context, perhaps the most important relationship was between region and monarchism. As indicated by Table 5, our Quebec respondents are somewhat less monarchist than their peers in the rest of the country, and the British Columbian children are notably more monarchist than other predominantly Enlgish-speaking regions. It must be pointed out that the unusually high affection for the Queen in the British Columbian sample may be simply an artifact of the data. The B.C. respondents are all in one area of the province, and the sample was atypical in many ways. There was a higher percentage of rural children, generally lower cognition scores, and generally fewer partisans than in other regional samples, and because all of these variables correlate with monarchism, the impact of "region" as an independent predictor is virtually washed out when we insert the controls.

In the case of Quebec, our selected schools were all in the Trois Rivières area and there were no anglophones in the sample. Thus, one might be tempted to conclude that the lower affection for the Queen among these children is a reflection of ethnic and not regional differences. However, when the variables "region" and "language spoken at home" are combined, as in Table 6, we discover that the non-Quebec franco-phones are at least as monarchist as their English-speaking peers. Thus, by themselves neither language nor region would seem to be very reliable

Table 5 Relative Affection: Head-of-State Roles By Region

Hierarchy of Affection with:	B.C.	West	Ont.	Que.	Atlantic
Queen First	73.7%	66.5%	67.3%	59.7%	68.5%
Governor General First	10.5	17.8	20.1	11.3	18.2
Prime Minister First	15.8	15.7	12.6	29.0	13.3
N =	(304)	(1036)	(1670)	(186)	(588)

Table 6   Relative Affection: Head-of-State Roles by Region/Language

Hierarchy of Affection with:	West	Ont.	Que.	Non Que. Francophones	Atlantic
Queen First	67.2%	67.4%	59.7%	73.8%	68.7%
Governor General First	16.6	20.0	11.3	13.4	18.4
Prime Minister First	16.2	12.6	29.0	12.8	12.9
N =	(1240)	(1640)	(186)	(149)	(572)

predictors, but when they are combined some significant variations emerge.

One possible explanation for the differences between Quebec and non-Quebec francophones is that because of the visibility of nationalism as an issue in provincial politics the Québécois are more likely to develop an "ethnic consciousness." As we saw in Table 1, French-Canadian adults are anti-monarchist (on the average) possibly because the monarchy is a symbol of the Britishness of our political community. While it is not likely that many of the children in our study have acquired an independent awareness of the British and therefore "alien" symbolism of the monarchy, it can be hypothesized that their lower affection for the Queen relative to anglophone children is as a result of a partial identification with their parents' views. Perhaps as they mature they will become ethnically conscious and reject the monarchy to as great an extent as do their parents.

The monarchism of the non-Quebec francophones is more difficult to explain. However, it seems possible that their high affection for the monarchy is related to their place as a minority in the process of being assimilated. It may be as a result of a conscious effort to become "more acceptable" to the English-speaking majority, or it may be an unconscious process resulting from a constant exposure to the values of the dominant culture.

CONCLUSION

Having dealt with children's attitudes to the Queen as an independent variable and having diligently pointed out the relationships between this variable and all of the standard independent variables, the single most startling finding is not the differences in attitudes but the similarities. Likely the most significant finding in this study is not that Québécois are less monarchist than their non-Quebec cohorts but that even in Quebec fully 59 per cent of our respondents have a higher affection for the Queen than for any other authority figure. Moreover, even when the Québécois who identified with the Parti Québécois are isolated, we find that 55 per cent of them prefer the Queen to any other authority figure. As political scientists we tend to focus upon conflict and the social and economic bases of that conflict. It is easy to forget that conflict *within* a political system is predicated on the pre-existence of general support for the system and consensus about its viability in the first place. We must recognize that compared to most other countries in the world our disagreements are settled amicably.

While we have by no means been able to demonstrate that the Queen is a symbol of either the regime or the political community in Canada, it is clear that a large percentage of Canadian children display greater affection for this particular authority role than for any other which we tested. Given that the Queen (or at least "the Crown") is in fact one of the formed authority roles of our system of government, positive affection for this role may be transferable to the regime or the political community as the child becomes more sophisticated.

Certainly it can be concluded on the basis of this evidence that symbols such as the monarchy are potentially significant in capturing the attention and affection of young Canadians. If this affection can be diverted from the symbol to the political object it represents, the result will be increased diffuse support for the system. If we accept this conclusion, it follows that we should perhaps be more cautious in our attempts to "rationalize" our system's remaining symbols, ceremonies and rituals which, to an adult mind, may appear inefficient and silly but which may be instrumental in creating a foundation for diffuse support in the young.

NOTES

1. David Easton, *A Systems Analysis of Political Life* (New York: Wiley, 1965), pp. 172–73. See also the introductory article in this volume.
2. This categorization is also elaborated in chapter 4 of R. Van Loon and

M. S. Whittington, *The Canadian Political System*, 2nd ed. (Toronto: McGraw-Hill Ryerson, 1976).
3. Easton, *Systems Analysis*, pp. 267–68; it must be noted that satisfaction with the outputs of the system over

a long time period can also build diffuse support (ibid., pp. 273–74).

4. Ibid., p. 273.

5. It might be argued that individual authorities such as John Diefenbaker have become associated with the monarchy because of a consistently favourable attitude to it. However, the connection here is not likely *symbolic*, for the monarchy to such individuals is viewed as a *policy matter*. The monarchy is in no way a symbol of John Diefenbaker, it is purely a policy matter with which we associate him.

6. Obviously this is only true in the short run, for if a series of elections were to produce a series of "Watergate administrations," eventually the system that placed such people in power would lose its credibility.

7. The possible combinations are Queen, Governor General, Prime Minister; Queen, Prime Minister, Governor General; Governor General, Queen, Prime Minister; Governor General, Prime Minister, Queen; Prime Minister, Queen, Governor General; Prime Minister, Governor General, Queen. The seventh possible combination is where the child does not perceive a hierarchical relationship at all—for instance, if the respondent liked the Queen better than the Prime Minister, the Prime Minister better than the Governor General, and the Governor General better than the Queen. It is interesting that fully 17 per cent of our respondents displayed this non-hierarchical or "confused" configuration with respect to affection and the figure increases to 20 per cent for both power and confidence.

8. The most commonly perceived hierarchy of power is still one having the Queen first (49.4 per cent) although the Prime Minister is viewed as most powerful by 35.9 per cent. Here the Governor General does not fare very well, being perecived as most powerful by only 14 per cent of the sample. As might be predicted, in the earlier grades the Queen is as likely to be viewed as powerful as she is to be liked, whereas by grade eight only 35 per cent of the respondents see her at the top of a power hierarchy as opposed to 53 per cent who see the Prime Minister as the most powerful.

9. Canadian Institute of Public Opinion Survey #331, 1968.

The Political Americanization of   13
Canadian Children

DONALD HIGGINS

While the extent of American penetration into the economic structure of Canada and into the Canadian academic community has received considerable attention,[1] the impact of American politics on the Canadian political culture has been virtually ignored. The fact that the majority of Canadians live within a hundred miles of the American border is well known and although the consequences of this for the future of the Canadian national identity may be of considerable importance, very little is known of the actual effect geographical proximity may have on the process of political socialization. However, because a continuous and heavy exposure of Canadians to American political phenomena through the U.S. media is an immediate consequence of geographical proximity, one can hypothesize, even in the absence of empirical evidence, that such exposure might figure prominently in the "political upbringing" of young Canadians.

It is now possible to empirically test some aspects of this hypothesis. The extent of American influence on the political upbringing of Canadian children was one of the concerns of a large-scale study of the political socialization process in Canada, some preliminary findings of which were reported earlier.[2]

It seems to be generally accepted that what is learned earliest is retained the longest, though the process of socialization generally, and political socialization in particular, is quite obviously life-long. As one ages, the basic political attitudes inculcated during the pre-adult years tend to be reinforced by knowledge and experiences acquired later in life, rather than fundamentally altered.[3] Because reality is often perceived in such a way as to be consonant with one's existing values, if Canadian school children acquire substantial American political orientations, then as adults it is to be expected that these American attitudes may be retained or even reinforced. For example, if it can be demonstrated that Canadian school children acquire orientations favourably disposed toward the United States, then they are unlikely to support highly anti-American causes later in life, and organizations like the Waffle will be unlikely to receive widespread support. Presumably, the election platforms of the Canadian political parties would tend to down-play nationalistic causes, and ideas like a continental energy policy would be played up.

The present analysis is based on but three geographic areas in Canada, and of course is limited to a single generation of Canadian children. With these two highly important limitations, it is clearly not possible to make consummate generalizations from the data, although the present analysis can likely serve as a base for subsequent studies.

The study focuses on political authority roles, specifically on both the level of knowledge the children have of authority roles, and their attitudes toward the political authority roles. Three types of attitudes are studied: affection, sanctions or power, and confidence, although because knowledge must logically precede the making of evaluations, we must look first at the cognitive development of the children.

COGNITION

The ability of children to provide the appropriate role title when given the name of one or more incumbents of the role is our operational test for the presence of some minimal degree of cognitive awareness. For example, the respondents were asked the question
Pierre Trudeau's job is:
  a) don't know
  b) Mayor
  c) President of the United States
  d) television star
  e) Prime Minister of Canada
and were asked to circle the answer they felt most appropriate. Similar questions were asked about other Canadian and American authority roles as well as the pictures of national flags as symbolic political objects. To minimize guessing, "don't know" was always the first answer option given, and the position of the correct answer was randomly selected so as to minimize response set bias.

Children in grades two and three were presented with a shortened version of the questionnaire, being asked to identify the role titles of only Pierre Trudeau, their provincial premiers, the Governor General, and Richard Nixon. They were also asked to identify the nationality of two pictures of flags, the Maple Leaf and the Stars and Stripes; in addition, children in grades three through eight were asked to identify the role titles of U Thant, local MLA's/MPP's, federal cabinet ministers, local M.P.'s, prominent M.P.'s, members of the United States cabinet, and prominent American Congressmen.

Clues to the extent to which Canadian children are "politically Americanized" can be found in comparison of correct identification of more or less equivalent Canadian and American roles and symbols, and in the confusion of Canadian roles (and flag) as American, and vice versa. Consistent with other studies, it is found that the flag is the earliest and most widely recognized political object among school children. In grade two, almost nine out of ten respondents correctly identified a picture of the Maple Leaf flag as the flag of Canada, and by grade eight, correct identification is virtually universal. What is surprising is not only the high frequency of correct identification of a picture of the Stars and Stripes, but the fact that in all of grades four through eight, the picture of the American flag is more often correctly identified than is the picture of the Canadian flag. The percentage differences are small, but they are consistent in all grades above grade three, as Table 1 indicates.

Also consistent with other studies is the finding that political authority roles occupied by a single person are more widely recognized at an early age than are group authority roles such as the cabinet and legislators.[4] It is not surprising, therefore, to find that Pierre Trudeau's role is more often correctly identified than that of any other political authority figure. Of great interest, however, is the finding that Richard Nixon's role as President of the United States is more often recognized than is any Canadian role other than the Prime Minister. In grade four, for example, the percentage of children correctly identifying Nixon's role is almost double the percentage correctly identifying the role of Canada's two most recent Governors General. Even in grade eight there is a percentage difference of almost 10 per cent between the two roles. Our findings therefore bear out the contention that awareness of personalized objects precedes awareness of institutional ones in the process of cognitive development, even when the personalized object is from another political system.

The two Canadian institutional political objects were more frequently identified than their American counterparts. Even in grade eight only one person in ten correctly identified the role of three prominent members of the American cabinet while more than half could recognize the role of three prominent members of the Canadian cabinet. Similarly, the names of three prominent American Congressmen were almost unknown, even at grade eight, while the three prominent Canadian M.P.'s were recognized by almost a third of the grade eight respondents.

Table 1   Recognition of Canadian and American Political Objects, by Grade (% correct identification)

	2	3	4	5	6	7	8
Canadian flag	86.4	91.8	92.4	92.0	95.7	95.5	97.4
American flag	71.7	87.7	95.8	96.7	98.2	97.1	98.8
Prime Minister	68.3	74.1	79.8	88.2	95.7	98.4	99.4
Governor General	14.3	27.8	29.3	44.0	61.7	71.1	84.8
U.S. President	25.7	42.8	57.9	69.8	89.2	89.3	93.3
Canadian cabinet	NA	NA	14.1	21.9	28.6	38.5	51.1
American cabinet	NA	NA	4.1	3.2	6.2	6.0	10.1
Canadian M.P.'s	NA	NA	9.5	13.6	18.0	22.9	32.0
U.S. Congressmen	NA	NA	3.3	5.2	5.2	6.0	6.8

NA: question not asked of children in grades two and three.

The high frequency of recognition of Richard Nixon as President of the United States contrasts sharply with the low frequency of recognition of the two American institutional authority roles. They tend of course to cancel each other out when aggregated in an index of correct recognition of the four American political roles and symbols. It is interesting to compare this index with an index of the four equivalent Canadian political authority roles and symbols—Prime Minister of Canada, the Canadian flag, prominent Canadian cabinet ministers, and prominent members of Parliament as indicated in Table 2.

From a comparison of this table with Table 1, it must be questioned whether we were very successful in discouraging the respondents from guessing at answers, for in all five grades presented in Table 2, the per-

Table 2   % Correct Recognition of All Four Canadian Political Objects Compared to % Correct Recognition of All Four American Political Objects, by Grade

	4	*5*	*6*	*7*	*8*
Correct all four Canadian*	2.8	4.7	7.9	14.3	24.3
Correct all four American†	0.2	0.4	1.6	1.9	3.8

*The four political objects are Prime Minister of Canada, the Canadian flag, prominent Canadian cabinet ministers, and prominent Canadian M.P.'s.

†The four political objects are President of the United States, the American flag, prominent members of the American cabinet, and prominent American Congressmen.

centages of respondents who correctly identified all four Canadian political objects are consistently lower than the percentages who correctly identified prominent Canadian cabinet ministers and prominent Canadian members of Parliament, the least frequently and latest learned of the four political objects involved. Thus, while it might be expected that the percentages in Table 2 would be at least the same as the lowest percentage for each grade in Table 1, because this expectation is not met it has to be admitted that our efforts to dissuade guessing were not entirely successful.

The fact remains, however, that the four Canadian political objects as a group are more often correctly identified than are their four American counterparts as a group, though to say that 2.8 per cent (in grade four) recognition of all four Canadian objects is greater than 0.2 per cent for the American counterparts is not saying much! The two tables suggest that between grades seven and eight the acceleration of cognitive development from the level of personalized objects to the level of institutional objects begins to take place and that cognition of the structural characteristics of political roles develops largely after grade eight or after the age of about fourteen. In this respect, the process of political socialization of our respondents seems to progress rather more slowly than in the United States. Greenstein found, for example, that in grade four, 29 per cent of the respondents had a reasonably accurate understanding of the role of President, and that the figure was 73 per cent by grade eight.[5] The take-off point for his respondents seems to have been between grades six and seven, at least for the role of President. In any case, our data indicate that in terms of being able to simply attach names to four political objects, our respondents cannot be characterized as highly Americanized. Only 3.8 per cent of the grade eight respondents correctly identified all four American objects, less than a sixth of the percentage who correctly identified all four Canadian objects. An interesting phenomenon which might be unique to Canada is the tendency for children to confuse Canadian and American authority roles. Identifying American political objects as Canadian tends to be more common than the opposite. The most impressive confusion is the identification of Richard Nixon as Prime Minister of Canada. Of our respondents in grade two, more than one in six made that connection, and even by grade five one in ten of the respondents still made that connection. The reverse confusion, that is identifying Pierre Trudeau as President of the United States, was made by 12 per cent of the grade two respondents and was virtually non-existent by grade eight (0.2 per cent). Correct recognition of the Canadian flag was so nearly universal, even in grade two, that only 2 per cent of those in grade two identified the picture of the Maple Leaf flag as being the flag of the United States. Correct recognition of the American flag was less universal, and one in ten of the grade two respondents identified it as the flag of Canada. Almost no one by grade eight made this confused identification.

The tendency to more often confuse American political objects as Canadian than vice versa applies also in regard to prominent legislators. About one in thirteen of the grade four respondents (the question was not posed to those in grades two and three) identified Mansfield, McCormack and Fulbright as Canadian M.P.'s, the percentage dropping to 2.9 per cent in grade eight. Only a small percentage (about 2 per cent) consistent from grades four to eight, identified David Lewis, George Hees, and Paul Hellyer as American Congressmen. The one exception to the more frequent tendency to confuse American political objects as Canadian is in regard to members of the cabinet, and even here the usual tendency is reversed only for grades four and five, as Table 3 shows.

If these findings are a function of genuine confusion rather than of guessing, some of the results are misleading in that they tend to under-state the full extent of cross national confusion. This obviously applies particularly to prominent legislators and prominent members of the cabinets, for there was such frequent correct identification of the flags and the names of Pierre Trudeau and Richard Nixon that confused nationality identification must be very small relative to correct recognition. But Table 1 indicated comparatively infrequent correct identification of prominent legislators and members of the cabinets. What is interesting is to find that in some grades the percentages of confused nationality actually exceed the percentages of correct identification. While it is of course quite possible that this reflects little more than simply a random distribution of responses the data in Table 3 do indicate the greater tendency to identify American political objects as Canadian than identification of Canadian political objects as American.

While it seems clear to this point that the level of awareness of Canadian children of a few American political objects (specifically the President and the flag) is high, cognition, especially when examined in relation to so few political objects, is certainly not an adequate indicator of the extent to which the respondents have acquired attitudes reflecting the

Table 3   Identification of Canadian and American Political Objects, by Grade*

	4	5	6	7	8
Rusk, MacNamara, Laird					
don't know	68.4	74.4	72.0	78.4	70.4
members of U.S. cabinet	4.1	3.2	6.2	6.0	10.1
members of Canadian government	9.4	7.3	7.1	4.0	6.0
Sharp, Turner, Munro					
don't know	53.1	44.2	40.3	34.3	27.1
members of Canadian cabinet	14.1	21.9	28.6	35.5	51.1
members of U.S. government	12.0	8.3	4.7	1.8	1.4
Mansfield, McCormack, Fulbright					
don't know	67.4	68.5	74.6	76.5	77.1
United States Congressmen	3.3	5.2	5.2	6.0	6.8
Members of Parliament	7.5	4.7	4.1	4.0	2.9
Lewis, Hees, Hellyer					
don't know	59.1	63.2	59.1	60.2	49.1
Members of Parliament	9.5	13.6	18.0	22.9	32.0
United States Congressmen	2.1	2.6	2.9	2.6	2.7

*The percentages do not total 100% because two additional categories for each question are not given here.

American political culture. More important than cognition in this regard are children's relative affection for and evaluations of American and Canadian political objects.

AFFECTION AND EVALUATION

A major purpose of the study was to examine children's relative affection for and evaluations of various authority roles. The three attitudinal dimensions we used can be termed affection, sanctions, and confidence, and these were operationalized by posing the questions "Which in each set is your favourite?", "Which in each set is more able to make people do what he wants?", and "If these people disagree, who do you think is more likely to be right?". After each question was posed, a series of pairs of authority roles followed, the respondents being asked to choose one or the other of the roles in each pair.

For example,

Which in each set is your favourite?

    a) Premier of Ontario—or—Local Mayor.

    b) President of the United States—or—Prime Minister of Canada.

    c) Member of Parliament—or—Congressmen

and so on. Respondents in grades two and three were posed at least seven such pairs for each of the three questions, while respondents above grade three were posed at least fifteen pairs for each question.

In gauging the Americanization of the respondents in terms of their affection for and evaluations of American authority roles relative to Canadian ones, it would be easy to simply add up the number of times an individual chose an American role over a Canadian one, and convert that number into a percentage. In preference to this simple technique, a rather complicated two-step procedure was used to enable characterizing each respondent as exhibiting an intensity of Americanization on each of the three sources of authority. The advantage of the more complicated technique lies in the fact that it takes into account the *relative importance* attached by the respondents as a whole to each of the authority roles. For example, in terms of affection, the Queen was rated higher than the Prime Minister of Canada by the respondents as a whole, and the Prime Minister of Canada in turn was rated higher than Member of Parliament by the respondents as a whole. The simple adding up of the number of occasions in which a respondent chose an American authority role in preference to any Canadian one cannot take the relative importance of the roles being compared into account. The more complicated technique that was used does accord a greater qualitative and quantitative difference to a child's choosing the President of the United States in preference to the Queen than to a child's choosing the President of the United States in preference to the Prime Minister of Canada, and so on.

For all respondents in grades four through eight, the role of President of the United States was compared with the Prime Minister of Canada, the Governor General, the Queen, and member of Parliament. The role of Congressman was compared with the Prime Minister of Canada and Member of Parliament. For children in grades two and three, only three comparisons were made, and they all involved President of the United States. Controls were built into the rating procedure to ensure that Americanization ratings were given only to respondents who made at least a minimum number of comparisons. Thus if a respondent gave an answer for only one pair of roles, and chose the American one in preference to the Canadian one, that respondent is coded "unrateable" rather than "100 per cent Americanized." The two-step procedure is described in the Appendix on page 263.

It is clear that the respondents as a whole display lower affection for American political roles than for Canadian political roles; seven in ten respondents had a "low affective Americanization" rating (less than 33 per cent Americanization) compared to only 10 per cent having a "high affective Americanization" rating (that is, more than 65 per cent Americanization). More importantly, almost four in ten respondents scored less than 11 per cent affective Americanization compared to only three in a hundred who scored more than 87 per cent Americanization.

Affective scores contrast quite sharply with Americanization scores on the other two attitudinal dimensions (sanctions and confidence), as indicated in Table 4. Thus, while the respondents as a whole do not like American authority roles as well as Canadian ones, they tend to be more inclined to ascribe high relative power to the American roles. It could be argued that with respect to perceptions of the power of political authorities, the respondents have a reasonably accurate perception of reality. However, this argument appears to be improbable in that it is generally the youngest of our respondents that demonstrate the greatest gap between very low affective Americanization and very low evaluative (power) Americanization. As has been argued elsewhere, younger children tend to perceive authority roles more in terms of the present incumbent than in terms of the structural characteristics such as the power implicit in the role *per se.*[6]

Table 4   Americanization Scores by Source of Authority

% Americanization	affection	sanctions	confidence
low (0 to 32%)	69.3	52.0	53.9
medium (33 to 65%)	20.9	37.4	36.4
high (66 to 100%)	9.9	10.6	9.6

It may come as a bit of a shock to some people to find that while our respondents display higher affection for Canadian political roles when compared with American ones, they are less inclined to impute confidence in the Canadian roles (see Table 5). Note particularly the responses for the comparisons between the Governor General of Canada and President of the United States. The percentage choosing Governor General dropped 20 per cent from the level on the affective dimension, so that only a bare majority chose the Governor General instead of the President on the confidence dimension.

Table 5   American Political Roles Versus Canadian Political Roles

	Affection*	Confidence†
Queen	78.8%	70.1%
President of the United States	15.8	22.0
don't know	5.4	7.9
President of the United States	28.8	34.3
Prime Minister of Canada	64.7	53.9
don't know	6.5	11.8
President of the United States	22.4	37.8
Governor General of Canada	70.6	50.7
don't know	6.9	11.5

*"Which . . . is your favourite?"
†"If these people disagree, who do you think is more likely to be right?"

Americanization ratings on none of the three sources of authority change much according to the school grade of the respondents in our sample. Even when the Americanization scores are collapsed into low, medium and high categories, differences by grade are not consistently acute; however, some interesting variations can be seen.

Table 6   Americanization Scores by Source of Authority, by Grade

American-ization*	2	3	4	5	6	7	8
affection							
low	60.6%	75.8%	71.8%	70.7%	69.2%	65.3%	71.9%
medium	21.0	15.5	20.7	21.9	22.1	·24.9	18.9
high	18.4	8.8	7.6	7.5	8.8	9.7	9.2
sanctions							
low	51.7	58.4	60.7	59.5	51.1	44.3	42.0
medium	31.2	29.6	33.2	33.6	41.7	45.4	44.5
high	17.1	12.0	6.1	6.9	7.1	10.3	13.5
confidence							
low	54.8	56.7	61.0	59.5	51.3	49.3	48.0
medium	29.6	30.6	33.6	33.2	41.4	41.5	42.8
high	15.6	12.7	5.3	7.3	7.2	9.3	9.2

*Low Americanization is less than 33%, medium is 33–65%, high Americanization is 66–100%.

For instance, there is a tendency for high Americanization ratings to drop off from the lower grades, reaching a low point in grade four, and then rising again through the higher grades. This is particularly the case on the power or sanctions dimension, but applies also to the two other sources. Conversely the number of respondents scoring low on the Americanization measure increases to grade four and then drops off through the higher grades. One does find that the grade eight respondents score high on each of the three sources of authority less often than the respondents in grade two, but the curvilinear trend perhaps suggests that if students beyond grade eight were studied, one would find them to be increasingly Americanized.

In most cases, the tables did not produce high coefficients of correlation. This indicates that our respondents are *selectively* Americanized politically, and it indicates further that our respondents could and did differentiate among the three questions relating to the dimensions of authority. There may well have been some incidence of response set, but it appears not to have been particularly serious. Correlation of attitudinal Americanization with cognition of all the American political objects examined in questions on cognition gives the following results, all of which are significant beyond the .05 level:

	index of American cognition
Americanization affection	.016
Americanization sanctions	.102
Americanization confidence	.102

These coefficients of correlation indicate that high attitudinal Americanization is associated with high cognition of American political objects, regardless of which dimension of authority one considers. But the figures are so low as to indicate that there is almost no connection at all between cognition and attitudinal Americanization. The ever-so-slight trend is to an increase in attitudinal Americanization as the respondent's knowledge of American political objects increases.

CONCLUSION

The findings noted earlier may be of both solace and concern to fervent Canadian nationalists, though probably more of the latter than the former. On the one hand we see that the American flag is actually more often correctly identified than is the Canadian flag in all but the two lowest grades and that Richard Nixon is more frequently correctly identified than is any Canadian political incumbent other than Pierre Trudeau. What may be considered a rather large proportion of the respondents thought that Richard Nixon is Prime Minister of Canada. While Canadian political roles are favoured rather than American ones, when posed with the not entirely hypothetical situation of an American political role in disagreement with a Canadian political role, considerable proportions of the respondents were prepared to put their confidence in the American. There is also the very slight tendency for the respondents more cognizant of American political objects to be attitudinally Americanized. On the other hand, correct identification of a picture of the Canadian flag and the name of Pierre Trudeau is almost universal; and though American political roles were often considered more powerful than Canadian ones, certainly the Canadian roles received more positive affection than did the Americans.

Appendix: Procedure for Constructing Attitudinal Americanization Scores

The two-step procedure enabled the characterization of each respondent as exhibiting a degree of Americanization on each of the three sources of authority.

The first step is to create an ordering of political roles by distance from the office of Prime Minister for each of the three sources of authority. Since the role "Prime Minister of Canada" was paired with each of the other eight authority roles, "Prime Minister of Canada" is placed at zero on a scale, and each of the other eight roles is placed between plus and minus one in comparison by subtracting the total number of respondents who have chosen the Prime Minister from a particular pair, from the total number who have chosen the other authority role in the pair. The resulting figure is then divided by the total number of people who answered the question. For example, if everyone chose the Queen over the Prime Minister, the Queen would be placed at plus 1 on the scale. If 75 per cent of the respondents chose the Prime Minister in preference to the Queen, the Queen would be placed at $-.5$. The scales thus show how the respondents as a whole rank the various authority roles in relation to the office of Prime Minister and thus in relation to each other for each of the three sources of authority. For example, the ratings for each role in relation to the Prime Minister on the affection source of authority are:

Queen	.5602
Governor General	.2318
Prime Minister	0.0
Member of Parliament	$-.2584$
Provincial Premier	$-.3499$
Cabinet Minister	$-.3692$
U.S. President	$-.3841$
Local Mayor	$-.4017$
Congressman	$-.5000$

The second step of the Americanization attitudinal rating procedure involves making the scale positions calculated in the first step positive for each role for each of the three sources of authority by adding plus one to each score. The range is now 0–2, with the Prime Minister at the position 1.0. Then, for each individual respondent, and for each source of authority, it is determined for each pair in which an American role is compared to a Canadian role whether the American was chosen in preference. If the American role is chosen the rating score of the Canadian role is added to a score for the respondent, and this procedure is repeated for each of the other pairs in which an American role is compared with a Canadian role. One eventually arrives at a final score for that respondent for that source of authority. This score is divided by the maximum possible score, that is the score that would have been obtained had the respondent chosen the American role in preference to the Canadian role every time, and converted into a percentage. Similarly for the other sources of authority for each respondent. Because of the large number of calculations involved, the procedure was programmed for computer tabulation.

NOTES

1. For example, Walter Gordon, *Final Report of the Royal Commission on Canada's Economic Prospects* (Ottawa: Queen's Printer, 1957); Melville Watkins, *Report of the Task Force on the Structure of Canadian Industry* (Ottawa: Queen's Printer, 1968); and Robin Matthews and James Steele, *The Struggle for Canadian Universities* (Toronto: New Press, 1969).

2. The study has been described in greater detail in the Introduction to this volume.

3. See, for example, Fred Greenstein, *Children and Politics* (New Haven: Yale University Press, 1965), and David Easton and Jack Dennis, *Children in the Political System* (New York: McGraw-Hill, 1969).

4. Ibid., pp. 115–17.

5. Greenstein, *Children and Politics*, p. 58; For a Canadian contrast to the Greenstein findings, see Jon H. Pammett, "The Development of Political Orientations in Canadian School Children," *Canadian Journal of Political Science*, vol. 4 (1971), pp. 132–41.

6. T. G. Carroll, D. J. Higgins, and M. S. Whittington, "The Development of Children's Perceptions of Political Authority Roles: Some Preliminary Findings," Paper delivered at the Annual Meeting of the Canadian Political Science Association, 1971, pp. 17–20.

The Socialization of Orientations Toward Canada:

14

A Study of Cape Breton Whites and Indians

STEPHEN H. ULLMAN

A. B. Hodgetts, a noted student of Canadian civic education, has characterized Canada as a "nation-state without firm [attitudinal] foundations."[1]

In 1867, we created a political regime—a set of federal and provincial institutions—without a stable political community to support it. No sooner had the Dominion of Canada been created than a growing emphasis on ethnic pluralism, compounded by expansion to the Pacific Coast, tended to obstruct the development of a social structure reinforced by a commonly shared group of values and beliefs, a consensus about what Canada is and what it means to be a Canadian. The question facing this country, then, is whether or not we have "built up a reservoir of support—frequently described as patriotism, love of country, loyalty, and the like—upon which it can count regardless of the particular trials and tribulations of its members."[2] Social scientists seem to agree that without this support, without a sense of community, a political system is vulnerable to collapse.[3]

Throughout the 1960s and 1970s, distinguished Canadian intellectuals have addressed themselves to Hodgetts' principal concern: is the Canadian political community vulnerable to collapse because the political socialization process does not produce sufficient nationalism?[4]

Analysts of Canadian nationalism agree that most Canadians are not fervently nationalistic. After examining Canadian Gallup Poll results from 1941 through 1963, Mildred Schwartz discerns only "a slow unfolding of a unified national sentiment," "a cautious and diffident search for identity," and an "absence of aggressive nationalism."[5] Peter Russell contends that, despite assertions to the contrary, Canadians are not the least nationalistic people in the world. At the same time, Russell also admits that many Canadians are torn by competing loyalties (to province, region, and linguistic group), thus diminishing Canadian nationalism.[6]

Although a number of scholars have investigated the extent of nationalism in mature Canadians, few have examined its socialization. This is unfortunate because the development of nationalism and continentalism as well as the effects of regional and cultural loyalties upon these orientations are questions of central interest to students of Canadian politics. In this article both topics are discussed.

In the socialization literature one finds at least three contrasting analyses of how young people acquire emotions and beliefs about political communities.[7] The "gradual appreciation" school asserts that they develop cognitive and affective orientations through a protracted process stretching from early childhood into late adolescence. The gradual appreciation theorists contend that only during adolescence do young people manifest a mature understanding of their society's character as well as full-fledged nationalism. Those espousing the "early attachment" approach focus on the socialization of affective orientations. They agree with the gradual appreciation school that six- and seven-year-olds have no more than fragmentary, poorly integrated knowledge of their country's geography, peoples and history. Nevertheless, young children still acquire highly positive, emotional bonds to their country and its symbols. These early affective ties are crucial, first, because of their supposed permanence, and, secondly, because of their hypothetical role as building blocks for the more sophisticated views acquired during adolescence and adulthood. Developmental psychologists have advanced the "centre-periphery" explanations of political socialization. These scholars assert that a child's intellectual operations evolve through several stages of ever-more-complex activity. When he learns about his neighbourhood, city, province or country, he is simply passing through phases of cognitive development. Initially the child only perceives the geographical entities closest to him, the neighbourhood and city (those at the centre); with subsequent cognitive maturation, he discerns the more distant entities, the province and the country (those on the periphery). The socialization of fundamental loyalties unfolds along the same centre-periphery path; after all, the young Torontonian cannot love Canada if he does not know it exists.

The discrepancies among the three approaches raise a number of critical questions: Do Canadians acquire nationalistic orientations (of whatever intensity) as a result of a gradual developmental process, or do they feel supportive of their country very early in life as the early attachment school asserts? Do Canadians develop orientations in the centre-periphery manner, becoming more devoted to Canada with greater maturity, or do they experience a "periphery-centre" progression, growing increasingly more parochial in their affective orientations? Are Canadians' sentiments about Canada as immutable as the early attachment theorists claim?

RESEARCH DESIGN

The survey data for this article were collected from 1,199 Canadians between the ages of nine and nineteen, all inhabitants of Cape Breton Island, Nova Scotia. The sample consisted of 149 Micmac Indian students and 1,050 white students. They completed paper-and-pencil questionnaires in their classrooms during January and February of 1970. The research design was quasi-longitudinal; respondents were selected at relatively close age-intervals in order to detect year-by-year changes in their political orientations. Most of the questionnaire items first appeared, in slightly different form, in the Hess-Torney and Easton-Dennis studies.[8] However, it was necessary to modify several because they presumed more knowledge on the part of economically deprived respondents than they possessed.

Seeking to evaluate the young Cape Bretoners' attitudes and beliefs about Cape Breton, Nova Scotia and Canada, I asked: Do you believe that Canada is the best country in the world? How strongly do you believe this? Are you proudest of your island, province, or country? Do you believe that Canada should give up its independence and join a hypothetical "United States of the World"? What are Canada's biggest problems? Do you spend any time discussing these problems with your family? What do you, as an individual, dislike about Canada?

The white respondents were students in the Sydney Public Schools.[9] Members of the sample ranged from the nine-year-old just barely able to express political opinions to the nineteen-year-old eligible to vote. The white sample was almost equally divided on the basis of sex (47.6 per cent male versus 52.4 per cent female) and quite representative of the general community economically. Some 45.3 per cent of the respondents came from unskilled, blue-collar family backgrounds; 20.6 per cent from skilled, blue-collar backgrounds; 15.0 per cent from clerical, white-collar backgrounds and 15.0 per cent from professional, white-collar backgrounds. The white sample slightly over-represented Sydney's Catholics; 61.5 per cent of the respondents were Catholic versus 35.0 per cent Protestant. In addition, the oldest white age-cohort (those aged seventeen, eighteen, and nineteen) over-represented females, persons from unskilled, blue-collar families, and Catholics. However, on balance, this contingent of whites did accurately reflect the school-age population of Sydney.

The questionnaire was also administered to Micmac pre-adults living on three Cape Breton reserves: the Eskasoni reserve, by far the largest in Nova Scotia with 1,348 residents; the Middle River reserve, population 274, located near the community of Baddeck; and the Membertou reserve, population 331, situated within the Sydney city limits. Because the Micmacs' school drop-out rate is so high, I was unable to administer the questionnaire to a sizable number older than sixteen. The Micmac sample was also closely divided on the basis of sex (46.3 per cent female versus 53.7 per cent male). Significant socio-economic distinctions were difficult to establish among the Indians; nearly all Micmacs share essentially the same economic status.

Before administering the questionnaire it was announced that this was not a test, that for most of the items there were no correct answers, that the respondents were part of a large group of students throughout Cape Breton who were answering the same items, and that their responses would be confidential. All the items were read to the white, grades four and six students but the older whites were allowed to do the questionnaire on their own. In order to minimize language problems, I read the entire questionnaire to all the Indian students.

RESEARCH SETTING

These Cape Breton data do not describe the political socialization of all Canadians; they pertain only to pre-adults maturing in the Maritime

Provinces, an economically and politically distinctive region. Extrapolating from Gallup Poll results, Mildred Schwartz concludes that of all the regions in Canada, the Maritime Provinces have the most homogeneous political sub-culture. Among the factors responsible for this relative unanimity of political perspective are: the absence of sizable non-Anglophone, non-British communities; the dearth of fundamentalist religious sects; the high proportion of native-born Canadians in the region (approximately 96 per cent of Maritimers are native-born versus 84 per cent for the entire country); and the economic deprivation which has afflicted eastern Canada since 1866.[10]

Sydney, like most other Maritime cities, must struggle to survive economically. Located on the northeastern tip of Cape Breton Island, it is a community of 32,000 residents, predominantly Scottish in ethnicity but containing sizable contingents of English, Irish, Ukrainians, Blacks and Jews. The economy of Industrial Cape Breton (a term applied to Sydney and its suburbs) is dependent, to a very large degree, on the coal and steel industries which account for about one-third of the area's total employment and constitute the base activities which support the other sectors of the area's economy. Unfortunately, the coal and steel operations are currently employing fewer people than in the past and only a small number of new businesses have arrived to take up the employment slack. Despite the heavy injection of both federal and provincial funds, the future for primary and secondary industry in Sydney does not appear bright.

To the casual observer, the Micmac Indians resemble other indigent Cape Bretoners except for their tribal language. No Micmacs live in the manner of their forebears. So many changes have occurred in their environment that it would be impossible to regain the aboriginal ways. The younger people have forgotten the traditional practices and most would view the old way of life as alien and uncongenial.[11] But there are significant differences between the Micmacs and other Cape Bretoners. Much more than whites, the Indians must endure inadequate sanitation, deficient housing, malnutrition, illness, drug abuse, alcoholism and violence. The fundamental problem—the Micmacs' wretched poverty—frequently precipitates and greatly exacerbates these other hardships.[12] Politically, the Micmacs have functioned on the fringes of the national and provincial systems. It was not until 1960 that they acquired the right to vote in federal elections. Although Nova Scotia was the only province to allow Indians to vote in provincial elections prior to 1960, there is evidence that election officers denied Cape Breton Micmacs the franchise until 1958. Hawthorn suggests that because of this disenfranchisement—this refusal by whites to consider Indians their political equals—the native people have failed to identify with the larger political community.[13]

HYPOTHESES ABOUT CAUCASIAN POLITICAL SOCIALIZATION

Two factors suggested the hypothesis that Cape Breton political socialization does not produce relatively intense support for Canada and its symbols. First, previous research had shown considerable disparity in the degree of nationalism developed by citizens of various states. Cross-cultural studies indicate that non-American children and adolescents become less nationalistic than comparable Americans. According to Jack Dennis, the English develop "a very restrained sense of political community identification."[14] With increasing maturity, Dennis's English respondents (ages eight to seventeen) do not manifest any significant growth in nationalism.[15] From his research on primary and secondary school students in two coastal Colombian towns, Reid Redding concludes that Colombians acquire less favourable attitudes toward their country than similar Americans surveyed by Hess and Torney.[16] Political socialization, thus, is not an inflexible process, invariably producing the highly supportive orientations which white Americans of the early 1960s displayed. Secondly, there exists in Cape Breton a complex of historical, economic, psychological and political factors which diminish Canadian nationalism. Some affect Canadians regardless of region: for example, the "colonial mentality" which Canadians supposedly acquired during their subordinate relationship with the United Kingdom; the power currently exercised by American governments, corporations and citizens in Canadian life; the scarcity of unifying political symbols and historical myths; and the Québécois' and Western Canadians' efforts to gain a special status for their provinces within Confederation. Other factors affect only Maritimers, Nova Scotians and Cape Bretoners: these include the long tradition of anti-Confederation activity in Nova Scotia dating from Joseph Howe's efforts to dissolve the British North America Act in the late 1860s; the Maritimes' economic backwardness which residents often blame on deliberate decisions by "Upper Canadians"; and the intense pride which many Cape Bretoners feel about their island.[17]

It was also hypothesized that increasing maturity produces ever-larger proportions of Cape Bretoners willing to exchange Canadian independence for membership in a hypothetical world government, a "United States of the World." Moreover, it was expected that political socialization in Cape Breton results in a rather parochial perspective on Canada's problems. When asked about Canada's biggest problem, white Cape Bretoners, therefore, manifest much greater cognizance of local problems, especially those of the economic variety, than of national or international problems. Finally, it was anticipated that the political socialization process does not produce a strong desire to discuss national problems. In other words, the Cape Bretoners' tepid nationalism begets relatively little nationalistic behaviour.

THE WHITE DATA

The data clearly demonstrate that white Cape Bretoners do not develop the intensely supportive attitudes toward the state which commensurate Americans do.

Hess and Torney report that a very high percentage of their fourth and fifth grade respondents (84 to 87 per cent) believe that the United States is the best country in the world. Americans, with increasing maturity, subscribe even more intensely to this notion. The American developmental pattern is not universal as English and Colombian responses to similarly phrased items show.

The white Cape Bretoners' high proportion of "don't know" responses is striking. They very much resemble Redding's Colombian students in their uncertainty about how they should react to strong nationalistic assertions. The Cape Breton sample differs from the American and British contingents which have less than 10 per cent of any age-cohort in the "don't know" category. Among the nine- to fourteen-year-old Cape Bretoners, a stable proportion (about 46 per cent) agrees that Canada is the best country in the world. An equally stable segment (approximately one quarter) disagrees. As Cape Bretoners enter middle and later adolescence, the percentage who think their country superior to all others does increase somewhat. However, at no stage of the socialization process do

Table 1   Responses to "Our Country Is the Best Country in the World"; Mean Scores of American, English, Colombian, and White Cape Breton Respondents[a]

Cape Breton Whites			Americans[b]			Britons[c]		
Age	N	Mean Score	Grade	N	Mean Score	Age	N	Mean Score
9–10	186	3.41	4	1735	4.33	8–10	140	3.10
11–12	199	3.37	6	1746	4.42	11–13	204	2.93
13–14	223	3.47	8	1689	4.57			
15–16	259	3.78				14–17	189	3.04
17–19	183	3.64						

Colombians[d]			
Grade	N	Equivalent to Canadians Aged:	Mean Score
3	76	11–12	4.32
5	67	13–14	3.85
II	70	15–16	3.20
IV	43	17–18–19	2.86

[a] The English, American, and Colombian mean scores are placed in Table 1 next to those of the Cape Bretoners most comparable in age. The Cape Breton mean scores are calculated on the basis of 1 point for a "strongly disagree" response; 2 points for a "disagree"; 3 points for a "don't know" or "no opinion" response; 4 points for an "agree"; and 5 points for a "strongly disagree."

[b] SOURCE: Robert D. Hess and Judith V. Torney, *The Development of Basic Attitudes and Values Toward Government and Citizenship During the Elementary School Years* (Washington, D.C.: United States Office of Education, 1965), p. 80. Students responded to the statement "America is the best country in the world." Mean scores were calculated in the same way as the Cape Breton scores.

[c] SOURCE: Jack Dennis, Leon Lindberg, and Donald McCrone, "Support for Nation and Government Among English Children," *British Journal of Political Science*, vol. 1 (1971), p. 30. Students responded to the statement "Britain is the best country in the world." Mean scores were calculated in the same way as the Cape Breton and American scores.

[d] SOURCE: Reid Redding, "Political Socialization in Colombia and the U.S.A.," *Midwest Journal of Political Science*, vol. 12 (1968), p. 361. Students responded to the statement "Colombia is the best country in the world." Mean scores were calculated on the basis of 1 point for a "very false" response; 2 points for a "false"; 3 points for a "don't know"; 4 points for a "true"; and 5 points for a "very true." Colombians are approximately three years older than North Americans in the same grade.

Table 2 Responses to "Canada Is the Best Country in the World"; White Cape Bretoners

Age	N	Strongly Agree	Agree	Total Agrees	Disagree	Strongly Disagree	Total Disagrees	DK
9–10	186	25.8%	21.0	46.8	24.7	3.2	27.9	25.3
11–12	199	19.1%	27.1	46.2	22.1	3.0	25.1	28.6
13–14	223	26.9%	19.3	46.2	21.1	2.7	23.8	30.0
15–16	259	33.6%	28.6	62.2	15.4	1.2	16.6	21.2
17–19	183	29.1%	28.0	57.1	19.2	1.6	20.8	22.0
Totals	1050	27.2%	25.0	52.2	20.2	2.3	22.5	25.3

Cape Breton pre-adults display the degree of certitude about their country's pre-eminence revealed by Americans. On the other hand, at no stage do Cape Bretoners exhibit the sharp decline in nationalism characteristic of the Colombian sample or the nearly equal division between respondents agreeing or disagreeing on the United Kingdom's superiority which typifies Dennis's sample.

Social scientists have emphasized the role of symbols, such as flags and anthems, in the growth and maintenance of nationalistic sentiments. Gordon Allport contends: "As a rule, personal loyalty can adhere to an abstraction only when the abstraction is richly symbolized. Christianity rivets upon the cross, nations focus on their respective flags."[18] Among Cape Bretoners, one would expect to find rather meagre support for the Maple Leaf flag, in part because of their lukewarm nationalism, and in part because of Maritimers' traditional anglophilia. Gallup polls indicate that adult Maritimers tend to be more supportive of British symbols (such as the former Canadian flag, the Red Ensign) than Canadians from other regions.[19] Adolescents and young adults aged thirteen to twenty share this same preference for British symbols, including the Canadian Ensign.[20]

Cape Breton pre-adults begin their political socialization relatively unenthusiastic about their national flag. The American and Colombian respondents are initially a great deal more supportive of their flags than their Cape Breton counterparts. Moreover, the Cape Bretoners' comparatively frail approval diminishes still further as they grow older. This decline, however, is not quite as pronounced as that manifested by the Colombian students.

Table 3   Responses to "Our Country's Flag Is the Best in the World": Mean Scores for American, Colombian, and White Cape Breton Respondents[a]

Cape Breton Whites			Americans[b]			Colombians[c]			
Age	N	Mean Score	Grade	N	Mean Score	Grade	N	Equivalent to Canadians Aged	Mean Score
9–10	186	3.75	4	1731	4.46				
11–12	199	3.42	6	1743	4.43	3	76	11–12	4.59
13–14	223	3.50	8	1688	4.46	5	67	13–14	4.34
15–16	259	3.35				II	70	15–16	4.14
17–19	183	3.33				IV	43	17–18	3.88

a The American and Colombian mean scores are placed in Table 3 next to those of the Cape Bretoners most comparable in age. The Cape Breton mean scores are calculated on the basis of 1 point for a "strongly disagree" response; 2 points for a "disagree"; 3 points for a "don't know" or "no opinion" response; 4 points for an "agree"; and 5 points for a "strongly agree."

b SOURCE: Hess and Torney, *The Development of Basic Attitudes*, p. 80. Students responded to the statement "The American flag is the best flag in the world." Mean scores were calculated in the same way as the Cape Breton scores.

c SOURCE: Redding, "Political Socialization in Colombia and the U.S.A.," p. 361. Students responded to the statement "The Colombian flag is the best flag in the world." Mean scores were calculated on the basis of 1 point for a "very false" response; 2 points for a "false"; 3 points for a "don't know"; 4 points for a "true"; and 5 points for a "very true." Colombians are approximately three years older than the North Americans in the same grade according to Redding.

Probing further into the Cape Bretoners' affective orientations toward Canada, the questionnaire asked: "Should Canada be willing to give up its independence and join a United States of the World?"[21] National surveys have unearthed a substantial vein of Canadian public opinion which favours American annexation. Since World War Two, between one-tenth and one-fifth of the Canadian public has been willing to renounce national independence. These data notwithstanding, very few Sydney students at any age level wish to relinquish Canadian autonomy in order to join a "United States of the World."

Although young Cape Bretoners do not believe in the superiority of their country and its symbols as profoundly as some non-Canadians; and although they increasingly feel greater pride in Cape Breton than in Canada,[22] they are generally reluctant to join a speculative world polity.

Table 4   Responses to "Should Canada Be Willing to Give Up Its Independence and Join a United States of the World?": White Students

Age	N	Yes	No	DK
9–10	186	7.5%	72.6	19.9
11–12	199	11.1%	73.9	15.1
13–14	223	4.9%	79.4	13.7
15–16	259	8.5%	81.9	9.7
17–19	183	6.6%	85.7	7.7
Totals	1050	7.7%	78.9	13.4

Several scholars have investigated Canadians' perceptions of their society's problems. Occasionally the Gallup Poll asks its samples to describe the main issues facing Canada. Mildred Schwartz examined the answers to four such items; she found that between 1957 and 1962 adult Canadians pointed to economic difficulties as the dominant national concerns.[23] Federal election studies have explored how issues shape voting behaviour. When asked which issues influenced their votes, 61 per cent of 1968 voters mentioned economic topics. The need for a majority government was the only matter with greater impact on electoral behaviour; 71 per cent of the 1968 voters cited it. Substantial proportions of the electorate pointed to unemployment, the cost of living, and welfare as the key issues in the 1972 federal election. Meisel maintains that national unity, bilingualism, and the host of other non-economic issues which agitated both politicians and pundits hardly made a ripple with the voters.[24] On the basis of these studies, plus Sydney's lamentable economic condition, it was hypothesized that when young Cape Bretoners enumerated Canada's biggest problems, they would refer most frequently to economic difficulties, particularly of the local variety. It was also assumed that they would mention only the most conspicuous non-economic topics—anglophone-francophone relations and Canadian-American relations. Furthermore, it was anticipated that Cape Bretoners, as citizens of an international middle power, would make few direct references to foreign policy.

Social problems (crime, alcoholism, violence, bad character traits) and pollution typify the nine- and ten-year-olds' conceptions of Canada's major difficulties. With increasing maturity, the proportion of "social problem" replies drops from 32 per cent of the nine- and ten-year-olds'

Table 5 Responses to "Canada's Biggest Problem Is ——?": White Respondents

Age	Total N of Responses	Social Problems	Economic Problems	Foreign Policy	Racial Problems	French Canada	National Identity and Unity	Government and Politics	Pollution	Other	N
9–10	125	32.0%	2.4	0.8	0.0	0.8	0.0	10.4	28.8	24.8	125
11–12	202	12.4%	22.8	8.9	0.5	3.5	0.0	7.5	34.7	9.9	202
13–14	240	12.5%	35.4	6.3	2.1	7.1	1.7	5.9	25.4	3.8	240
15–16	286	8.0%	37.1	7.0	2.4	11.9	6.6	7.6	12.9	6.3	286
17–19	231	5.6%	36.8	6.5	2.2	17.7	8.7	7.8	6.1	8.7	231
Totals	1084	12.1%	30.0	6.4	1.7	9.2	4.0	7.6	20.1	9.0	1081

responses and 12.2 per cent of the eleven- and twelve-year-olds' answers to 5.6 per cent of the oldest students' answers. To the youngest respondents, the problem of pollution, especially that emanating from the Sydney steel plant, is quite salient. This early stress on local pollution reveals the somewhat insular perspective previously hypothesized. Although very few nine- and ten-year-olds mention economic problems, they constitute the second most frequent theme among eleven- and twelve-year-olds, and the most common selection among those aged thirteen through nineteen. In this response pattern we see how Cape Breton's frail economic condition affects its young people's attitudes about Canada's afflictions. As the country's most significant problem, they cite local strikes, other examples of labour unrest, the failures of the Sydney Steel Corporation, the possibility of the steel plant's closing, regional economic disparities, and emigration of the talented out of Cape Breton. These data confirm the proposition that economic issues, mainly of the local variety, grow increasingly relevant to Cape Bretoners during political socialization.

Until the thirteen- and fourteen-year-old stage, there are very few answers bearing upon francophone-anglophone relations. Among the fifteen- and sixteen-year-olds, francophone-anglophone relations are the third most frequently listed problem and among the seventeen-, eighteen-, and nineteen-year-olds, the second. Still, the oldest age-cohort names economic difficulties twice as often as strife between the two founding peoples. Political and governmental issues generally do not strike Cape Breton students as being Canada's most crucial burdens. Only 10.4 per cent of the answers from the nine- and ten-year-olds relate to topics such as the Prime Minister, various public policies, and police-community disagreements. With further political socialization, the proportion of political-governmental answers declines. As hypothesized, Cape Breton pre-adults do not believe that foreign entanglements constitute their country's most significant predicaments. Most young Cape Bretoners also do not hold issues of national identity and unity very important. No respondent mentions these questions until ages thirteen-fourteen and the percentage of responses dealing with these topics peaks at only 8.7 per cent. A final note: practically no whites mention racial discrimination or prejudice.

Demonstrating causal linkages between psychological orientations and political behaviour is a challenge for all who investigate public opinion.

This task is particularly difficult for students of pre-adult political socialization. Nevertheless, the Cape Breton questionnaire did try to discover
how much nationalistic behaviour results from the respondents' mild form
of nationalism. It asked: "Have you talked with your mother or father
about our country's problems?" This item seeks to determine whether the
child expresses concern for his country by discussing its difficulties within
the nuclear family. As the reader may recall, it was hypothesized that
political socialization in Cape Breton does not produce a strong desire to
thrash out national problems. The data confirm this hypothesis. Cape
Breton high school seniors do not talk about national issues with their
families as frequently as, for instance, American fourth-graders.[25]

Table 6   Responses to Item on Discussion of National Problems Within
the Family: Cape Breton White and American Respondents

Cape Breton Whites			Americans[a]		
Age	N	% of Yes Answers	Grade	N	% of Yes Answers
9–10	186	30.1	4	1733	58.8
11–12	199	38.2	6	1740	71.4
13–14	223	40.8	8	1687	71.7
15–16	259	46.7			
17–19	183	52.2			
Total	1050	41.8			

[a] Hess and Torney, *The Development of Political Attitudes in Children*, p. 71.

HYPOTHESES ABOUT RACIAL VARIATIONS

The second objective of this article is to examine sub-cultural variations
in the socialization of whites and Indians. In particular, this research
explores whether the Micmacs begin political socialization as devoted to
Canada as whites; and if the Micmacs do, whether their supportive
orientations remain intact through adolescence. Greenberg's research on
black and Caucasian elementary and junior high school students suggests
the developmental patterns which one can anticipate in the Micmacs.[26]
Greenberg finds that black children are slower in learning about the
national community than comparable whites. In addition, he demonstrates

that although blacks initially feel as favourably disposed to the United States as whites, they progressively become somewhat less nationalistic. Greenberg thus challenges the thesis that those orientations which one acquires earliest in life (such as nationalism) are perforce the most permanent. Racism and poverty partially erode the black child's initial loyalty to the national community. However, these black-white differences are a matter of degree; they do not indicate racial polarization. Greenberg's data reveal some racial differences in support for the United States; however, his black respondents certainly do not reject that country as totally repugnant. For instance, he finds an 11 per cent difference between black and white seventh- and ninth-graders in their appreciation of the American flag; 76 per cent of the blacks (as compared to 87 per cent of the whites) selected the American flag as the best flag in the world. Similarly, the proportion of seventh- and ninth-grade blacks agreeing with the statement "Sometimes I'm not very proud to be an American" is only 6 per cent higher than among whites.

Extrapolating from the Greenberg study, it was hypothesized that Cape Breton Indians resemble their white counterparts until the onset of adolescence (about thirteen years old or so) primarily because they gain political knowledge more slowly than do whites.[27] However, after learning more about Canadian society and their position within it, Indians become less supportive of the national community and its symbols than whites. It was also anticipated that the political socialization process on Micmac reserves produces greater propensity to relinquish Canadian sovereignty in order to join a "United States of the World." In addition, it was hypothesized the Micmac socialization process results in an insular, alienated view of Canada. Therefore, when asked to describe the country's greatest problem or its distasteful aspects, the Indians at each age level should refer more frequently to reserve problems or racial discrimination than whites. Finally it was hypothesized that Cape Breton Indians acquire less inclination to discuss national problems within the family than whites.

What is the justification for these hypotheses? It appears that the Micmacs, living in poverty-stricken isolation, come to perceive themselves as a separate people: marginal members, at best, of the Canadian commonwealth. They resent their inferior economic and political statuses and tend to blame white Canada (with ample reason) for their multitudinous hardships. Naturally, these attitudes affect the Indians' political socialization.

THE INDIAN DATA

During the early years of political socialization (from ages nine to twelve), the Micmacs are slightly more convinced than the whites of Canada's superiority to other countries. However, in middle adolescence, the Indians diverge somewhat, growing a bit less likely than the whites to assert that Canada is the best country in the world. For instance, at the fifteen-sixteen-year-old age-level, 16.8 per cent fewer Micmacs than whites are willing to proclaim Canada's greatness. According to these data, the direction of the socialization process differs for the two racial groups. From ages nine-ten to fifteen-sixteen, the percentage of whites agreeing on Canada's superiority increases 15.4 per cent while the percentage of Indians decreases 8.6 per cent. The Micmac "don't know" percentages are comparatively high on this and the subsequent flag item. While it is impossible to present a single, definitive explanation for this phenomenon, two alternative explanations will be offered. On the one hand, these

Table 7   White and Indian Responses to "Canada Is the Best Country in the World": Percentages and Mean Scores

Cape Breton Whites			Cape Breton Indians			Americans[a]		
Age	N	Mean Score	Age	N	Mean Score	Grade	N	Mean Score
9–10	186	3.41	9–10	25	3.68	4	1735	4.33
11–12	199	3.37	11–12	44	3.82	6	1746	4.42
13–14	223	3.47	13–14	47	3.45	8	1689	4.57
15–16	259	3.78	15–16	33	3.48			
17–19	183	3.64						

Indian Responses

Age	N	Strongly Agree	Agree	Total Agrees	Disagree	Strongly Disagrees	Total Disagrees	DK
9–10	25	40.0%	12.0	52.0	16.0	4.0	20.0	28.0
11–12	44	38.6%	15.9	54.5	2.3	4.5	6.8	38.6
13–14	47	21.3%	25.5	46.8	19.1	2.1	21.3	21.3
15–16	33	12.1%	33.3	45.4	9.1	0.0	9.1	45.5
Totals	149	27.5%	22.1	49.6	11.4	2.7	14.1	36.2

[a] Hess and Torney, *The Development of Basic Attitudes*, p. 80.

unusual proportions of "don't knows" may indicate that the Indians who hold negative attitudes about Canada are reluctant to reveal them to an unfamiliar social scientist. On the other hand, the large number of "don't knows" may connote not an active rejection of the Canadian political community but only ambivalent feelings and, therefore, refusal to express either hostility or support.

Only at ages eleven and twelve do the Micmacs express more approval for the Canadian flag than whites. As the Indians gain greater political knowledge, they become more critical of the flag than the white respondents. The most visible racial contrast is at the fifteen to sixteen-year-old level when 14.2 per cent fewer Indians concur on the flag's superiority than whites. The Micmacs, as they grow older, become noticeably more reluctant to respond in any way to this item.

The Indians react less nationalistically than whites to the question of whether Canada should surrender its independence in order to join a "United States of the World." At all age levels, the Micmacs are more

Table 8   White and Indian Responses to "The Canadian Flag Is the Best Flag in the World": Percentages and Mean Scores

Cape Breton Whites			Cape Breton Indians			Americans		
Age	N	Mean Score	Age	N	Mean Score	Grade	N	Mean Score
9–10	186	3.75	9–10	25	3.32	4	1731	4.46
11–12	199	3.42	11–12	44	3.86	6	1743	4.43
13–14	223	3.50	13–14	47	3.23	8	1688	4.46
15–16	259	3.35	15–16	33	3.18			
17–19	183	3.33						

Indian Responses

Age	N	Strongly Agree	Agree	Total Agrees	Disagree	Strongly Disagree	Total Disagrees	DK
9–10	25	28.0%	16.0	44.0	24.0	8.0	32.0	24.0
11–12	44	34.1%	27.3	61.4	4.5	2.3	6.8	31.8
13–14	47	10.6%	34.0	44.6	14.9	8.5	23.4	32.0
15–16	33	12.1%	21.2	33.3	21.2	3.0	24.2	42.5
Totals	149	20.8%	26.2	47.0	14.8	5.4	20.2	32.9

likely to assent to Canada's linking up with the conjectural "U.S.W." More importantly, at each stage of socialization, they are less inclined to disagree with the proposal. The differences between Indians and whites are quite substantial throughout the socialization process.

Table 9   White and Indian Opposition to Surrendering National Independence and Joining a "U.S.W."

	Cape Breton Whites			Cape Breton Indians	
Age	N	% Opposing U.S.W.		N	% Opposing U.S.W.
9–10	186	72.6		25	48.0
11–12	199	73.9		44	52.3
13–14	223	79.4		47	66.0
15–16	259	81.9		33	60.6
17–19	183	85.7			
Totals	1050	78.9		149	57.7

The Micmacs, from ages nine-ten to fifteen-sixteen, are either less willing or less able to outline Canada's biggest problems. While 1,050 white students point to 1,084 problems, the 149 Micmac residents specify only 66. Furthermore, many Micmacs do not define themselves as full-fledged members of the Canadian national community, as Table 10 indicates. Not one Micmac respondent alludes to the Canadian Indians' unique tribulations as Canada's biggest problems. In their eyes, these are *Indian* problems, not *Canadian* problems.

Like the white students, the Indians are most distressed by economic problems. With greater age, the proportion of Micmac responses devoted to economic topics also increases. The Indians develop less anxiety over pollution than whites. Environmental degradation may seem inconsequential to them because they are more worried about basic concerns, such as their family's next meal or decent shelter. At each age level, the proportion of Indian responses about government and politics is higher than for whites. However, the percentage of Indian political-governmental answers declines among students aged thirteen through sixteen as it does in whites of similar ages. It is possible that the older Indians may believe the problems of politics and government are so intractable that they are not worth describing. Issues of national identity do not worry Micmac

Table 10 Responses to "Canada's Biggest Problem Is ——?": Indian Respondents

Age	Social Problems	Foreign Policy	Racial Problems	French Canada	National Identity and Unity	Government and Politics	Economic Problems	Pollution	Other	N
9–10	9.1%	9.1	0.0	0.0	0.0	18.2%	27.3	18.2	18.2	11
11–12	9.1%	18.2	0.0	0.0	0.0	27.3%	18.2	4.5	22.7	22
13–14	15.0%	10.0	0.0	0.0	0.0	10.0%	35.0	15.0	15.0	20
15–16	15.4%	15.4	0.0	7.7	0.0	7.7%	38.5	7.7	7.7	13
Totals	12.1%	13.6	0.0	1.5	0.0	16.6%	28.8	10.6	16.7	66

respondents at all. Quebec surfaces as a national imbroglio only in the fifteen- and sixteen-year-olds' replies.

The students were also asked to complete a second open-ended item: "What I do not like about Canada is ———." This wording personalizes the request to evaluate the national community. Rather than soliciting judgments about the entire country's dilemmas, it seeks to discover what the respondents, as individuals, dislike about Canada. This item elicits interesting racial variations. In their answers, the Micmacs frequently mention race-related poverty and discrimination. They do not do so when enumerating Canada's biggest problems. These contrasting response patterns suggest that the Micmacs do not believe their burdens to be relevant to other Canadians.

CONCLUSION

In Cape Breton, race does influence the socialization of orientations toward Canada and its symbols. As the Micmac Indians mature and learn more about Canadian society and their standing within it, they become less supportive of their country than whites. They thus parallel American blacks in their moderate deviations from white socialization patterns. As in the case of the Caucasian-black differences in the United States, the white-Indian differences are matters of degree; they do not betoken sharp racial polarization insofar as attitudes toward Canada are concerned. At various points in the data many Micmacs reveal that they do not consider themselves integral parts of the Canadian political community. In addition, more Indians than whites state that they are willing to surrender Canadian independence. The Micmacs are also less likely to engage in nationalistic behaviour, such as discussing Canada's problems, than whites.

The data confirm that Cape Breton whites and Indians undergo contrasting socialization experiences which produce somewhat divergent results. While the gradual appreciation approach seems to explain the socialization of whites, a new model (perhaps we should call it the gradual disaffection approach) is needed to explicate that of the Micmacs.

White Cape Bretoners do not acquire the intensely supportive attitudes toward the state which, for instance, white American pre-adults develop. On the items concerning country and flag, the Cape Breton respondents at all five age levels manifest only a gently nationalistic developmental pattern. Most do not express the very approbative views which early attachment theorists predict. In their tendency to report local problems (the Sydney steel plant, its pollution, and so on) as Canada's biggest tribulations, one sees evidence of their growing parochial loyalties. Sydney's young people do not, by and large, conceptualize national unity and identity as important problems. In addition, relatively few white respondents discuss the country's difficulties with their parents. Nonetheless, very few white Cape Bretoners are willing to surrender Canada's independence in order to join a hypothetical world government. In summary, the Sydney data cast doubt on the cross-cultural validity of the early attachment thesis that children as young as nine possess highly positive emotions toward their country. The gradual appreciation approach provides the most accurate description of this phase of Cape Breton political socialization.

NOTES

1. A. B. Hodgetts, *What Culture? What Heritage?: A Study of Civic Education in Canada* (Toronto: The Ontario Institute for Studies in Education, 1968), p. 11.
2. David Easton, *A Systems Analysis of Political Life* (New York: John Wiley, 1965), p. 125.
3. Hodgetts, *What Culture?*, p. 11.
4. Many scholars have examined the consequences of nationalism for the polity. Many agree with Hodgetts that without a sense of nationalism a political system is vulnerable to collapse. For instance, Paul Rosenblatt contends that the degree of support for the national political community is related to its ability to survive emergencies and crises. Paul C. Rosenblatt, "Origins and Effects of Group Ethnocentrism and Nationalism," *Journal of Conflict Resolution*, vol. 8 (1964), p. 131. In addition, nationalism "makes it easier to cheat, to fight, or to kill an outsider," and increases one's motivation to go to war. Ibid., p. 141. Sidney Verba maintains that national identity is the "most crucial political belief" which an individual ever acquires, the societal equivalent to the personal concept of self-identity. Verba also asserts that if citizens are not particularly nationalistic, illegal and violent patterns of social and political change are more likely to occur. Furthermore, Verba points out that a country's aggregate degree of nationalism is related to the leaders' ability to mobilize citizens and to commit them to achieving national goals. Sidney Verba, "Comparative Political Culture," in Lucian W. Pye and Sidney Verba, eds., *Political Culture and Political Development* (Princeton: Princeton University Press, 1965), p. 529.
5. Mildred A. Schwartz, *Public Opinion and Canadian Identity* (Berkeley: University of California Press, 1967), pp. 119–20.
6. Peter H. Russell, "Nationalism in Canada," *Your Canada: Complete Series* (Toronto: Toronto-Dominion Bank, 1968), p. 6.

7. The labels given the three analyses first appeared in Edward S. Greenberg, "Children and the Political Community: A Comparison Across Racial Lines," *Canadian Journal of Political Science*, vol. 2 (1969), p. 474.

8. Robert Hess and Judith Torney, *The Development of Political Attitudes in Children* (Chicago: Aldine, 1967), and David Easton and Jack Dennis, *Children in the Political System* (New York: McGraw-Hill, 1969).

9. There is no separate school system as such in Sydney, although children are assigned to schools along Catholic/non-Catholic lines.

10. Schwartz, *Public Opinion and Canadian Identity*, p. 147.

11. Fred Gross, "Indian Island: A Micmac Reserve," in Jean Leonard Elliot, ed., *Native Peoples* (Scarborough, Ontario: Prentice-Hall, 1971), pp. 89–98.

12. The Extension Department of St. Francis Xavier University did a survey which shows how impoverished Cape Breton's Indians really are. During February and March 1967, the Eskasoni reserve had an unemployment rate of 32 per cent. When retired and pensioned householders are added, the percentage of unemployed increases to 64 per cent. Only 12 per cent of the Membertou householders said they were unemployed; the Membertou figure rises to 28 per cent when retired and pensioned people were added. When we analyse how many Micmacs were steadily employed—that is, worked for at least eight months during the previous year—we get a bleaker picture of the Indians' economic situation. Only 26 per cent of the Eskasoni householders were steadily employed; Membertou, 33 per cent. Only 38 per cent of Eskasoni families had incomes above the 1967 poverty line; 40 per cent of the Membertou families were above this line. Alex A. MacDonald, *Community Resources and Dimensions of Alienation on Indian Reserves* (Antigonish, Nova Scotia: Extension Department, St. Francis Xavier University, 1967).

13. H. B. Hawthorn, ed., *A Survey of Contemporary Indians of Canada* (Ottawa: Indian Affairs Branch, 1966), vol. 1, pp. 360–84.

14. Jack Dennis, Leon Lindberg, and Donald McCrone, "Support for Nation and Government Among English Children," *British Journal of Political Science*, vol. 1 (1971), p. 30.

15. Ibid., pp. 25–47.

16. Reid Redding, "Political Socialization in Colombia and the U.S.A.," *Midwest Journal of Political Science*, vol. 12 (1968), p. 360.

17. Many of the Sydney respondents seem to think of themselves as residents of the "Province of Cape Breton" rather than of Nova Scotia. In informal conversation, one notices the distinction which Cape Bretoners often draw between Cape Breton and the "Mainland." Further evidence of this local patriotism is the manner in which several respondents wrote their addresses on the questionnaire. Instead of writing "Sydney, Nova Scotia" they put "Sydney, Cape Breton" or "Sydney, C.B." This insular identification, I believe, detracts from the development of Canadian nationalism.

18. Gordon W. Allport in T. H. Pear, ed., *Psychological Factors in Peace and War* (London: Hutchinson, 1950), p. 153.

19. Schwartz, *Public Opinion and Canadian Identity*, p. 106.

20. John C. Johnstone, *Young People's Images of Canadian Society: An Opinion Survey of Canadian Youth Thirteen to Twenty Years of Age* (Ottawa: Information Canada, 1971), p. 13.

21. Unfortunately, the wording of the question creates some possibility of misinterpretation. Respondents may think that they are being asked whether they are favourably inclined to renouncing their independence in order to associate themselves with

the United States of America. Whatever the interpretation the schoolchildren put on the term "United States of the World," the query definitely requests their opinion on whether Canada should yield its autonomy. I suspected that Cape Bretoners might be unusually amenable to this suggestion. After all, Maritimers have long considered themselves the economic victims of Confederation. What would they have to lose?

22. I asked the respondents whether they are most proud of Cape Breton, Nova Scotia, or Canada. What appears in their responses is a "periphery-centre" pattern. Among the white respondents, 61.6 per cent of the nine- and ten-year-olds choose Canada as the entity of which they are most proud; this figure declines to 48.4 per cent among the seventeen-, eighteen-, and nineteen-year-olds. In contrast, the proportion of white respondents who choose Cape Breton increases steadily from 13.4 per cent among the nine- and ten-year-olds to 34.6 per cent among the seventeen-, eighteen-, and nineteen-year-olds. The monotonic nature of the decline in pride in Canada and of the increase in pride in Cape Breton connotes an increasing parochialism and a rejection of Canada as the primary object of community loyalty.

23. Schwartz, *Public Opinion and Canadian Identity*, pp. 228–31.

24. John Meisel, *Working Papers on Canadian Politics* (Montreal: McGill-Queen's Press, 1973), pp. 19–22 and 218–22.

25. Hess and Torney, *Development of Political Attitudes*, p. 71.

26. Greenberg, "Children and the Political Community."

27. See Stephen Ullman, "Cross-Cultural and Sub-Cultural Variations in Political Socialization: A Study of Caucasion and Indian Canadians" (unpublished PH.D. thesis, University of Minnesota, 1973).

Conflicting National Identities Among Canadian Youth*

15

H. D. FORBES

Canada, like the United States, is a nation of immigrants; its people come from many different lands. Most Canadians today assume that a distinctive nationality is in the process of formation in Canada. They assume that a transformation will take place in Canada similar to the one that made Americans out of Yankees, Virginians, Germans, Czechs, Poles, and Italians. Only the result will be *Canadians*. Talking about this new nationality—anticipating the national identities of future Canadians and trying to discern the outlines of this new national character—is a national pastime of Canadians.

A main theme in recent discussions of Canadian nationality has been Canada's commitment to cultural diversity: to bilingualism and multiculturalism. The Canadian mosaic is contrasted with the American melting pot.[1] Fifty or one hundred years ago there would have been greater emphasis on "Britishness" in defining Canada. Allegiance to the British crown symbolized, for many Canadians, "an inchoate desire to build . . . a society with a greater sense of order and restraint than freedom-loving republicanism would allow."[2] Canada was British North America: North American opportunity with British liberty and constitutional government. Thus Canada stood for the inhibition of anarchic impulses and the refusal to pander to the passions of the mob. It would have been identified with orderly progress, high standards of public morality, and respect for authority and tradition. Canadians would have been presented as a less sinful, more austere and more refined people than their brash, self-indulgent, vulgar neighbours to the south. Canada's role in the world, and

*Research support from the H. P. Kendall Fund and from the Izaak Walton Killam Fund of the Canada Council is gratefully acknowledged. For criticism of an earlier draft of the paper I am grateful to R. A. Manzer and John Terry.

its contribution to world history, would have been discussed in relation to the British Empire.[3]

Today we hear only the faintest echoes of these once popular themes. Donald Smiley expresses the contemporary attitude when he says that "we have had too much of racial nationalism—of French-Canadian delusions of a providential mission, of notions of British Imperial destiny, of latter-day Anglo-Saxon assimilationism."[4] What we need, and what we shall see we have, if only we examine our traditions with the proper care, is "a Canadian political nationality divorced from cultural considerations."[5] Canadians have always been united by allegiance to a monarch, and this is a political bond that is inherently more tolerant of diversity than is commitment to the abstract principles of republican democracy. "One of the blessings of Canadian life," Professor Morton tells us, "is that there is no Canadian way of life, much less two, but unity under the Crown admitting of a thousand diversities."[6] Ramsay Cook endorses this emphasis on diversity when he distinguishes between the nationalist-state and the nation-state:

> The nationalist-state is one in which the ideological demands of one cultural group or nation are forced upon all other groups within its borders. . . . A nation-state is a political and juridical concept which seeks to protect the individual and collective rights of its inhabitants without reference to cultural or national ideological claims. . . . The Fathers of the Canadian Confederation understood this distinction perfectly well and sought to express it in their concept of "a new nationality." It has too often been forgotten by Canadian politicians and intellectuals since.[7]

Despite his skepticism about attempts to discover the Canadian identity, Cook allows that "perhaps it is the heterogeneous pluralism itself that is the Canadian identity."[8] Many Canadians are convinced that it is this heterogeneous pluralism that gives Canada a role to play on the world stage. For example, Prime Minister Trudeau: "Better than the American melting-pot, Canada could offer an example to all those new Asian and African states . . . who must discover how to govern their polyethnic populations with proper regard for justice and liberty. . . . Canadian federalism is an experiment of major proportions; it could become a brilliant prototype for the moulding of tomorrow's civilization."[9]

For more than a decade, however, discussions of Canadian nationality have betrayed considerable anxiety about the future. Two great problems threaten the successful completion of the process of nation-building upon which Canadians launched more than a century ago. The vigorous separatist movement in Quebec has revived fears of fragmentation, of the break-up of Canada into its regional components and the collapse of the federal government. This is the contemporary form of the perennial problem of national unity. More recently, disillusionment with the United States has stimulated concern about economic and cultural domination analogous to the older fear of outright annexation. Economists have pointed to the increasing American ownership and control of Canadian industry and resources. Philosophers have lamented the impact of the American mass media on the Canadian mind. Many Canadians fear that Canada is rapidly becoming a duplicate United States, America North, a nation unable and unwilling to give any real content to its formal political sovereignty. This is the current problem of national independence.

The growing celebration of cultural diversity is obviously related to the growing fear of separatism and American control. Respect for diversity provides a basis for cooperation between Canada's diverse ethnic groups, particularly the English and the French, and it also provides a justification for Canadian independence vis-à-vis the United States. Insistence on Canada's pluralist virtue is a way of simultaneously discrediting the "racial nationalism" of Quebec's separatists and the false internationalism of English Canada's continentalists.

But are Canadians in fact committed to respect for diversity? The question is obviously complex. What is meant by diversity? What would be the signs of such a commitment? How can we possibly generalize about the political ideals of twenty-two million people? Plainly it is not just a matter of adding up the opinions of all Canadians, indifferently setting alongside the views of a prime minister, let us say, those of a teenager who may have only the haziest ideas about Canada and its political traditions. Yet it is equally plain that the answer must depend in some way upon how citizens talk about their country.

This paper examines the responses to questions about national identity of a sample of Canadian youth in 1968. The questions were part of a paper-and-pencil questionnaire given to students in 23 schools in three provinces in the spring of 1968. The data have all the usual limitations and imperfections of mass survey data, and some less common ones as well. The respondents were all students in grades eleven and twelve in public high schools. Their opinions were garnered by means of anonymous questionnaires filled out in the classroom during regular classroom time. Two questionnaires were used in the study, one in English and the other in French. The French questionnaires were used only in French Catholic high schools in Quebec. Most of the questions were the same in both questionnaires, but some of the questions were asked in only one of the questionnaires, and sometimes the order of questions was different. All the basic questions we shall be concerned with were in both questionnaires and occurred in the same sequence in both.

The sample of schools was drawn unsystematically (not randomly) from five urban areas: Winnipeg, Oakville, Toronto, Montreal, and Quebec City. Altogether 1,825 students completed questionnaires, but the proportions from different cities bear no relationship to the sizes of these cities. There are approximately equal numbers of males and females in the sample. The median age of the English students was 17.9 years; of the French students, about 17.6 years.[10] The students came from a wide range of backgrounds, though disproportionately from the upper social strata. Thirty-nine per cent of the English students and 4 per cent of the French students reported that one or both of their parents were born outside Canada. Thus the sample is representative, at best, of older high school students in urban areas in the central regions of the country, and perhaps only of those urban areas, moreover, where there are relatively few recent immigrants.

Despite the limitations of the data, they will, I hope, throw some light on the Canadian identity. The youthfulness of the sample is an advantage, of course, in so far as we are interested in trends and in anticipating how the problems of nation-building will be seen by the next generation of Canadians.

CHOOSING LABELS

A series of questions midway through the questionnaire asked each student to describe himself from the standpoint of nationality and ethnicity. The first of these questions asked the student to check, from a list of commonly used labels, all those that applied to him personally.

How many of the following terms do you ever use to describe yourself?
(Check as many as apply to you personally).

– Canadian	– German
– English Canadian	– Irish
– French Canadian	– Italian
– American	– Polish
– Belgian	– Scandinavian
– British	– Scottish
– Dutch	– Ukrainian
– English	– Welsh
– French	– North American

The question in the French questionnaire was the same except that six of the terms less likely to be chosen by the French students (Dutch, German, Polish, Scandinavian, Ukrainian, and Welsh) had been edited from the list of responses and two terms (Acadien and Québécois) had been added. The second question in the series was open-ended and was the same in both questionnaires: "How do you prefer to think of yourself—as English Canadian, or French Canadian, or German or Italian Canadian, as simply a Canadian, or how?" This was followed by a question which forced a choice between three basic alternatives.

Of the three terms below, which one comes closest to describing you?

– Canadian
– English Canadian
– French Canadian

It was the same in both questionnaires.

Table 1 shows the distribution of responses to the first question. To simplify the table, the proportions choosing a particular label are shown only for those labels chosen by at least 10 per cent of either the English or the French sample. Two results may be noted at once. First, there is some variation from city to city in the responses of the English students, though not a great deal. The students in Montreal and Quebec City are more likely than those in Winnipeg to describe themselves as "English Canadians," and less likely to describe themselves as "Canadians." Secondly, fewer than a third of the students in either group indicate that

Table 1   Free Choice of Descriptive Terms by Language and Province*

Term	English Students			French Students
	Manitoba	*Ontario*	*Quebec*	
Canadian	95%	92%	88%	65%
English Canadian	29	34	39	4
French Canadian	4	4	8	78
English	19	26	25	1
French	6	5	6	15
Irish	12	12	11	3
Scottish	12	11	12	2
North American	23	25	22	30
Québécois	N.A.	N.A.	N.A.	79
	(N = 371)	(N = 507)	(N = 203)	(N = 744)

*The percentages sum to more than 100 per cent because the respondents could check more than one term. The percentages are computed from the total number of respondents, not from the total number of responses.

the term "North American" describes them. Since all the students are presumably aware that Canada is part of North American and are also aware of the close connections between Canada and the United States, the low proportion checking "North American" may indicate unwillingness to identify personally with the wider continental or American dimension of Canadian life.

The most striking feature of Table 1 is the relatively large proportion of the English sample who check the description "Canadian." The English students are far more likely to check this description than are the French students, who favour "French Canadian" and "Québécois." The term is also far more likely to be checked than any of the other descriptive terms available in the English questionnaire. The diversity of the "English" sample (only about one third of whom are the offspring of emigrants from England) is obviously one reason for this preponderance of "Canadian" choices. The table would look quite different if the English respondents had been classified by ethnic or national origin rather than by province. For in general, of course, there is a strong correlation between (objective) origin and (subjective) identity. Thus 64 per cent of the students in the English sample who report German ancestry (maternal, paternal, or both) check the description "German"; 50 per cent of those with Polish ancestry check the description "Polish"; and 72 per cent of those with Ukrainian ancestry check "Ukrainian."[11] Even by comparison with these figures, however, the proportion who check "Canadian" is strikingly high: regardless of origin, about nine out of every ten students in the English sample say that they think of themselves as Canadians.

The first question about national identity did not demand that the relation between different identifications be made clear: the respondent simply checked as many of the terms as he thought applied to himself. The second, open-ended question did implicitly demand a ranking of different loyalties. Answers to this question were grouped in seven main categories: Emphatically Canadian, Simply Canadian, Qualified Canadian, Hyphenated Canadian, Another Nationality, Provincialist, and Internationalist. The first four categories, having to do with different styles of Canadian identification, demand further explanation:

1) Emphatically Canadian: those who put a special emphasis on the idea that they were simply Canadians and nothing else.

2) Simply Canadian: those who wrote down, in ordinary script, the word "Canadian" (or "Canadien").

3) Qualified Canadian: those who indicated that they were Canadians, but with some qualification or elaboration, for example, "Canadien de langue française," "Canadian of German descent," "Canadian citizen and British subject."

4) Hyphenated Canadian: those who said "English Canadian," "Canadien français," "German Canadian," etc.

The seventh category, Internationalist, includes those who said that they did not think of themselves as any particular nationality, that they were human beings, that they did not believe in national distinctions, and so on.

Table 2 shows the distribution of responses to this question. Again the similarity of the English-speaking students from different cities is striking. It is also striking that only about one out of a hundred students took the opportunity provided by this question to declare that they thought of themselves as citizens of the world rather than as members of any particular nation. The English and French students did not differ in this respect. Where there is a clear difference between the two linguistic groups is in how they relate themselves to the Canadian community. Seven out of

Table 2 Basic National Identity by Language and Province

Identity	English Students			French Students
	Manitoba	Ontario	Quebec	
Emphatically Canadian	32%	34%	30%	10%
Simply Canadian	38	42	41	9
Qualified Canadian	12	7	8	10
Hyphenated Canadian	14	11	16	61
Another Nationality	2	4	4	3
Provincialist	0.0	0.2	0.5	5
Internationalist	1	1	0.5	1
	(N = 367)	(N = 498)	(N = 203)	(N = 719)

ten English students say, with greater or less emphasis, that they are simply Canadians; by comparison, only two out of ten French students do so. About seven out of ten French students draw attention to their identification with the French third of the Canadian population, most of them by putting down that they are "Canadien français." About 15 per cent of the French students indicated that they were Québécois, as compared with a minuscule proportion of the English students who drew attention to their provincial loyalties.[12]

The contrast between the English and the French students is clearest in their answers to the last of the three questions (Table 3). Most English-speaking students call themselves "Canadians," while most French-speaking students call themselves "French Canadians."

Taking these data at face value, they suggest two generalizations. First, Canadian youth rarely identify with any group other than Canada or one

Table 3 Best Term for National Identity by Language and Province

Identity	English Students			French Students
	Manitoba	Ontario	Quebec	
Canadian	87%	81%	78%	29%
English Canadian	11	17	20	1
French Canadian	1	2	2	70
	(N = 367)	(N = 501)	(N = 199)	(N = 731)

of its component parts. Canada is the outer limit, so to speak, of their conscious loyalties. Specifically, they manifest little inclination to think of themselves as North Americans. Secondly, there are marked differences in the national loyalties of French and English students. It is not clear how these differences should be described. We could say that the French students tend to identify with one particular region and ethnic group, while the English students tend to identify with the nation as a whole. Or we could say that the English students have a single dominant loyalty, while the French students have multiple loyalties, so that their identifications are more ambiguous.

It is debatable, of course, whether we should take these data at face value. They may be purely conventional responses that reveal little about the real loyalties and self-images of the students. It is important to take into account their answers to a variety of other questions before deciding what significance the responses examined so far have.

CHOOSING HEROES AND COUNTRIES

Nationalism is associated with devotion to symbols of the nation such as flags, slogans and national anthems. Common admiration for heroic national figures is also supposed to fortify and express the sentiment of national solidarity. At the beginning of the questionnaire the students were asked "What great people, living or dead, do you most admire?" The question said that they should try to think of two or three whom they really admired. Most named two, and when their responses were classified by nationality, the results provided some support to the generalization made earlier about differences in national identity of English and French students, but the most surprising result was the large number of Americans chosen by both groups. Table 4 shows the distributions by nationality for the first, second, and third choices for each linguistic group separately.[13] The more imaginative youth—those who put down more than one hero— were more likely to name a Canadian, but even among the third choices the Americans outnumber the Canadians. It might be objected that the small number of Canadians is only to be expected, as Canada has pro- duced few world-historical figures. But world-historical figures are not prominent among the heroes of our youth. Plato, Caesar, Shakespeare, or Beethoven were admired by a tiny fraction of the students; most chose

Table 4 Nationality of Great Men by Language of Respondents

Nationality	English Students			French Students		
	First Choice	*Second Choice*	*Third Choice*	*First Choice*	*Second Choice*	*Third Choice*
English Canadian	6%	8%	7%	0.2%	2%	2%
French Canadian	6	8	5	5	13	8
American	52	38	19	74	31	14
British	15	15	5	3	9	4
French	3	3	2	7	11	7
Other	11	8	8	8	17	11
No Response	7	19	55	4	17	55
	(N = 1049)	(N = 1042)	(N = 1042)	(N = 740)	(N = 731)	(N = 730)

less remote figures: Pope John, Billy Graham, Timothy Leary, Dag Hammarskjöld, or Frank Zappa, for example. About three-quarters of the first choices were political figures. Although no records were kept of individual choices, John Kennedy was obviously the most frequently chosen single person.

These results suggest that the first generalization about national identities—that Canadian young people have little identification with the United States—needs to be modified. True, there is little conscious identification with the United States, and "American" or "North American" are not important parts of the Canadian's self-image, but there is also little inclination to emphasize differences between Canada and the United States and there is, of course, considerable actual involvement in American politics and culture.[14]

The low salience of differences between Canada and the United States is clearly apparent in the responses to another question that was part of a short series about living in countries other than Canada. The students were asked to indicate, from a list of ten possible choices, which they thought were "the main advantages of being a Canadian." Table 5 repro-

Table 5   Advantages of Living in Canada by Language of Respondents*

Advantages	English Students	French Students
The freedom and the democratic government	80%	62%
The opportunity here for anyone who wants to get ahead	69	47
Canada is rich—most people have good jobs	59	46
The beautiful scenery here in Canada	55	48
We can be proud of the achievements of many great Canadians	49	29
Canada has done a lot to preserve peace in the world	43	35
Canada has two main cultures and two languages	32	31
The power that Canada is going to have in the future	22	53
Canada is protected by the power of the United States	20	23
Being part of the British Commonwealth under the Queen	12	3
	(N = 1081)	(N = 744)

*See note to Table 1.

duces the list from which they chose, though the items have been re-arranged so that they are in decreasing order of popularity among the English students. The students were instructed that they should check as many as they though were "important advantages" and that "most people" check 3 or 4. The average number checked by the English students was 4.4, and by the French students it was 3.8. What is most striking about the data in Table 5 is the great popularity of the advantages which express the North American ideology of freedom and opportunity. The advantages that implicitly contrast Canada with the United States—"two main cultures," "Canada a peace-keeper," and "being part of the Commonwealth" —are less frequently chosen. "Being part of the British Commonwealth under the Queen" comes in last, substantially behind the advantage that "Canada is protected by the power of the United States."

Lack of enthusiasm for the monarchy is also shown by the answers to a direct question, "Do you think that Canada should continue to pay allegiance to the Queen, or do you think that we should become a Republic with an elected President?" A slight plurality (42 per cent to 36 per cent) of the English students favoured retention of the monarchy, while 21 per cent were undecided or did not care. Among the French students the corresponding percentages were 16 per cent in favour of the monarchy, 62 per cent in favour of a republic, and 21 per cent indifferent or undecided.

Finally, Table 5 suggests that the English and French students are inclined to emphasize different advantages of living in Canada. The French students are evidently less impressed by the freedom and opportunity in Canada,[15] and less inclined to bask in the reflected glory of "many great Canadians" than are the English students. They are more concerned than their English compatriots with the future power of the country. It is as if the French students saw the virtues of Canada as those of a good ally.

SIMILARITIES AND DIFFERENCES

Perhaps the simplest way to estimate one group's feeling of distance from or identification with another is to ask them whether the others are similar or different from themselves. This question was asked in a variety of ways in the questionnaire, with interesting results.

About three-quarters of the way through the questionnaire the students were asked to rate pairs of groups on a five-point scale from very similar to very different. The instructions said that "although a pair of groups may seem similar in one way and different in another," they should "try to make an overall judgement of their similarity." Some of the results from this question are summarized in Table 6. A little more than a third of both the English and the French students, when rating the similarity between "English Canadians and French Canadians," place this pair at the similar end of the scale, checking the points corresponding to "very similar" or "fairly similar." Thus on the average both groups of students say that "English Canadians and French Canadians" belong in the middle of the scale—about as similar as they are different. These ratings shall be our point of reference in what follows. As the figures in the first column of Table 6 show, the English students tend to see English Canadians as much more similar to Americans and to British (from Britain) and much less similar to French (from France). Conversely, they tend to see French Canadians as being quite unlike Americans and British (from Britain), but quite similar to French (from France)—all by comparison with how they rate English Canadians and French Canadians. Turning to the

Table 6   Ratings of Similarity by Language of Respondents*

Groups Compared	English Students		French Students	
	"English Canadians"	"French Canadians"	"English Canadians"	"French Canadians"
"English Canadians"		35%		36%
"French Canadians"	35%		36%	
"Americans"	71	7	58	25
"British (from Britain)"	70	5	45	7
"French (from France)"	5	56	4	38
	(N = 1081)	(N = 1081)	(N = 744)	(N = 744)

*The figures in the table are the percentage of each group of students who rate the given pair of groups "Very Similar" or "Fairly Similar." Thus 71 per cent of the English students checked one of these responses for the comparison of "English Canadians" and "Americans," and 58 per cent of the French students did likewise. Comparing "French Canadians" and "Americans," the corresponding proportions rating these groups very or fairly similar were 7 per cent and 25 per cent respectively.

ratings by the French students, we see essentially the same pattern of perceived similarities and differences, but less clearly. The French students, like the English students, see English Canadians as being relatively unlike the French (from France). Like the English students, they see more similarity between French Canadians and English Canadians than between French Canadians and Americans. The British (from Britain) are seen as clearly different than French Canadians. Unlike the English students, the French students tend to see approximately the same degree of similarity or difference between French Canadians and French (from France) as they do between French Canadians and English Canadians. It is perhaps not surprising that the French students, by comparison with the English, should minimize the differences between themselves and Americans, and should see greater differences between themselves and Frenchmen. Nor is it surprising that they should be struck by the similarities between English Canadians and Americans. What is more surprising is that the English students, too, tend to emphasize the similarities between English Canadians and Americans.

Different ways of asking essentially the same question produce somewhat different results, and an impression of greater solidarity among Canadians vis-à-vis foreigners. At an earlier point students were asked who they thought had "more in common," French Canadians and English Canadians or French Canadians and French people from France. The distributions of responses are shown in Table 7. Despite the greater similarity they perceive between French Canadians and French from France, the students in both groups clearly tend to say that French Canadians have more in common with English Canadians.

Table 7 Group Having More in Common with French Canadians by Language and Province

Group	English Students			French Students
	Manitoba	Ontario	Quebec	
English Canadians	66%	66%	64%	62%
French from France	18	20	22	26
Not Sure	16	14	14	12
	(N = 365)	(N = 498)	(N = 198)	(N = 734)

Table 8   Group Having More in Common with English Canadians by Language and Province

Group	English Students			French Students
	Manitoba	Ontario	Quebec	
French Canadians	36%	30%	36%	40%
Americans	54	60	55	48
Not Sure	10	10	9	12
	(N = 366)	(N = 498)	(N = 199)	(N = 737)

A similar question involved the comparison of English Canadians, French Canadians and Americans. Both groups of students tended to say that English Canadians and Americans have more in common, rather than English Canadians and French Canadians (Table 8). This is in line with the results of the rating scales of similarity/difference, but the results are not nearly so clear-cut as with the rating scales. Here, too, there is apparently a tendency to say that English Canadians and French Canadians have much in common despite their dissimilarities.

Response to these "more in common" questions is evidently a function not just of perceived similarities and differences, but also of the political institutions which unite groups or which leave them formally independent of one another. In the case of the French Canadians and the French from France, the absence of these political ties is evidently more salient than the cultural and linguistic similarities. But in the comparison of English Canadians and Americans the cultural and linguistic similarities are so striking that they override the formal political independence of the two groups.

NATIONALISM AND NATIONAL IDENTITY

Lord Durham's "two nations warring within the bosom of a single state" is a tempting summary of the findings presented so far. The questions about self-image seem to show that Canada is two nations not just sociologically, but also psychologically. The questions about similarities and differences reveal that both language groups regard Canada as artificial in the sense that there is a greater natural affinity between English Canadians and Americans than between English Canadians and French Canadians.

Yet the handy formula of "two nations" is in some ways quite misleading. It does not indicate the kind of nationalist conclusions the students draw from the cultural similarities and differences they perceive. This is particularly so for the English-speaking students, but it is also true for the French-speaking students.

The English students are overwhelmingly against the separation of Quebec from the rest of Canada and they are equally opposed to a political union between Canada and the United States. In response to a question about separation, 78 per cent said that they were "strongly opposed to separation"; only 6 per cent said that they were slightly or strongly in favour of separation. The next question asked whether they thought "that Quebec will decide to separate from the rest of Canada some time in the future." Only 14 per cent said that they thought it would. On the question of Canadian independence vis-à-vis the United States, only 9 per cent said that they were in favour of "Canada and the United States joining together as one country."

The assumption implicit in these opinions is that cultural differences need not be a barrier to national unity, nor cultural similarities necessarily grounds for political union. Such an attitude is symbolized, in a sense, by their choice of "Canadian" to describe their national identity. It is reflected in the demand that others, too, recognize that they are Canadians first and only secondarily members of a particular ethnic group. Eighty-six per cent of the English students agreed with the statement that "it would be better if everyone in Canada called themselves simply Canadians, instead of saying English Canadian or French Canadian."

What is unclear is whether the English students should be regarded as proponents of the "mosaic" or the "melting pot." Both symbols stand for conceptions of nationality divorced from traditional ethnic differences. No current issue clearly tests allegiance to one or the other conception. The closest thing we have to a touchstone of devotion to cultural diversity is the issue of bilingualism.

The English questionnaire contained four questions having to do with language policy. From the answers to these questions we can say that the English students tended to regard Canada as "basically English" (about four out of five say this), but also to support bilingualism (about two out of three do so).[16] In response to an open-ended question about what Canada should be in the future—the question followed immediately after the question whether Canada is "equally French and English" or "basically an English country"—about four out of ten of the students evaded the linguistic issue, declaring that Canada should be united, stronger, independent, more nationalistic, a peacekeeper, etc. About one out of ten gave an answer suggesting multiculturalism (e.g., "the homeland of many different people") or one classified as Pan-Canadian (e.g., "Canadian"). Another two out of ten said that Canada should be English. The remaining three in ten said that Canada should be both French and English (e.g., "bilingual," "more French," "equally French and English," etc.). The only generalization that seems realistic in light of these figures is that English-speaking youth, like their elders, are divided and ambivalent about bilingualism.[17]

Perhaps the most revealing question of the series about language was the following: "Out of every hundred Canadians, how many would you say are able to speak *only* French?" Estimates ranged from 0 to 90 but the modal estimate was 5 out of 100. The medians of the estimates of the Winnipeg, Toronto/Oakville, and Montreal/Quebec City students were 7.9, 9.7, and 10.3 respectively. The proportions guessing 5 or fewer out of 100 were 46 per cent, 40 per cent, and 36 per cent respectively for the three groups of students. Thus even the English students living in the heart of French Canada tend to underestimate greatly the number of unilingual francophones. From these estimates one would infer that bilingualism is a big fuss about a small problem. Canada is "basically English."

The political attitudes of the French students are harder to describe. From the propensity of the French students to say that they are French Canadians and Quebecers one might reasonably infer that a large fraction of them are alienated from English Canada and disposed to demand political independence for Quebec. Many no doubt are. But the relationship between nationalism and national identity is complex, and in some ways the political attitudes of the group seem to be remarkably similar to those of the English students.

The federal government is identified in the minds of many French Canadians with the interests of the numerically larger English community. Yet the French students in 1968 did not seem to be any more inclined

Table 9 Preferred Government by Language and Province

Government	English Students			French Students
	Manitoba	Ontario	Quebec	
Federal	14%	11%	41%	10%
Provincial	55	52	28	54
Both	17	27	20	24
Neither One	14	10	11	12
	(N = 323)	(N = 423)	(N = 167)	(N = 663)

than their English counterparts to regard it as serving interests opposed to their own. Both groups were asked "Which government do you think takes the best care of the interests of people like you?" Table 9 shows that the francophones from Quebec and the anglophones from Ontario gave almost identical distributions of responses. The group that is out of line— in the direction of alienation from the provincial government—is the English-speaking Quebecers.

A divergence between the English and French students appears when the questions about government touch on feelings of personal involvement in federal politics and the correlative sense that the federal government is responsive to popular demands. The difference is sharpest in response to the question "How much attention do you think the federal government pays to what people think when it decides what to do?" The English students from all three provinces responded to this question in approximately the same way: between 58 and 63 per cent of them answered "Very much" or "Some." The French students responded quite differently: only 29 per cent checked one of the answers favoured by the English students, and 71 per cent said "Not much" or "None."

The English and French students also differ in the political significance they attribute to cultural differences. As we have seen, the English students tend to deny that cultural differences have any political significance. The French students tend to take the opposite view. This difference between the two groups is illustrated by their answers to a question about the "foreignness" of the other group. Students in both groups were asked whether they ever thought of the other language group—English Canadians or French Canadians—"as being like foreign people." About six out of every ten of the English students replied that they never thought of

Table 10 Tendency to Regard Other Group as Foreign People by Language and Province

Response	English Students			French Students
	Manitoba	Ontario	Quebec	
Yes, always	4%	4%	4%	11%
Yes, sometimes	34	40	25	56
No, never	62	56	71	34
	(N = 366)	(N = 496)	(N = 199)	(N = 738)

French Canadians in this way, while more than six in ten of the French students said that they sometimes or always thought of English Canadians as foreigners. As Table 10 shows, there is a particularly striking contrast between the attitudes of the French students and those of the anglophones in Quebec. In the abstract, as we saw earlier, the English-speaking and French-speaking have very similar perceptions of the relatively great differences between English Canadians and French Canadians, and of the greater similarity of English Canadians and Americans. Yet most of the English students describe themselves as "Canadians" and, it seems, do not think of themselves as members of a group which is foreign vis-à-vis French Canadians. The French students, by contrast, generally think of themselves as "French Canadians" and do regard English Canadians as somewhat foreign. When questions about similarities and differences have clear political overtones, the English students tend to emphasize similarities between the two groups, while the French students tend to emphasize differences.

These feelings of distance from the federal government and from English Canadians obviously underlie support for the movement for Quebec independence. It is difficult to estimate how extensive is support for separation among francophones in Quebec. A straightforward question —"Are you for or against separation?"—tends to underestimate the level of support because independence is regarded as something to be attained in the future, not something that is immediately practicable. Thus only 14 per cent of the students checked "independence of Quebec" in response to a question about which "constitutional option" they favoured. But a few seconds later 30 per cent of them agreed with the statement that "The best way for Quebecers to progress is for them to become a distinct and independent nation." And 48 per cent agreed that "Quebecers should be ready to make greater sacrifices to obtain their national independence." The most revealing question regarding separatism was very simple: "What is your opinion on the subject of independence for Quebec?" The alternatives available were various combinations of desirability and feasibility. The distribution of responses was as follows:

Desirable and feasible immediately	2%
Desirable, but not feasible immediately	38
Desirable, but not feasible at all	6
Not desirable	46
Undecided	7

Independence by evolution rather than revolution might be a good motto for the separatist movement in Quebec.

There is, of course, a strong relationship between a person's national self-image and his response to these questions about separatism. It is simplest to compare those who described themselves as "Canadians" and those who described themselves as "French Canadians" in response to the last of the national identity questions (see page 292). Table 11 shows the correlation (Gamma = .64) between this variable and response to the question about the desirability and feasibility of independence. The responses to the other questions about separation have a similarly strong relation to variations in self-description. A narrow identity is, in this sense, the psychological basis for separatist nationalism. Thus the number of respondents who call themselves "French Canadians" is one measure

Table 11   Opinion about Quebec Independence by National Identity, French Students Only

Opinion	National Identity	
	Canadians	French Canadians
Desirable and feasible immediately	—	3%
Desirable, not feasible immediately	15%	47
Desirable, not feasible at all	7	6
Not desirable	74	35
Undecided	5	8
	(N = 205)	(N = 505)

of the latent support for independence. By this test separatist sentiment is very widespread, for seven out of ten of the French students choose the label "French Canadian" rather than "Canadian" (see Table 3).

The feeling of separateness of the French students should not be exaggerated, however. They were asked which they thought of as their country, all of Canada or only Quebec. Seventy-seven per cent said Canada; 20 per cent said Quebec; the remaining 3 per cent were undecided. It is not clear whether we should say *fully* or *only* 20 per cent chose Quebec. The proportion is certainly higher than it would be among the English students (no comparable question was included in the English questionnaire). It is too low to support any simple generalization about the disaffection of Quebec youth from Canada.

Nor should we exaggerate the Canadian nationalism of the French-speaking "Canadians." The "Canadians," by comparison with the "French Canadians," are more likely to say that they would be willing to go to the United States to seek employment. They are also more likely to approve of a political union between Canada and the United States. They are more likely to say that Americans "treat other people as equals" rather than "acting as if they were above others." None of these relationships is very strong (the coefficients of association are .24, .25, and .19 respectively), but they are statistically significant and they are the opposite of what you would expect if you thought of the French-speaking "Canadians" as ardent Canadian nationalists. It would be truer to say that the "Canadians" are continentalists: having transcended provincial ethnic loyalties, they are not disposed to confine their expanding consciousness within the boundaries of Canada. This is understandable, given the similarities they perceive between English Canadians and Americans.

These findings draw attention to the ambiguity of the label "French Canadian" and to the ambivalence of those who choose it to describe themselves. This ambivalence is what stands out in the responses of the French students. For example, 60 per cent of them endorse the statement that "it would be better if everyone in Canada called themselves simply Canadians. . . ." This is a substantially smaller proportion than the 86 per cent agreement among the English students, but it is still surprisingly high, compared to the 70 per cent who call themselves "French Canadians." Evidently many of the French students are drawn to the ideal of a Canadian nation in which ethnic loyalties are subordinated to an over-arching national identity, but they evidently also find the ideal more equivocal than do the English students.

CONCLUSION

When asked to describe themselves from the standpoint of nationality, English-speaking students typically respond quite differently than do French-speaking students. The English students call themselves "Canadians," while the French students prefer to set themselves apart as "French Canadians." Both groups agree, however, that English Canadians are more similar to and have more in common with Americans than they do with French Canadians. Many of the French students look forward to the eventual attainment of sovereignty by Quebec. The English students are opposed to separation and do not believe that it will happen.

"Two nations" was earlier considered and rejected as a summary of these attitudes. The formula distorts the nationalism of the English students, which is symbolized by loyalty to Canada as a whole, not just to English Canada. It also suggests that the English students are "English Canadians" in the traditional sense, when in fact they reject such an identity, they are far from being staunch monarchists, and they are more American than British in their choice of heroes.

"Two nationalisms" is an alternative interpretation of the findings. One might hypothesize that English-speaking Canadians have attained a fundamentally different conception of nationality than have French-speaking Canadians. Kenneth McNaught, for example, has written that

English-speaking Canadians take a non-racial view of nationality. . . . The English-speaking view has always anticipated a Canadian nationality in which the significance of racial origin will diminish rather than increase. . . . English-speaking Canadians [have always] thought of Canadian nationality as something that included people of French, British and other origins and which would move steadily toward its own sense of identity. That identity was not to be homogenous in the American sense, but diverse. . . . Tradition has planted firmly in the minds of English-speaking Canadians the idea that their national loyalty is to national diversity.[18]

The implied contrast is with the narrow "racial" or "ethnic" nationalism of French-speaking Canadians, which McNaught refers to as "a kind of psychological neo-colonialism" aiming at "security and identity by closer integration in French or Latin civilization."[19] It would be conceded, of course, that not all English-speaking Canadians have transcended a narrow conception of nationality and not all French-speaking Canadians have failed to do so. In this respect, the students in our sample are probably typical of the communities from which they are drawn. About one out of five English students say that they are "English Canadians" and about three out of ten French students say that they are simply "Canadians." It is the communities which differ in their balance of views, not necessarily every individual member.

Many of the findings are consistent with, and thus support, this interpretation. The hypothesis of a Canadian political nationality accepted in differing degree by the English and French communities explains why the two groups draw different conclusions, on balance, from the commonly accepted facts of ethnic diversity. The English students, it seems, de-emphasize ethnicity in describing themselves, deplore it in others, and attach little significance to it politically. The French students, by contrast, seem to be preoccupied with ethnicity, not only in describing themselves but also in evaluating political institutions.

Yet the familiar distinction between broad (English) and narrow (French) conceptions of nationality becomes less and less clear the more one studies the kind of data presented above. Where is the pluralism among the English students? Where is the enthusiasm for diversity? The group is pretty clearly ambivalent about bilingualism and hostile to hyphenated Canadianism. The qualified and seemingly contradictory loyalties of the French students may be closer to what would be involved in a genuine political nationality than the single-minded Canadianism of the English students. Perhaps what distinguishes the English from the French students is not their broader conception of nationality, but their greater equanimity about the new nationality that is developing in Canada out of the present diversity of Canada's population.

Where the hypothesis of a Canadian political nationality seems to be on weak ground is in implicitly drawing a sharp contrast between English Canadian and American attitudes toward ethnic diversity. English Canadians, it is suggested, believe in the mosaic—"their national loyalty is to national diversity"—while Americans believe in the melting pot.

It is worth recalling that in the American lexicon "the melting pot" is an alternative to, not a synonym for, the ideal of conformity to Anglo-American cultural norms.[20] It symbolizes the ideal of an American nation which has incorporated the distinctive contributions of a great many nations, in addition to those of the English, and which has thus clearly outgrown its colonial relationship with Great Britain. Stated in this way, the melting pot is obviously an ideal with considerable appeal to English-speaking Canadians.[21]

A distinction between ideal and reality is, of course, crucial in discussing these matters. Casual observation suffices to establish that in the United States there has been a great deal of behavioural assimilation (or acculturation) to Anglo-American cultural norms, despite widespread acceptance of pluralist/melting-pot ideology. Closer investigation shows that assimilation is far from complete, and ethnic boundaries are still very salient in regulating the more intimate forms of association, particularly marriage and the family. These residual ethnic loyalties are correlated with some differences in tastes, occupations, education, residence, political attitudes, and political behaviour.[22] In other words, the melting pot is a poor description of American life, despite its popularity as a symbol. This is not to deny that there has been some melting: one thinks, for example, of the eclectic menu of the all-purpose roadside restaurant. None the less, what must be emphasized in any thumbnail description of the United States is the mixture of Anglo-American conformity in the public sphere and structural pluralism in the private sphere.

How does this differ from what we observe in Canada? One outstanding difference between the two countries is, of course, the existence of Quebec within Canada. The French-speaking community in Quebec, partly because of its limited political autonomy, remains distinct and relatively isolated from the English civilization of the rest of North America. To notice this distinctiveness is not to be blind to Quebec's sixty years' experience with an urban industrial way of life. Nor is it to deny the long-term implications of the recent expansion of advanced technical education, the sharp decline in the role of the Church in Quebec society, and the growing determination of ambitious young Quebecers to participate as managers and not just workers in the North American economy. None the less, "two solitudes" still exist; Canada as a whole still exemplifies cultural and not just structural pluralism.

But what about English Canada? Does the difference of symbols—mosaic rather than melting pot—correspond to any real difference in the way English-speaking Canadians and Americans live? Do not Germans, Italians, and French Canadians learn to speak English here? Are not our political and economic institutions those of England and the United States? Have we not become votaries of practically the same "civil religion" (or American Shinto) described by Herberg and Bellah?[23] What, after all, does multiculturalism amount to other than folk-dancing on the weekends? Do we propose to accommodate the Greeks in our midst by instituting military rule, or the Turks by establishing *medrese*? We can scarcely point to our ghettos and our separate schools to defend our self-image of diversity, for the Americans have these in abundance too.

The hypothesis that English Canadians have developed a political conception of nationality, while clearly attractive, seems to underestimate English Canada's continuity with some aspects of its past and also, curiously, to miss the implications of its deep commitment to the ideals of reason and progress. Thus it implicitly denies the extent to which Canada's vertical mosaic has functioned as a melting pot, transmuting non-British immigrants into good English-speaking Canadians. It overlooks the tremendous assimilating power of English North America, and the very considerable involvement of English Canadians in American politics and culture. It exaggerates the ability (not to mention the willingness) of English Canadians to abandon ethnic particularisms, such as language, that are not really challenged in the present circumstances. It puts the most generous possible interpretation on the Diefenbaker-like antipathy to ethnic diversity implicit in the statement that "it would be better if everyone in Canada called themselves simply Canadians, instead of saying English Canadian or French Canadian." In short, the rhetoric of the Canadian mosaic may be no more than sugar coating on the bitter pill of assimilation.

The hypothesis of a Canadian political nationality also minimizes, as we are in the habit of doing, the disruption of tradition implicit in modernization. The hypothesis exemplifies our propensity to ignore the fact that affluence and technology are themselves a culture, and that this new culture threatens the integrity of the customs and values we pretend to preserve in a culturally neutral nation-state.

Whatever the shortcomings of the concept of a Canadian political nationality, it does draw attention to the fact that English Canadian youth today are not traditional "English Canadians"—not in their self-images, not in their allegiance to symbols like the monarchy, and not in the heroes they choose. On these points the data reported above provide convincing evidence. What remains unclear is whether the English-speaking youth have transcended their "Englishness" or only their "Britishness." In our English respondents we may have the same combination of pluralist ideology and unconscious assimilative power that Americans exemplify. And in our French respondents we may have the ambivalent reaction to this combination of a group large enough to entertain the ideal of the nationalist-state, but not yet fully convinced that sovereignty is practicable or relevant, and thus inclined to put off its realization to the future. The prognosis would be a turbulent future.

NOTES

1. For an excellent discussion of this theme, with references to the relevant literature, see Allan Smith, "Metaphor and Nationality in North America," *Canadian Historical Review*, vol. 51 (1970), pp. 247–75.
2. George Grant, *Lament for a Nation* (Toronto: McClelland and Stewart, 1965), p. 70.
3. See especially Carl Berger, *The Sense of Power: Studies in the Ideas of Canadian Imperialism, 1867–1914* (Toronto: University of Toronto Press, 1970). There is also interesting material in S. F. Wise and R. C. Brown, *Canada Views the United States: Nineteenth Century Political Attitudes* (Toronto: Macmillan, 1967), and in S. M. Lipset, "Revolution and Counterrevolution: The United States and Canada," in *Revolution and Counterrevolution* (New York: Basic Books, 1968).
4. D. V. Smiley, *The Canadian Political Nationality* (Toronto: Methuen 1967), p. 130.
5. Ibid., p. 131.
6. W. L. Morton, *The Canadian Identity* (Toronto: University of Toronto Press, 1961), p. 111.

7. Ramsay Cook, *The Maple Leaf Forever* (Toronto: Macmillan, 1971), pp. 5–6.
8. Ibid., p. 214.
9. P. E. Trudeau, *Federalism and the French Canadians* (Toronto: Macmillan, 1968), p. 179.
10. English and French refer to those who filled out the English and French versions of the questionnaire. This convention is followed throughout the paper. Less than 1 per cent of the English students come from homes in which French is normally spoken; similarly less than 1 per cent of the French students come from homes in which English is the main language. As subsequent tables show, a slightly larger fraction of each group have a subjective identity which is at odds with the classification by language, but the differences are very slight.
11. National origin was determined by means of two questions near the end of the questionnaire: "From which country outside Canada did most of your father's ancestors originally come?" and "From which country outside Canada did most of your

mother's ancestors originally come?" The numbers of those in the English sample with German, Polish, and Ukrainian ancestry are 80, 70, and 75 respectively.

12. These results are in line with the results of other surveys, for example, Marcel Rioux and Robert Sevigny, *Les Nouveaux Citoyens* (Montreal, 1967), where it is reported that 75 per cent of a sample of French-speaking Quebec youth describe themselves as primarily or exclusively French Canadian. See also D. M. Taylor, L. M. Simard, and F. E. Aboud, "Ethnic Identification in Canada: A Cross-Cultural Investigation," *Canadian Journal of Behavioural Science*, vol. 4 (1972), pp. 13–20.

13. Three names were classified according to nationality. Only 6 per cent of the English students and 8 per cent of the French students wrote in four or more names of admired people. There were no substantial differences by province in the relative frequencies with which the English students chose heroes of different nationalities, hence to simplify the table the English students are treated as a single group.

14. In this connection Jean Laponce makes the very interesting point that his Vancouver-Burrard respondents tended to react to American presidential candidates as Americans would rather than as Canadians concerned with each candidate's policies toward Canada. See Jean Laponce, *People vs. Politics* (Toronto: University of Toronto Press, 1969), pp. 166–67.

15. J. C. Johnstone, *Young People's Images of Canadian Society: An Opinion Survey of Canadian Youth Thirteen to Twenty Years of Age* (Ottawa: Queen's Printer, 1969), reports essentially the same difference between English and French youth.

16. The questions were: "Do you think of Canada right now as *equally French and English* or do you think of it as *basically* an English country?" and "Do you think that both French and English should be official languages in Canada, or do you think that English should be the only official language in Canada?" For both questions it was possible to answer "I'm not sure."

17. "The reactions of Anglophone youth indicate what could at best be assessed as a modest level of linguistic tolerance. . . . All in all, [their answers] suggest that they generally recognize and accept Canada's other language but are not inclined to favour its spread." J. C. Johnstone, *Young People's Images*, pp. 56, 58.

18. Kenneth McNaught, "The National Outlook of English-Speaking Canadians," in Peter Russell, ed., *Nationalism in Canada* (Toronto: McGraw-Hill, 1966), pp. 63–66.

19. Ibid., p. 69.

20. See M. M. Gordon, *Assimilation in American Life* (New York: Oxford University Press, 1964), for a penetrating discussion of the different theories of assimilation which have influenced American political thinking.

21. So much appeal, in fact, that we sometimes confuse enthusiasm for the melting pot with devotion to the mosaic. Consider the following declaration of faith in the melting pot: "British political wisdom, Jewish cosmopolitanism and realism, French lucidity of mind and expression, German emotional depth and capacity for work, Slavonic spontaneity and verve—all these are there in the riches of our Canadian life and each set of qualities can be learned and assimilated by all." Porter quotes this passage to "represent the often expressed value of the Canadian mosaic." John Porter, *The Vertical Mosaic* (Toronto: University of Toronto Press, 1965), p. 70.

22. In addition to the book by Gordon cited above, see Nathan Glazer and Daniel Moynihan, *Beyond the*

Melting Pot (Cambridge, Mass.: Harvard University Press, 1963), and Edgar Litt, *Ethnic Politics in America* (Glenview, Ill.: Scott Foresman, 1970), and the literature cited there.

23. See Will Herberg, *Protestant-Catholic-Jew* (New York: Doubleday, 1955), and R. N. Bellah, "Civil Religion in America," in *Beyond Belief* (New York: Harper Row, 1970).

Notes on Contributors

Terrance Carroll is Assistant Professor in the Department of Politics, Brock University. Besides his work in political socialization, he has done a detailed study of ethnic conflict and political violence in Northern Ireland.

Harold Clarke is Associate Professor in the Department of Political Science, University of Windsor. He has co-authored numerous articles in the field of legislative behaviour, which have appeared in, among other places, the *Canadian Journal of Political Science*, the *American Journal of Political Science*, *Legislatures in Comparative Perspective* (Allan Kornberg, ed.), and *The Provincial Political Systems* (David Bellamy, Jon Pammett, and Donald Rowat, eds.). He was co-investigator of the 1974 Federal Election Study and is currently engaged in work on Canadian voting behaviour.

Jack Cramer is an Educational Systems Planning Officer with the Public Service Commission of Canada. He is author of *The Monteith Vocational Preparatory Program: The Road Back to Society*, published by the Department of Manpower and Immigration.

Donald Forbes is Associate Professor in the Department of Political Economy, University of Toronto. He is co-author of "Party Loyalty and Electoral Volatility: A Study of the Canadian Party System," in the *Canadian Journal of Political Science*. He is currently completing a study, based on Canadian data, of the relations between nationalism, ethnocentrism, and personality.

Magnus Gunther is Associate Professor in the Department of Politics, Trent University. He has specialized in research into the relations between personality and democratic theory and has publications in the fields of Canadian government, political socialization, and philosophy of science.

Donald Higgins is Assistant Professor in the Department of Political Science, St. Mary's University. His article on Nova Scotia and New

316

Brunswick will appear in Donald Rowat, ed., *Recent Reorganizations of Local Government Around the World*. He is pursuing research on the development of city councils in Canada and is writing a book on urban government and politics.

Robert Krause is Assistant Professor in the Department of Political Science, University of Windsor. He is co-author of articles in the *Canadian Journal of Political Science, Cost and Management*, and *The Provincial Political Systems*. His current research interests involve the leadership selection process in Canadian political parties and the socialization and recruitment of Canadian M.P.'s.

Ronald Landes is Assistant Professor in the Department of Political Science, St. Mary's University. He has published articles in the *Dalhousie Review* and the *International Journal of Comparative Sociology*. He is currently completing a province-wide study of the political socialization process in Nova Scotia.

Thelma Oliver is Assistant Professor in the Department of Political Science, Simon Fraser University. Her interest in problems of political dissent has centred on empirical investigation of political attitudes and activism in western Canada. She is currently engaged in a study of twelfth- and thirteenth-century France, with special attention to the Albigensian Crusades.

Jon Pammett is Assistant Professor in the Department of Political Science, Carleton University. He has published articles in the *Canadian Journal of Political Science* and is co-editor of *The Provincial Political Systems*. He was co-investigator of the 1974 Federal Election Study and is working in the field of Canadian electoral behaviour.

Richard Price is Assistant Professor in the Department of Political Science, University of Windsor. He is co-author of articles on legislative behaviour in the *Canadian Journal of Political Science* and *The Provincial Political Systems*. His current research includes projects dealing with the political socialization, recruitment, and careers of Canadian legislators and party activists.

Stuart Proudfoot is Assistant Professor in the Faculty of Administrative Studies, York University. He is co-author of *Public Land Ownership:*

Frameworks for Evaluation, and his research interests lie in the fields of urban planning and development, and the public policy process in Canada.

John Shiry is Assistant Professor in the Department of Political Science, University of Alberta. He has been primarily interested in the theoretical and methodological problems involved in doing research in the fields of public policy and political behaviour. He is currently preparing an instructional manual in techniques of data analysis using Canadian survey data.

Stephen Ullman is Associate Professor in the Department of Political Science, State University of New York at Brockport. He has published several articles on Canadian political culture and socialization. He is currently doing research on regional and linguistic variations in press coverage of the 1974 federal election.

Michael Whittington is Associate Professor in the Department of Political Science, Carleton University. He is co-author of *The Canadian Political System* and is currently doing research in the fields of public policy and northern development.

John Woods is Associate Professor in the Department of Political Science, University of Calgary. His research is at present directed toward a lengthy study of Canadian ideology, as distinct from political theory, and a subsequent consideration of contemporary policy problems and political alignments in that context.